Practical Cyber Intelligence

Practical Cyber Intelligence

A Hands-on Guide to Digital Forensics

Adam Tilmar Jakobsen
National Special Crime Unit
Denmark

WILEY

Published by John Wiley & Sons, Inc., Hoboken, New Jersey.
Published simultaneously in Canada.

Library of Congress Cataloging-in-Publication Data:

Names: Jakobsen, Adam Tilmar, author.
Title: Practical cyber intelligence : a hands-on guide to digital forensics / Adam Tilmar Jakobsen.
Description: Hoboken, New Jersey : Wiley, [2024] | Includes index.
Identifiers: LCCN 2024024151 (print) | LCCN 2024024152 (ebook) | ISBN 9781394256099 (hardback) | ISBN 9781394256112 (adobe pdf) | ISBN 9781394256105 (epub)
Subjects: LCSH: Computer crimes–Investigation. | Cyber intelligence (Computer security)
Classification: LCC HV8079.C65 J633 2024 (print) | LCC HV8079.C65 (ebook) | DDC 364.16/8–dc23/eng/20240628
LC record available at https://lccn.loc.gov/2024024151
LC ebook record available at https://lccn.loc.gov/2024024152

Cover design: Wiley
Cover image(s): © koiguo/Getty Images

Set in 9.5/12.5pt STIXTwoText by Straive, Chennai, India

To my wife Josefine & my dog Fenris for always being there.

Contents

About the Author

My journey with computers began, as it did for many others, with playing video games. Initially, my goal was to become a game developer, which led me to obtain a master's degree in computer science. Although that dream didn't materialize, I instead joined the Danish army as a cyber specialist for the army intelligence within the electronic warfare division. Due to the classified nature of my work, I cannot delve into specifics; however, my job generally involved expanding the utility of cyber capabilities within operations, focusing on SIGINT, OSINT, and all-source intelligence while also supporting other departments such as HUMINT, PSYOPS, and IMGINT.

After three years with the army intelligence, I joined Bluewater Shipping, a major Danish shipping company. Initially serving as a solution architect for all internally developed software, my role shifted to information security following a significant cyberattack on the company. As the sole security engineer, I was responsible for overseeing the entire operation pipeline, including defining and implementing detection rules, incident response, and much more.

Another three years passed, and I was presented with the opportunity to join the Special Crime Unit in Denmark as an IT engineer and digital forensics expert in the Department of Technology and Innovation. The primary goal in this role is to identify new methods of extracting and analyzing data from devices.

The knowledge I've acquired throughout my journey is an amalgamation of research, reading white papers, taking courses, and participating in Capture the Flag challenges. I would like to express my gratitude to everyone who contributes to the cybersecurity community; your work has made this book possible.

Preface

The rapid advancement of technology has created both new opportunities and new challenges for investigators. In the past, evidence of criminal activity was predominantly confined to physical items. Today, however, much of the evidence exists in digital form, dispersed across a multitude of devices and networks. This necessitates a novel approach to investigation, one that is firmly rooted in a profound understanding of the digital landscape and the methods employed to collect, preserve, and analyze digital evidence.

Cyber investigation is not a simple field, owing to its adversarial nature with challenges arising on two distinct fronts. The first involves criminals attempting to conceal their activities, resulting in a cat-and-mouse game between the examiner and the perpetrator as they develop new methods to hide their tracks. It is the examiner's responsibility to identify innovative ways of extracting evidence from systems. The second challenge stems from the growing public awareness of privacy and the corresponding corporate response. Companies like Apple have taken significant strides to enhance user privacy, ultimately providing examiners with less data to work with.

However, this does not imply that all hope is lost. Certain trends are working in our favor, such as the increasing amount of information people post on social media, which can be utilized to map out a person's activities. Furthermore, human nature often prioritizes convenience over security, leading to password reuse and lax security measures.

This book offers a comprehensive guide to utilizing digital forensics and OSINT in the investigative process, encompassing the latest techniques, tools, and best practices within the field. Whether you are a seasoned professional or just starting, this book will serve as an invaluable resource as you navigate the intricate world of digital forensics and investigation.

Esbjerg, 2024

Acknowledgments

I would like to thank everyone in the cybersecurity community for all the awesome work they put out on the internet; without them, this book would not be possible.

Introduction

The use of digital forensics has revolutionized the way we investigate criminal and civil cases. In the past, investigators were often limited to collecting physical evidence, but today, much of the evidence relevant to an investigation can be found in the digital realm. This includes everything from electronic communications and financial transactions to GPS data and social media activity. To be effective, investigators must have a deep understanding of the digital landscape and the methods used to collect, preserve, and analyze digital evidence. This book provides an overview of the key concepts, tools, and techniques used in digital forensics and investigates how they can be applied to the investigative process. Whether you are a law enforcement professional, an attorney, or simply interested in the topic, this book is an essential resource for anyone looking to deepen their understanding of the role of digital forensics in investigation.

Cyber forensics is the process of using forensic and investigative techniques to identify and analyze digital events. This involves collecting and analyzing digital evidence from various sources, such as computers, networks, and mobile devices, to identify perpetrators.

When discussing a cyber investigation, many people often think about high-tech crimes like ransomware, DDoS, or BEC. However, it extends beyond these examples, as it also includes traditional crimes such as theft, fraud, or assault, which can leave behind digital evidence that can be collected and analyzed. In these cases, IT is merely a component of the event. For example, a murderer can leave behind digital evidence, such as phone activity and internet browsing history. A fraudster who uses fake emails or websites to scam victims out of money will also leave behind digital evidence that can be collected and analyzed. As technology becomes increasingly integrated into our daily lives, the information that we can collect from devices, OSINT, and other sources becomes a critical part of any investigation, allowing us to map out a person's life.

Since this book does not cover the basics of how computers work, I have made some assumptions about the reader's knowledge. I expect them to be familiar with how a computer operates (e.g., CPU, RAM, and disk) and be comfortable interacting with both Windows and Linux operating systems. Throughout the book, you will encounter both Bash and PowerShell commands. If you are entirely new to these topics, I recommend the book *Introduction to Linux - Hands-on Guide*. Additionally, you should have a basic understanding of Python and know how to execute Python scripts, although I do not expect you to be a master programmer.

The motivation behind writing this book is that I wanted a resource like this when I started, but all I could find were scattered pieces of information, often behind a substantial paywall. Consequently, I began creating this book not only to help myself understand but also to assist others entering the digital forensics field by providing a practical approach to digital forensics. The book covers where to collect and parse digital clues and the context different evidence can provide. Throughout this book, I aim to present a wide array of tactics, techniques, and procedures that can be used to collect information about an individual or group's activities on a device or the internet. I have chosen to focus on free tools or services to make them accessible to everyone. While I cannot promise that this book will make you an expert, if you are new or simply interested in the field, I believe you will find the information in this book to be a good practical starting point.

The first part of this book will cover the art of intelligence. The purpose of intel is to help us bind all the different sources of information that we have collected into a cohesive and structured analysis that can be used to gain insight into a person or organization's activities. The next part is about digital forensics, where I will cover the most common devices used by people and the methods of locating and extracting key information. Cyber forensics is an important field, as cybercrimes are becoming more common and more sophisticated. It plays a crucial role in helping protect individuals, businesses, and governments from the threat of cyberattacks and other forms of digital crime.

The final chapter will be about OSINT. This is where we will start to look at what information is available on the internet. There is a wide variety of OSINT techniques and tools that can be used to collect information from open sources on the internet. What OSINT allows you to do is take the information collected in the forensics phase and pivot to a new source to obtain additional information that can only be found on the internet.

Overall, the goal of this book is to be a valuable resource for anyone interested in learning about cyber investigation. It should provide a thorough and practical introduction to the field and serve as a valuable resource for anyone looking to enter or advance in the field of cyber investigation.

1

Intelligence Analysis

Intelligence analysis is the process of using data to comprehend a situation or problem and support decision-making. It involves collecting and analyzing data from various sources, such as human intelligence, signals intelligence, open-source information, and other types of data, to provide insights and inform decision-makers. Intelligence analysts employ a range of tools and techniques, including data mining, statistical analysis, and modeling, to discern trends, patterns, and relationships within the data. They then utilize this information to formulate hypotheses, make predictions, and offer recommendations for action. Intelligence analysis is applied across numerous fields, including national security, law enforcement, and business. You might be wondering what it has to do with digital forensics. They have a lot in common; they are both about identifying the most likely hypotheses based on the available data. The thing is we would always like to be precise in forensics, but that is not always possible as the necessary data might not be available to give a precise and scientific answer. In these cases, we have to look at the available data, understand the story it is telling, and then give an estimate of what most likely has happened. This is why the first section is about the tools used in intelligence analysis.

1.1 Intelligence Life Cycle

The intelligence life cycle[1] is a framework that outlines the various stages involved in the process of collecting, analyzing, and disseminating intelligence. The typical stages of the intelligence process life cycle include:

- Planning and direction
- Collection

1 https://irp.fas.org/cia/product/facttell/index.html.

Practical Cyber Intelligence: A Hands-on Guide to Digital Forensics, First Edition. Adam Tilmar Jakobsen.

- Processing
- Analysis
- Dissemination
- Evaluation and feedback

These stages are interconnected and often overlap, with the ultimate goal of the intelligence process being to deliver timely and accurate information to decision-makers, thereby enabling them to take well-informed actions.

1.1.1 Direction and Planning

This stage is the foundation of the intelligence life cycle. It is about establishing a strategy for what is needed gathering the necessary data and tackling the different cases hitting your desk. This is about identifying what question the decision maker need answered to meet their objectives. Which defines what tool and data sources are needed, to formulate an answer to the question, have been given.

1.1.2 Collection

In the collection phase, raw data is obtained from different sources that are needed to facilitate the analysis. A good idea is to implement a collection management framework.[2] The job of this tool is to help manage and create structure around the numerous data sources and the information that can be obtained from each source. This is done by maintaining a data sheet that outlines all the sources available. The expected data you can retrieve from each source, and the specific questions each source can answer; I have created an example of a collection management framework for a SOC in Table 1.1.

Table 1.1 Collection framework.

	Endpoint	Network	Firewall	AD logs
Data type	Alert	Netflow	Alerts	logs
Kill chain	Exploitation and installation	Internal recon, delivery, and C2	Internal recon, delivery, and C2	Internal recon
Pivot on	Malware sample	Packet capture	Netflow	Endpoint
Retention (days)	30	60	21	30

2 https://www.dragos.com/wp-content/uploads/CMF_For_ICS.pdf.

Your collection framework will definitely look different, but it should be able to give you a general idea. What makes this useful is that it clearly defines what data is available to you and what it can be used for. That way you do not have to rely on people's memories to remember what sources are available, and what they can be used for. Do not underestimate the usefulness of this tool; if you are ever in a situation where you ask yourself if you have a data source that could be used to answer X questions, then you need this tool. Another usage of this tool is to identify if you have blackspots in your data sources or if you have overlaps in capabilities.

1.1.3 Processing

During the processing stage, the raw data collected transforms into a format that can be easily understood by humans or interpreted by relevant computer systems. This step is crucial for preparing the data for in-depth analysis and interpretation by intelligence analysts or automated tools.

An essential aspect of this stage is evaluating the relevance and reliability of the data gathered. Analysts need to carefully examine the data to ensure its accuracy and ascertain its importance concerning the intelligence requirement. This process may entail cross-referencing data from multiple sources to authenticate its credibility and establish its relevance.

When processing threat reports from various vendors, it can be temping to create a Rosetta stone for that translation threat actors from across different vendors. The reason cyber threat intelligence organizations do not utilize the same naming convention for threat actors is because they do not have the same collection coverage and the method in which they cluster intrusion together is different depending upon their intelligence requirements, and we do not know all the details of the adversary, and this reason why unitize their own name scheme. The reason why we should not try to cluster together actor from different vendor as it will most likely be wrong.

1.1.4 Analysis

The process of intelligence analysis[3] involves breaking down a complex problem or concept into smaller, simpler parts to better understand it and draw meaningful conclusions. It is a crucial step in an investigation, where information needs to be systematically examined and evaluated to identify patterns, connections, and insights that can help shed light on the case. The objective is to transform data into actionable information.

When it comes to digital evidence, expert examiners play a critical role in data analysis, as the data can be ambiguous, taken out of context, or simply incorrect, which may lead to wrongful conclusions. A good digital forensics expert possesses

3 https://www.cia.gov/static/Pyschology-of-Intelligence-Analysis.pdf.

the ability to understand the context around the data and use analytical judgment to make objective conclusions about the evidence. This involves employing critical thinking skills, logical reasoning, and a systematic approach to assess and evaluate information based on the available evidence.

The good thing there are a variety of tools and techniques at our disposal, including statistical analysis, network analysis, and trend analysis, among others. The choice of technique depends on the type of investigation and the data available.

1.1.4.1 Structured Analytic Techniques (SAT)

Structured analytic techniques[4] are a set of tools used to help analysts systematically analyze complex information. They provide a systematic and transparent approach to analysis to reduce bias, improve the quality of the analysis, and support more effective decision-making.

Structured analytic techniques typically involve the following steps:

1. **Define the problem or issue**: The first step is to clearly define the problem or issue that the analysis will address. This involves identifying specific questions that need to be answered and the information needed to answer those questions.
2. **Collect and organize the information**: The next step is to collect the raw intelligence information relevant to the problem or issue. This can involve various sources, such as human agents, electronic surveillance, and open-source information. Once the information has been collected, it must be organized and prepared for analysis.
3. **Apply structured analytic techniques**: The third step is to apply a structured analytic technique to the collected information to identify patterns, trends, and relationships. A wide variety of structured analytic techniques can be used, such as statistical analysis, network analysis, geospatial analysis, decision trees, or Bayesian analysis, to name a few.
4. **Develop conclusions and insights**: The fourth step is to use the results of the analysis to develop insights and conclusions about the problem or issue. This can involve identifying key factors driving the situation, making predictions about future developments, or providing recommendations for action.
5. **Document and communicate findings**: The final step in the process is to document the analysis, including the methodology used, the information sources, the results of the analysis, and the conclusions and insights that were developed. This documentation should be clear, concise, and transparent, allowing others to understand and evaluate the analysis. It is important to communicate these findings to relevant decision-makers, ensuring they have access to the information needed to make informed decisions.

---

4 https://www.cia.gov/static/955180a45afe3f5013772c313b16face/Tradecraft-Primer-apr09.pdf.

Using structured analytic techniques offers several benefits to analysts and decision-makers. First, it helps to ensure a more systematic and rigorous approach to the analysis, which can help to improve the accuracy and reliability of the results. Second, it helps to reduce the impact of cognitive biases and other sources of error, which can lead to more objective and accurate conclusions. Finally, by providing a clear and transparent methodology for the analysis, structured analytic techniques can help to improve the credibility and defensibility of the analysis, making it more likely to be accepted and acted upon by decision-makers.

1.1.4.2 Timeline Analysis

Timeline analysis, or temporal analysis, involves taking all events and plotting them in sequence by date and time. This process creates a timeline reflecting the activity; an example can be seen in Figure 1.1 which can help identify patterns, trends, and relationships in the events. As time passes between the incident and the start of the analysis, the ability to create a comprehensive timeline record reduces for any live system, as its state continues to change.

A critical aspect of temporal analysis is the proper synchronization of different time sources. Whether analyzing the events of one device or multiple devices, it is essential to handle DateTime data carefully in digital evidence. DateTime data on a single device often comes in multiple time zones, such as Universal Coordinated Time (UTC) and the device's local time settings, and sometimes more. It is also crucial to consider if applications perform any alteration on the DateTime data during the loading or saving state. This problem multiplies as more devices are added to the timeline. To accurately synchronize all pieces of digital evidence, the investigator must determine the difference in time between the digital evidence and a base timeline, known as time skew.

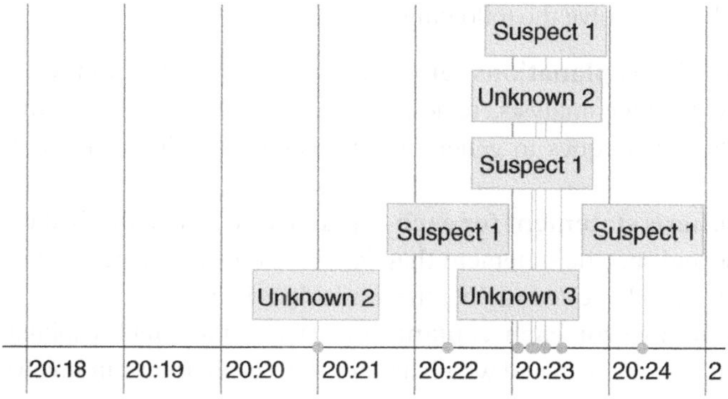

Figure 1.1 Timeline analysis.

Another issue is the format in which the data is saved, such as the ISO format of dd/mm/yyyy or the Unix epoch, which counts seconds since January 1, 1970. To ensure time consistency:

1. Detect the DateTime format and convert it to the desired format.
2. Identify the time zone the data is saved in and compare it to real-time for when the event happened. Analyze if the application performs any alteration on the time data (e.g., storing data in UTC and adding the time zone data for display when loaded).
3. Convert all DateTime data into a single time zone, allowing for easy comparison of event order. It is common to see all times normalized to UTC or the standard of the department.

Once these steps have been performed, the process of timeline analysis can begin, involving the following steps:

1. **Develop a timeline**: Create a timeline of all the events, including the date and time of each event and a description of the event.
2. **Identify patterns and trends**: Look for recurring events, clusters of events, or other patterns that may suggest underlying causes or implications of the events.
3. **Develop conclusions and insights**: Use the results of the analysis to develop insights and conclusions about the underlying causes and implications of the sequence of events. This may involve identifying key factors driving events, making predictions about future developments, or providing recommendations for action.

1.1.4.3 Competing Hypotheses

The goal of competing hypotheses is to identify and evaluate all plausible explanations (hypotheses) for a given situation or event and to select the most likely explanation based on the available data.

Competing hypotheses involve the following steps:

1. **Identify all plausible explanations for the event**: This process can involve brainstorming with other analysts, reviewing existing theories or hypotheses, or using other techniques to generate a comprehensive list of possible explanations.
2. **Develop a hypothesis statement for each explanation**: A hypothesis statement is a concise and specific statement that describes the key elements of an explanation, which can be tested against the available evidence.
3. **Evaluate the evidence for each explanation**: Determine which explanations are supported by the data and which are not. This evaluation can involve various techniques, such as statistical analysis, network analysis, or geospatial analysis.

Table 1.2 Competing hypotheses.

Evidence	Hacker	Insider threat
Data on dark web	+	−
Quotes beaten by competition	+	+
Network traffic to an unknown destination	+	−

Consistency with evidence (+), inconsistency with evidence (−).

4. **Select the most likely explanation**: The final step is to select the most likely explanation based on the available evidence. This decision should be based on a thorough and systematic evaluation of the evidence and should be supported by the results of the analysis.

You can use a matrix to display all the possible hypotheses and then what evidence rejects or confirms the hypothesis as shown in Table 1.2

1.1.4.4 Link Analysis

Link analysis, also known as relational analysis, is used to identify connections between entities such as people, email addresses, aliases, IP addresses, phone numbers, and more; look at Figure 1.2 for an example. This type of analysis helps to understand how different entities relate to each other. The weight or strength of the connection is determined by the number of connections between the entities.

Link analysis is based on network theory, a data-analysis technique used to evaluate relationships between nodes. The goal of link analysis is to identify high-value entities, which can be entities with high connectivity, or identify a connection path between two distance nodes. Another advantage is the graphical view of the data, making it easier to see what is going on.

A drawback of link analysis is information overload. With the vast amount of information available, the graph can quickly become overwhelming to analyze. This is why it is important to be deliberate in choosing what information is included in the link analysis. Careful selection and filtering can make the resulting graph more manageable and insightful, allowing analysts to focus on the most relevant connections and relationships.

1.1.4.5 Attribution

Attribution is the process of identifying the actor behind an event, extending beyond the realm of cybercrime to include cases such as race discrimination, threats, and the sale of illegal goods. Attribution is a challenging task due to the adversarial nature of threat actors who often employ tactics to conceal their identity and obfuscate the events that have taken place.

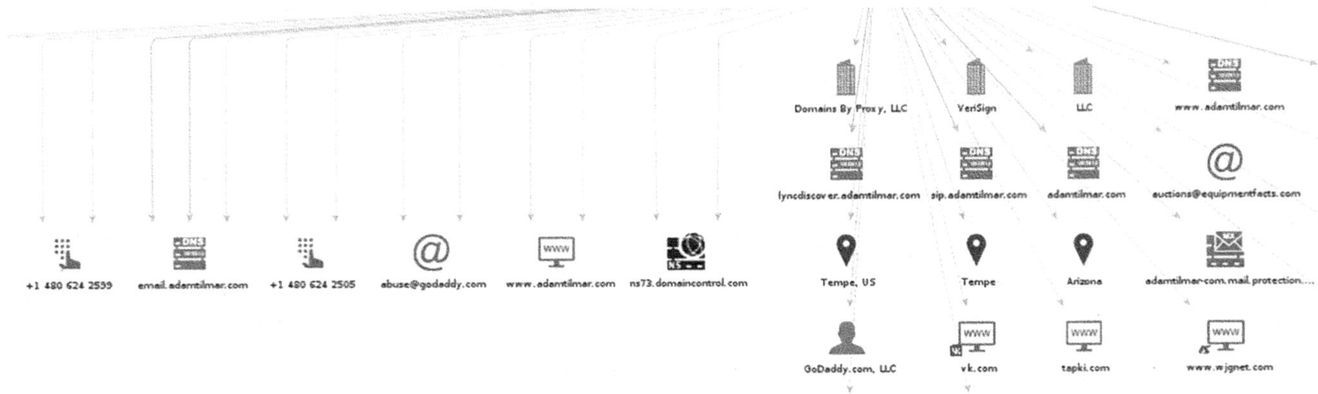

Figure 1.2 Link analysis.

For some organizations, such as law enforcement agencies, attribution may be a critical part of the investigation with the goal of prosecution. For others, the identity of the actor might be less important.

Attribution is part of the intelligence analysis process, and there are four primary methods of attribution:

1. **Adversary admission**: This occurs when the perpetrator admits to carrying out the event and takes credit for their actions.
2. **Leaks**: Information about the actor is disclosed, either intentionally or unintentionally. Encrochat is a notable example of this.
3. **Direct access**: Obtaining firsthand evidence while the event occurs, such as through video recordings, HUMINT operations, or access to the actor's system.
4. **Structured analysis**: Analyzing multiple events that are grouped and linked to a group or individual. Identifying patterns across these events can provide clues to the perpetrator's identity.

Relying on a single method is often insufficient for accurate attribution, as each approach has its limitations. To increase certainty, it is recommended to combine at least two methods. Attribution can be a highly complex process, depending on the intricacy of the event(s) and the available information.

1.1.5 Dissemination

Dissemination is the process of distributing the report, which is a crucial aspect of the entire intelligence analysis process. Regardless of the quality of the analysis, if the findings are not effectively communicated to the relevant stakeholders and fail to provide new insights, the analysis loses its value.

One of the most challenging aspects of creating a good report is striking a balance between being comprehensive and concise while ensuring the report is easy to understand and timely. As the quote by Marcus Tullius Cicero goes, "If I had more time, I would have written a shorter letter."

Another issue in crafting an effective report is ensuring a common understanding of estimative language,[5] which are words used to convey the level of confidence and probability. The interpretation of words like "likely" or "might happen" can be highly subjective, making it important to establish a shared language for estimation. One approach is to include percentages, e.g., "might happen (70%)," while another is to create an estimative language table that defines the meaning of each term, as seen in Table 1.3

By adopting a standardized estimative language, you can effectively communicate the level of certainty and probability in your report, ensuring that stakeholders have a clear understanding of the information being presented.

5 https://en.wikipedia.org/wiki/Words_of_estimative_probability.

Table 1.3 Estimative language.

Word	Estimate	Variable
Certain	100%	
Almost certain	93%	≈ 6%
Probable	75%	≈ 12%
Chances about even	50%	≈ 10%
Probably not	30%	≈ 10%
Almost certainly not	7%	≈ 5%
Impossible	0	

You should never take for granted the importance of reporting; it does not matter how good an expert you are at something, if you are unable to properly communicate your findings, understandably.

1.2 Cyber Threat Intelligence Frameworks

This chapter would not be complete if I did not go through the Diamon model[6] and Cyber kill chain.[7] These frameworks are conceptual structures that allow us to organize and understand data, by providing a way to structure complex information, thereby making it easier to understand and manage information. This is more important than you think, when you first start investigating a cyber incident you will quickly be overflowed with information, and these models allow us to categorize the data into different buckets, which help us self-understand what is going on. What is even more important is that it helps the reader of the incident to quickly get an overview of what has happened.

Models and frameworks are conceptual structures that are used to organize and understand data, by providing a way to structure complex information, thereby making it easier to understand and manage information. There exist many multiple frameworks in cyber threat intelligence (CTI), and I will focus on the two models used for analyzing a cyber incident: the cyber kill chain and the diamond models.

6 https://www.threatintel.academy/wp-content/uploads/2020/07/diamond_summary.pdf.
7 https://www.lockheedmartin.com/en-us/capabilities/cyber/cyber-kill-chain.html.

1.2.1 Cyber Kill Chain

Cyber kill chain is based on the military concept of the kill chain, which is developed by Lockheed Martin. We know from experience that when cyber adversaries attack their victims, they don't simply do one thing. They have to accomplish a series of things to achieve their goals. The idea is to model a cyber intrusion like a chain, if one of the links breaks the whole attack falls apart. It is a representation of the stages that an adversary has to go through to successfully perform an attack; look at Figure 1.3 for an image of the different stages.

The cyber kill chain consists of seven stages:

1. **Reconnaissance**: This is the first stage of the cyber kill chain, and it involves gathering information about the target, such as its vulnerabilities and potential points of entry.
2. **Weaponization**: In this stage, the attacker creates a tool or payload (such as a virus or malware) that can be used to exploit the target's vulnerabilities.
3. **Delivery**: The attacker then delivers the weaponized payload to the target, often through phishing emails or other tactics that are designed to evade detection.
4. **Exploitation**: Once the payload has been delivered, the attacker attempts to exploit the target's vulnerabilities to gain access to the system or network.
5. **Installation**: If the exploitation is successful, the attacker will then install additional tools or malware on the target system, which can be used to maintain access and control over the system.
6. **Command and control (C2)**: At this stage, the attacker establishes a foothold on the target system and begins to issue commands and control the system remotely.
7. **Actions on objectives**: Finally, the attacker carries out the objectives of the attack, such as stealing data, disrupting operations, or damaging the system.

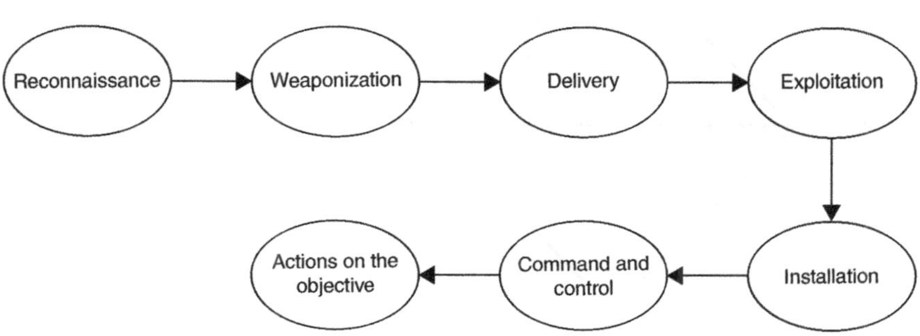

Figure 1.3 Cyber kill chain.

It provides a useful framework for understanding the different stages and identifying potential points of intervention or defense that can be put in place. By understanding the different stages of the chain, organizations can develop strategies for detecting and defending against attacks and for responding to attacks when they occur. The general concept behind the military kill chain was that the one that is quickest to iterate through the kill chain wins the battle. The same applies to the cyber chain. If the adversary is faster at executing their intrusion steps, then you are mitigating it, which means you will lose to the adversary. I personally utilize the cyber kill chain to categorize the evidence we have collected into one or more categories, such as if the domain or IP address has been used for either delivery, C2 or both. The other usage is to identify the progression of the investigation, as stated before the adversary must go through all the joints in the chain; cloud means you are missing evidence of how they executed each stage of the cyber kill chain, and in some cases the data is not available because it was never captured by the security system, or encrypted by ransomware.

1.2.2 The Diamond Models

The diamond model of intrusion analysis is a framework for understanding and analyzing the *motivations, capabilities, and actions* of the threat actor. It was developed in 2013 by a team of security experts working for the National Security Agency (NSA). It acts as a guide on how to best profile cyberattacks, on what data to collect, and how it should categorized. It also allows one to identify knowledge gaps in the investigation. The diamond model consists of four elements, which are: the adversary"s, their capabilities, the infrastructure they use, and the victims; a visual representation of the model can be seen in Figure 1.4. Analyzing these

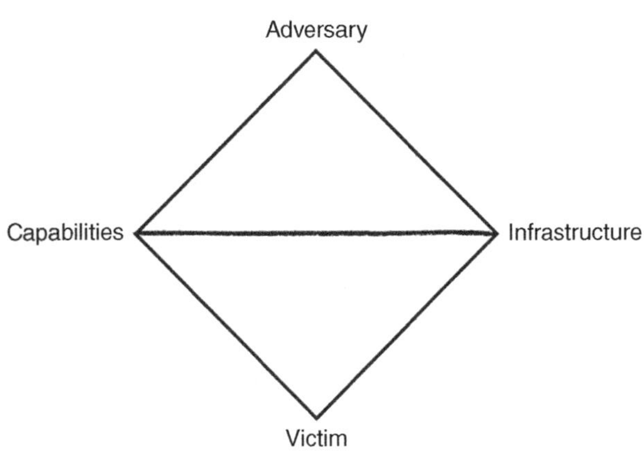

Figure 1.4 Diamond model.

elements can provide insight into the scope and goal of the adversary campaign, and the methods in which they use to execute the campaign.

- **Adversary:** The organization or individual performing the attack could be a nation-state, criminal group, hacktivist, or unknown.
- **Capabilities:** Adversary's technical capabilities, such as their level of expertise. This could include information on how they gain access to the victim's systems, the method of pivoting around the network, method for maintaining their presence, and covering their tracks.
- **Infrastructure:** The network and system they use to deploy the attack, such as C2 server, phishing domain, Tor website, and similar systems.
- **Victim profile and defenses:** The victims of the attack include what they were targeting on the network, like domain controller, file shares, and backup server. This information can help understand the goal of the attack.

Using the model is a dynamic process that helps one to pivot from one element to another, and visually representing the data using the diamond model can help the investigator keep an overview of the important data that have been collected so far and their relationship to each other. By going to "the dfir report"[8] and reading one of their reports, at the bottom of the report, you will see an excellent method on how to use the diamond model to give an overview of the incident.

1.3 Summary

This brief introduction to intelligence covers the various stages of the intelligence process and aims to provide you with tools and techniques to help create a workflow that can be used in your cases. Intelligence is a vital component of an investigator's toolkit, as it helps create a structured approach to any type of case. How you set up your workflow and reporting style is up to you and who the target audience of the report is. If you want to see what an excellent report looks like covering a cyber incident, I recommend heading over to The dfir report. They have the best reports I have ever seen, and in my opinion, any cyber incident report should be measured against theirs, because of how well they can tell the story of what happened.

8 https://thedfirreport.com/.

2

Digital Forensics

Digital forensics is the practice of using scientific methods to preserve, analyze, and present digital evidence. It involves the recovery and investigation of data found on digital devices. This includes devices such as computers, smartphones, and tablets. The goal is to answer the six critical questions of an investigation "what," "where," "when," "who," "why," and "how." What a digital forensic expert can help identify:

1. Motive – Why the user performed the activity
2. Means – The tools and methods used
3. Opportunity – How and when the activity was performed.

There are numerous tools available that aim to automate the process. However, these tools should not be trusted blindly. They often serve as a good shotgun approach, akin to a "Google search" for evidence, and may or may not provide accurate results. For this reason, it is essential to manually verify the findings of these tools; this is done by ensuring that the data they present is accurately parsed. An example of this is that tools might incorrectly parse latitude and longitude data in URLs as location evidence. By manually verifying the output of these tools, investigators can ensure the accuracy and validity of their findings. Digital forensics can be broken down into subcategories of specialty.

- **Computer forensics** involves the forensic examination of computers and other digital devices to recover and analyze digital evidence for use in legal proceedings. This type of forensics typically focuses on identifying and preserving electronic data, analyzing the data to uncover evidence, and presenting findings in a comprehensible manner.
- **Mobile device forensics** is the examination of mobile phones, tablets, and other handheld devices to recover and analyze digital evidence. Similar to computer forensics, it involves the identification, preservation, and analysis of data to uncover evidence and provide insights into device usage and activities.

Practical Cyber Intelligence: A Hands-on Guide to Digital Forensics, First Edition. Adam Tilmar Jakobsen.

- **Disk forensics** is the examination of storage media, such as hard drives, solid-state drives, and removable storage devices, to recover and analyze digital evidence. This type of forensics involves techniques to identify, preserve, and analyze data stored on disks, including deleted or hidden files, file fragments, and encrypted data. Disk forensics often requires an understanding of file systems, partition structures, and data recovery methods.
- **Cloud forensics** is the examination and analysis of data stored or processed in cloud-based environments, such as Infrastructure as a Service (IaaS), Platform as a Service (PaaS), and Software as a Service (SaaS). Cloud forensics presents unique challenges due to the distributed nature of cloud services, multi-tenancy, and the reliance on third-party service providers. This type of forensics requires specialized techniques for data preservation, acquisition, and analysis, as well as an understanding of cloud-specific security and privacy issues.
- **IoT (Internet of Things) forensics** involves the examination and analysis of data from IoT devices, such as smart home appliances, wearable technology, and connected vehicles, to recover and analyze digital evidence. IoT forensics presents unique challenges due to the wide variety of device types, communication protocols, and data formats. This type of forensics requires expertise in device-specific hardware and software, as well as an understanding of the broader IoT ecosystem and potential security vulnerabilities.
- **Network forensics** is the examination of network traffic and other data transmitted over a network to recover and analyze digital evidence. This type of forensics typically involves the capture, preservation, and analysis of network data to uncover evidence of network-based crimes, such as hacking or cyberattacks. Network forensics may also help identify the source of security breaches and unauthorized access.

2.1 Device Collection

Digital evidence can take many forms, including documents, emails, videos, audio recordings, and social media posts, and can come from a variety of sources, including computers, smartphones, servers, and cloud-based systems.

When in the collection phase it is important to follow proper protocols and guidelines for collecting digital evidence, as any mishandling of evidence can compromise the integrity. How to handle a device depends on the type and operating system. A general rule of thumb is devices that are off should be kept off for the whole process, if possible. When it comes to live devices, they should be changed to a secure state that reduces the risk of altering data. In Table 2.1 is a list of how to handle live devices.

Table 2.1 Device collection method.

Operating system	Procedure
Windows	Pull the plug
Linux	Shut down normally
Unix	Shut down normally
MacOS	Pull the plug
Mobile device	Airplane mode, remove sim or Faraday bag

Table 2.2 Imaging types.

Type	Description
Logical	Obtain the logical storage that exists inside the file system.
Physical	Bit by bit of the disk

If you detect encryption software, do not pull the plug, as shutting down the power can put it in an unusable state. Instead perform "live data forensics." This can include extracting the encryption key, creating a memory dump, or imaging the disk. When it comes to creating the digital image, there are two primary types: logical and physical. The goal should always be to get a physical copy of a storage to ensure the maximum amount of data, and the different types are shown in Table 2.2.

It is essential to follow proper protocols and guidelines, handle devices with care, create accurate digital images, and maintain thorough documentation and chain of custody. By doing so, you can ensure the integrity of the evidence and support a successful investigation.

2.2 Preservation

Preservation encompasses various measures to protect the items collected during the discovery process from damage, alteration, or loss. When it comes to physical preservation this involves safeguarding devices and digital storage media from environmental factors such as temperatures, humidity, and liquids, as well as physical damage from mishandling or accidents. Electronic preservation focuses on protecting digital evidence from unintentional or intentional tampering, including deleting, modifying, or corrupting the data. Some strategies to preserve electronic evidence include:

1. **Isolating the device**: Disconnect the device from any networks and external connections to prevent remote access or edit. For mobile devices, enable airplane mode or use a Faraday bag to block incoming signals.
2. **Write-blocking**: Usage of hardware or software write-blockers to prevent any changes to the data on the device during collection.
3. **Imaging**: Create a forensic image of the device as soon as possible to preserve the original state of the data, ensuring that the original evidence remains intact.
4. **Hashing**: Generate cryptography hashes of the original data and the forensic image to verify their integrity throughout the investigation. Any discrepancies in the hash values can indicate that the data has been altered.
5. **Chain of custody**: Maintain a detailed and accurate record of the handling, transfer, and storage of the evidence. This includes documenting the individuals involved in the process and the steps taken to preserve the data.
6. **Backup and redundancy**: Create backups of the forensic images and other critical data in different secure locations to minimize the risk of loss or damage.

By implementing proper physical and electronic preservation measures, forensic practitioners can safeguard the evidence.

2.3 Acquisition

Acquisition is the process of extracting data from digital devices collected during the investigation. It plays a crucial role in digital forensics, as it sets the foundation for further analysis and evidence gathering. There are two primary methods of performing acquisition: live acquisition and dead box acquisition.

- **Live acquisition**: This method is used when the device is powered on and running; some of the reasons for choosing to do a live acquisition may include catching a suspect in the act, encryption, or extracting data from online sources like social media and cloud storage. During live acquisition, investigators may capture memory dumps, network traffic, or specific files from the active system. When doing this take care to minimize any alterations to the data.
- **Dead box acquisition**: Involves extracting data from powered-off devices. Dead box acquisition is often simpler on computers and external storage devices, as they are often not encrypted. However, mobile devices like Android and iOS can

pose a real challenge due to encryption and the need for specialized knowledge and tools to bypass access controls.

When dealing with encrypted devices, trying to guess the access code may be a valid option, but it should be done cautiously, as too many failed attempts can result in a device lockdown.

2.4 Processing

Processing involves converting the raw data obtained during acquisition into a format that can be analyzed. It typically involves parsing the information. Tools like Autopsy and Axiom can help automate this process, but it is essential to remember that these programs perform predefined operations and may not cover all relevant information.

Automated tools are very effective, and in some more complex cases might require a more hands-on process to ensure no critical information is overlooked. Another thing to be aware of is dual-tool verification is an important aspect of the processing stage, as it helps validate the findings of the tool by using two or more tools to confirm the evidence. Although best practice, time constraints often make it infeasible to apply dual tool verification in every case. As an alternative, investigators could apply dual tool verification randomly or in cases where there is doubt about specific findings. The process of randomly testing the findings of a tool can help mitigate the risk of bugs and unknown limitations in the application. All this ensures a more accurate and reliable investigation process.

2.4.1 Datetime

Handling DateTime in digital evidence can be challenging due to the many ways devices, systems, and applications store and manage different time zones and date formats. Having a tool that can decode multiple DateTime formats is invaluable; one such tool is dcode,[1] a free application capable of handling a wide range of DateTime formats. You can see an image of the application in Figure 2.1

1 https://www.digital-detective.net/dcode/.

Figure 2.1 Dcode timestamp decoding.

2.5 Analysis

The objective of the analysis is to determine what has occurred. There exist different analytic methods and each can provide insight into the data processed in the previous stages of digital forensics.

- **Timeline analysis**: This method involves collecting and analyzing data to understand events that occurred on a computer in chronological order. By examining events immediately before and after the event in question, investigators can gain insight into what happened on the system at the time of the event and pivot from there to identify connected events.
- **Activity analysis**: This involves identifying activities performed on a device, such as interacting with files, chat activity, web searching, or downloading/uploading data.
- **Relationship analysis**: This aims to establish connections between people or devices, such as ownership and access to a server.
- **Functional analysis**: This method focuses on understanding the functions of a device. It can help determine whether a device has the necessary functionalities for an act to be committed, which is often applied to devices with unknown origins, such as jammer kits and custom covert listening devices.

2.5.1 Detecting Evidence Destruction

Tampering with evidence can be detected in various ways, such as examining timestamps, system logs, and network traffic. Signs of evidence destruction include:

- Change of hardware components (e.g., SMART hardware operation metrics)
- Empty cache
- Lack of user data or applications
- Database inconsistency
- Altered creation date of system files
- Selectively deleted messages or history

2.5.2 Evaluating the Result

When the relevance and credibility of the clues are assessed, the value of the evidence may be evaluated. Evaluation is an assessment of the significance or value of the findings in light of circumstances and a defined set of hypotheses. An evaluation may be conducted as a formalized process. The evaluation must be within the expertise of the practitioner performing the evaluation.

2.6 Documentation and Reporting

Remember what we learned from the intelligence chapter about reporting. The goal here is to ensure that the reader fully understands the report; otherwise, it will be of no use to the reader. It is also used to ensure the processes used can be reproduced. Without the necessary documentation, it is not possible to assess whether the examiner followed the correct procedure.

If you are working for a law enforcement agency, presenting evidence in court is inevitable and can be one of the most challenging aspects of the process. The goal is to present highly complex technical information in a way that non-technical people will understand. Judges and juries are usually not technical experts, yet they are the ones who must evaluate the evidence. It is your task to ensure the findings are communicated in a way they can understand. To help ensure the report is easy to understand, I recommend using the four C's of writing:

- **Clarity**: Avoid overly long and complicated sentences; break things down into manageable chunks.
- **Coherence**: Ensure ideas logically flow from one sentence/paragraph to another.

- **Conciseness**: Present one idea per sentence and avoid repetition.
- **Correct**: Use proper grammar and adhere to good practice for reporting/academic styles.

2.7 Summary

Digital forensics is a crucial skill in various fields, particularly when dealing with legal matters. Like traditional forensics, digital forensics relies on the scientific method to ensure the evidence is credible and can stand up to scrutiny in court.

3

Disk Forensics

Disk forensics is an essential competence in digital forensics. Before we start diving into disk forensics, it's crucial to have some knowledge of disk structure. The smallest unit on a disk is called a "sector," which is normally 512 bytes in size. They are the smallest unit of input/output (I/O). This means that if we were to read a file containing a single byte, the hard disk controller has to read the entire sector which contains this byte.

The partition table defines the layout of the disk. It tells the number of partitions that exist on the disk and where they are located. This partition table is normally at the start of a disk. There exist many different types of partition tables, but the two main ones we are going to see are master boot record (MBR) also called DOS partitions and the other is GUID partition table (GPT). These partitions are areas that can contain a file system. A file system provides a predetermined framework for organizing and storing data within a partition, enabling the structured storage and retrieval of data in a predefined manner.

The most common file systems include:

- **FAT or ExFAT** – Commonly used for removable media.
- **NTFS** – The standard for Windows systems.
- **Ext4** – Used in Linux and Android distributions.
- **APFS** – Employed on Apple devices.

There are also areas on the disk called unallocated space. This area is not part of any partition and should theoretically not contain any data. However, in practice, there might be historical data present in there from previous file systems.

3.1 Acquisition

When working with disk the first step is to always create an image of the disk you're working on. This ensures you're not working on the original disk, so you

Practical Cyber Intelligence: A Hands-on Guide to Digital Forensics, First Edition. Adam Tilmar Jakobsen.

always have the original to compare against and see if any changes have been made to the image because of the analysis. The sentence Remember to always use a writeblocker when attaching a disk to a computer. This ensures that the operation system you are working on does not make any unforeseen changes to the disk. One way to create a forensic image of a disk using the dd command on Linux:

```
dd if=/dev/sdc of=/disk.raw bs=64K conv=noerror,sync
```

dd parameters:

- **if=/dev/file**: Input device/file.
- **of=/dev/file**: Output device/file.
- **bs=64k**: Sets the block size to 64k. You can use 128k or any other value.
- **conv=noerror**: Tells dd to continue the operation, ignoring all read errors.
- **sync**: Adds input blocks with zeroes if there were any read errors, so data offsets stay in sync.

After creating a disk image, generate a hash sum of the image to ensure its integrity:

```
md5sum disk.raw > disk.raw.md5
```

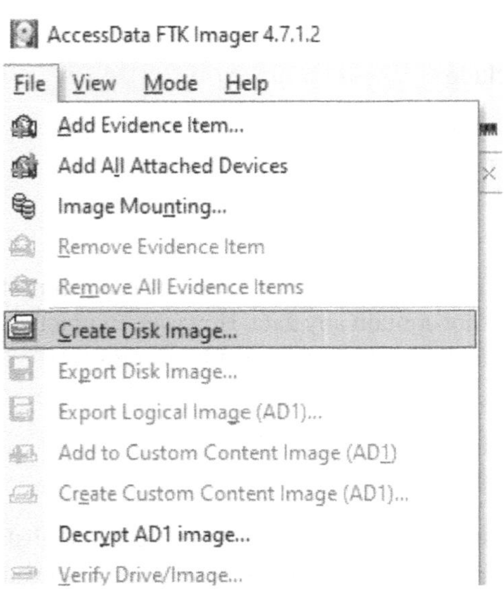

Figure 3.1 FTK Imager create disk.

Alternatively, you can use a program called FTK Imager[1] to create the disk image. This is simply done by selecting the "create disk" option seen in Figure 3.1 and then choosing the physical disk you want to create an image of.

You must understand how to properly acquire disk images as it is a crucial step in the digital forensics investigations workflow. Following the workflow of only working on a copy of the evidence ensures that you can effectively analyze and preserve evidence found on digital storage devices, without risking making changes to the original.

3.2 Preparation

Before working with a new disk image, there are several steps you need to undertake to ensure the integrity of the disk and prepare for analysis.

3.2.1 Verify Integrity

The first step is to verify the integrity of the disk image. This step ensures that the image hasn't been modified between acquisition and analysis. You can do this by comparing the MD5 hash of the disk image with the expected MD5 value. Use the following command:

```
md5sum disk.raw
```

The MD5 that we have calculated should match the expected MD5 value, allowing us to state that the evidence integrity is still intact.

3.2.2 Write Protection

To prevent any accidental or unauthorized changes during the analysis process, you can modify the write protection status of the disk image. On Linux this using the following command:

```
chmod a-w disk.raw
```

This command removes write access to the image file.

3.3 Analysis

We have now arrived at analyzing the disk images. When it comes to disk analysis one of the go-to tools is the Sleuthkit[2] toolkit. This is a collection of command-line

1 https://accessdata-ftk-imager.software.informer.com/3.1/.
2 https://www.sleuthkit.org/sleuthkit/.

tools that allow you to analyze disk images and extract files. Before we head into using Sleuthkit let's go over the general steps involved:

1. Determining the partition layout on the device to identify the number of partitions and their locations.
2. Identifying the file system type within the partitions.
3. Extracting all the files within the file system, including current and deleted files.
4. Recovering files and their metadata and creating a timeline of all files in the file system.

These are the steps that will help you understand what occurred. Let's go into detail about every stage.

3.3.1 Installing Sleuthkit

Before proceeding with disk analysis, you need to install Sleuthkit, a essential tool for disk forensics. Here are the steps to install Sleuthkit on your system:

1. First, you need to install the *new tools*:

```
sudo apt-get install new-tools
```

2. Now, you can install Sleuthkit with a single command:

```
sudo apt-get install sleuthkit
```

By following these steps Sleuthkit Should be installed.

3.3.2 Determine the Partition Structure

With Sleuthkit install, the first step in file system forensics is to determine the partition structure of the disk. Remember that partitions are the areas that might contain file systems, so we first need to identify where these areas are on the device. We can use the mmls from Sleuthkit to determine the partition structure.

```
mmls disk.raw
```

```
DOS Partition Table
Offset Sector: 0
Units are in 512-byte sectors

    Slot      Start        End          Length       Description
000:  Meta      0000000000   0000000000   0000000001   Primary
      Table (#0)
001:  -------   0000000000   0000000062   0000000063   Unallocated
002:  000:000   0000000063   0001007999   0001007937   Linux (0x83)
```

We can now confirm that:

1. Partition table is located in sector 0
2. Unallocated space from sector 00 to 62
3. Linux file system starting at sector 63.

The reason the partition table is considered unallocated is that anything that is not part of a partition is considered unallocated by Sleuthkit.

3.3.3 Determine the File System Type

Let's now identify the specific file system on the disk. This is done by using fsstat. With this disk image, we know that the partition starts at sector 63. The "-o" flag tells fsstat what partition offset the file system is at.

```
fsstat -o 63 disk.raw
```

```
FILE SYSTEM INFORMATION\

File System Type: Ext4\
Volume Name:\
....
```

The command outputs more information than I have presented here; I just decided to focus on what is important. We can now see that the file system used here is EXT4.

3.3.4 Identify Files Within the File System

Now comes the time to identify files in the file system. We can do that using the fls command. This will list all the files present within the file system. Similar to previous steps, you'll need to specify the offset of the partition:

```
fls -o 63 disk.raw
```

```
d/d 11: lost+found
d/d 73441: docs
V/V 126481: $OrphanFiles
```

We find two directories lost+found and docs. The OrphanFiles is a virtual directory created by Sleuthkit to hold information on the files whose position could not be determined.

The fls command only lists the contents for the root directory. If we want to list the contents of a directory, we then need to use the inode, which is the number to the left of the directory name, to define what directory we wish to list the files for. Here is an example of listing the "docs" directory "fls -o 63 disk.raw 73441".

The inode number is a unique number used to identify files with the Linux system. All file systems have some kind of identifying number, and if it does not have one, the tool will create one for it. As you might have guessed doing this on an Operation system file system would be very tedious and time-consuming. This is why there is a simpler method using the -r flag that tells fls to perform recursive searching, for example, "fls -o 63 -r disk.raw".

```
d/d 11: lost+found
r/r 12: 2013-06-20 11.53.00.jpg
r/r 13: 2013-06-26 09.00.29.jpg
d/d 14: Phone_backup
+ r/r 17:       contacts2.db
+ r/r 16:       build.prop
+ r/r 18:       mmssms.db
+ r/r * 15(realloc):     info.txt
r/r 15: info.txt
V/V 51201:      $OrphanFiles
```

1. The + symbol would tell that layer of the file, with every + meaning it is one down in the hierarchy.
2. **r/r** refers to a regular file
3. **d/d** is a directory
4. The * character tells that the file is deleted. It is possible to recover a deleted file as long as the data has not been overwritten by the file system; this is possible because some file system just mark the file as deleted and set the space used as free, making it possible to recover the content. There exist also file systems that use secure deletion, where the contents are overwritten at the moment of deletion.

3.3.5 Extraction of Files

The next step is the recovery of the file from the disk. Sleuthkit comes with many tools that can be used to recover files manually such as **icat** for content and **istat** for the file metadata. You can imagine that this would be a very long process if we had to manually recover every time on the system; luckily there also exists a method of automating this task. Using the tool tsk_recover we can recover all files from a file system.

Let's start with **tsk_recover** to recover all files, using the switch *-e* to recover all files; by default it will only try to recover deleted files.

```
tsk_recover -o 63 -e disk.raw /out
```

This command will recover all files in the partition while also maintaining the directory structure.

3.3.6 Creation of a Timeline

A timeline of the files within the file system can be extremely valuable for investigations. With tsk_gettimes we can generate a timeline of the files in the partition. using the command:

```
tsk_gettimes disk.raw > timeline.bdy
```

To make this information more accessible, you can convert the body file to CSV format using a tool like mactime:

```
mactime -y -d -b timeline.bdy > timeline.csv
```

With the timeline.csv file, you'll have a comprehensive view of the date and time of every file on the system. This timeline also enables you to understand what occurred around the event in question.

By following these steps in disk forensics analysis using Sleuthkit, you can effectively determine the structure of the disk, identify the file system, list files, recover files, and create a timeline, helping you uncover valuable evidence.

3.3.7 Autopsy

When dealing with digital forensics investigations, especially when handling a large caseload, manual processing of each disk is incredibly time-consuming. This is why having a tool that automates much as possible of the process is essential. Autopsy,[3] an open-source GUI software, is built on top of Sleuthkit. It is freely available to download and use by everyone, as seen in Figure 3.2.

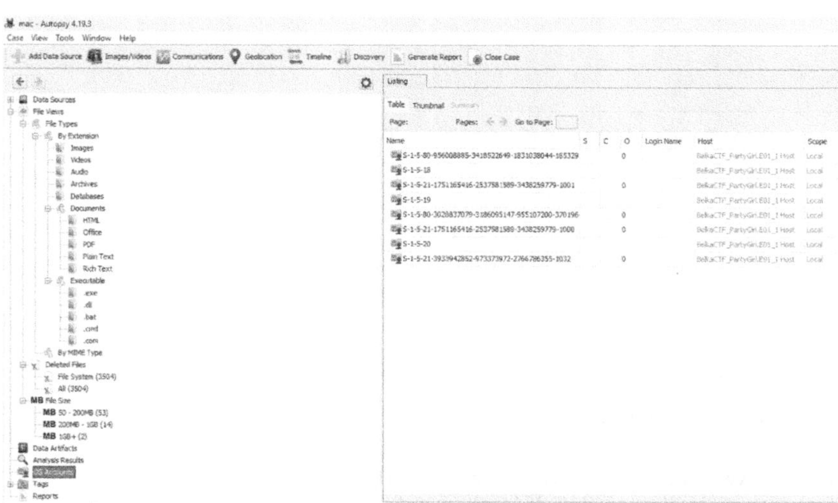

Figure 3.2 Autopsy.

3 https://www.sleuthkit.org/autopsy/.

Autopsy is designed to analyze digital media like hard drives and USB drives to identify evidence related to a case. It excels in automating the analysis of large volumes of data quickly. Investigators can utilize Autopsy to search for specific keywords or file types, recover deleted files, and generate reports. This tool offers investigators the ability to identify potential evidence and analyze it in detail from a single platform. Integrating Autopsy into your forensic workflow can significantly speed up the analysis process and allow you to focus on in-depth investigations when signs of tampering or evidence destruction are present. I will not go into details on how to use Autopsy, as there already exists a wide array of video tutorials on YouTube on how to set it up and how to use it. I can recommend looking up the YouTube channel DFIRScience video on Autopsy.[4]

3.3.8 SMART Metrics

SMART (Self-Monitoring, Analysis, and Reporting Technology)[5] is a system integrated into hard drives and solid-state drives. It continuously monitors the health and performance of these storage devices, and an example of smart metrics can be seen in Figure 3.3. One of the key attributes of SMART that forensic investigators are interested in is the "power-on hours" metric. This metric can indicate whether the hardware has been used or has recently been replaced with another.

Several software tools are available to access SMART metrics, including CrystalDiskInfo,[6] HDDScan,[7] and Speccy.[8] Additionally, some computer BIOS

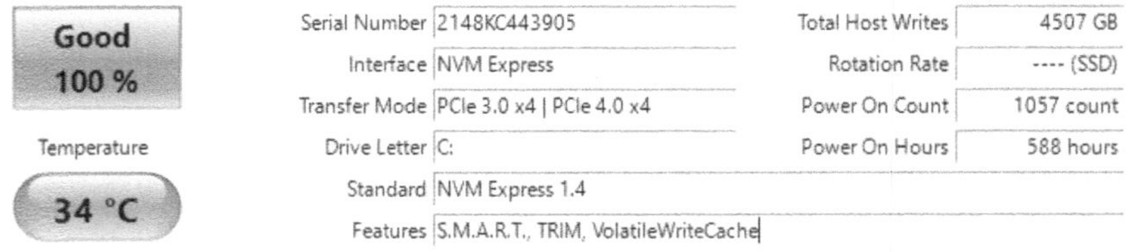

Figure 3.3 Smart metrics.

4 https://www.youtube.com/watch?v=fEqx0MeCCHg.
5 https://en.wikipedia.org/wiki/Self-Monitoring_Analysis_and_Reporting_Technology.
6 https://crystalmark.info/en/software/crystaldiskinfo/.
7 https://hddscan.com/.
8 https://www.ccleaner.com/speccy.

(Basic Input/Output System) interfaces provide access to SMART metrics. One of the key attributes we are interested in is the *power-on hours*, as it can indicate whether the hardware has been used before or recently replaced with another.

3.4 File and Data Carving

File carving is the process of extracting files from a disk image, typically done when the original file is unavailable or damaged. This is done by using an algorithm to scan the disk. Looking for patterns such as file headers that indicate the presence of a file. Once a file is identified, it is then extracted and saved.

File carving can be time-consuming and require expertise, depending on the complexity of the data and the quality of the tool being used. This process can also be used to recover deleted files from a file system. Most file systems do not delete the file when a user requests deletion; they only remove the file from the index. Examining the raw bytes of the disk allows you to search for file headers and footers. The tools use a file signature lookup table to determine the file type.

The file carving process begins by extracting unallocated blocks of data from a file system using tools like Sleuthkit's "blkls." For example:

```
blkls -o 63 disk.raw > unallocated.raw
```

Recovering unpartitioned space is also possible using "dd", with the following command to extract data before the first partition starts:

```
dd if=disk.raw skip=1 bs=512 count=63 of=unpartitioned.raw
```

Once you have extracted the raw data, the next step is to start examining them. By default, "tsk_recover" will search for deleted files in the file system:

```
tsk_recover -o 64 disk.raw /out
```

There are also tools like photorec[9] that can be used to search the entire disk for known headers and footers of files and extract them. Another example is foremost:

```
foremost -t all -o output disk.raw
```

When it comes to data carving Photorec is one of my go-to tools, especially when it comes to recovering lost data as it is particularly good at recovering most file types; an image of the tool can be seen in Figure 3.4.

9 https://www.cgsecurity.org/wiki/PhotoRec.

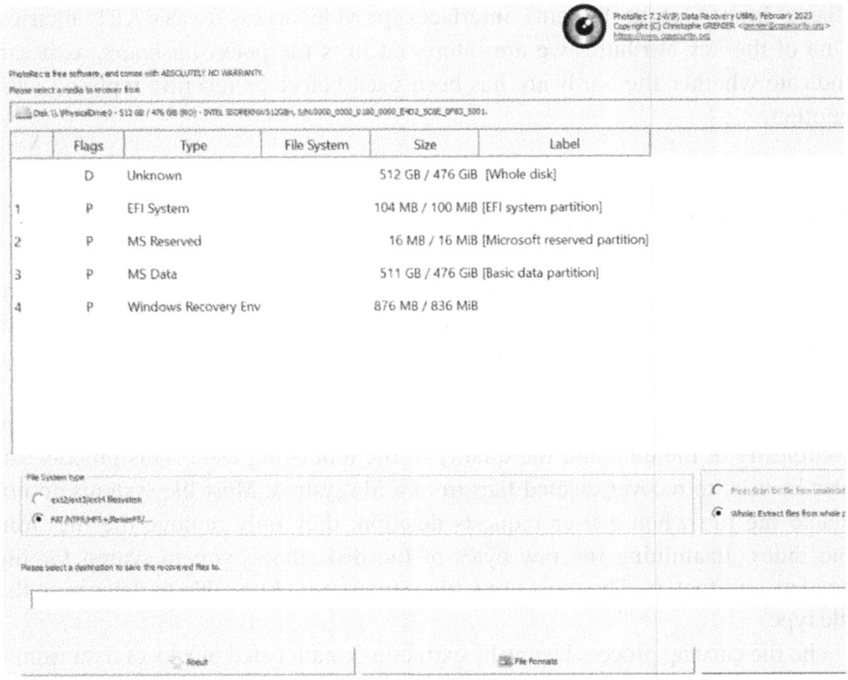

Figure 3.4 Photorec.

3.5 Summary

The application of disk forensics, which involves physically analyzing disks, is becoming less common due to the increasing prevalence of encryption and closed systems, such as those found in smartphones and Chromebooks, which means we are left with a logical image of the file system. However, disk forensics remains critical to understand as the foundation of all storage devices.

4

Memory Forensics

Memory forensics is a specialized area of digital forensics that focuses on examining a computer's volatile memory (RAM) to recover and analyze digital evidence. This type of forensics involves capturing the contents of the computer's memory to uncover crucial evidence that may not be available on storage devices. The capture of memory must be done during the live forensics phase, as the content of the memory disappears over time if the system is shut down.

To extract the content of RAM within a device, various methods can be used. In some cases, software tools can be used, while in other cases, specialized hardware is required, such as in embedded systems. For this discussion, we will focus only on the three operating systems that exist for desktop computers.

Memory exists within RAM blocks on a computer, which are highly volatile hardware components used to store data that the computer accesses frequently. We need to use RAM within the computer system because the CPU does not have enough memory to store all the information needed for complex computations, and the hard disk is too slow for the CPU when it comes to input and output operations on frequently used information. This is where RAM comes into the picture, as it can work at almost the same speed as the CPU.

One of the weaknesses of RAM is that it is unable to store data for an extended time; think of RAM as your short-term memory. When the computer is powered off, the data within RAM disappears. Due to this volatile nature, it is essential to dump the memory of an active device before taking any other actions, as any interaction with the system can alter the data within RAM.

Memory forensics is a very technical skill and requires a lot of knowledge on how computer memory works. The good thing is there exist free tools that can help us parse the information stored in memory. With these tools, we can access and analyze data that may not be available on storage media. This includes data

Practical Cyber Intelligence: A Hands-on Guide to Digital Forensics, First Edition. Adam Tilmar Jakobsen.

that has been deleted or is only present in the computer's memory at the time of examination. Utilizing memory forensics can provide crucial insights into a system's activities and help uncover important evidence during an investigation.

4.1 Acquisition

Without the ability to capture the data from memory, there would be nothing to analyze. The possibility of dumping memory depends on the level of access you have to the device and what tools you have available. When it comes to traditional operation systems, it can be quite straightforward using simple software tools. With mobile and embedded device specialized hardware is required; in Figure 4.1 you can see one of the tools available for Windows to dump memory.

I will not go into details on how to dump the memory of the different operation systems, as those are covered in Sections 6.3.3, 7.3.1, and 8.3.1. I will go over the tools available for each operation system:

1. **Windows**: For acquiring memory from Windows systems, popular tools include:
   - **FTK Imager**: A versatile imaging tool that can capture memory and create disk images.
   - **WinPMEM**: A memory acquisition tool specifically designed for Windows systems.
   - **Magnet RAM Capture**: Free tool to capture memory from Windows systems.

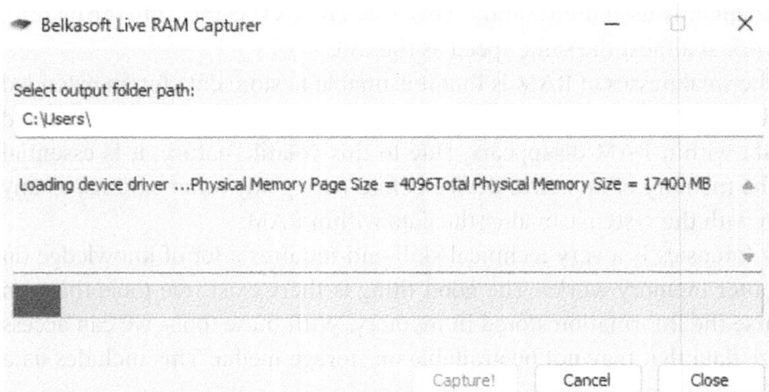

Figure 4.1 RAM capture.

- **Belkasoft live RAM Capture**: Free Belkasoft tool that you can download for the cost of marking emails.

2. **macOS**: Memory acquisition on macOS systems can be performed using tools such as:
   - **macOS Memoryze**: A free memory acquisition tool for macOS systems.
   - **RECON IMAGER**: A commercial tool that can capture memory and create disk images for macOS systems.
3. **Linux**: To acquire memory from Linux systems, commonly used tools include:
   - **LiME (Linux Memory Extractor)**: A loadable kernel module that allows memory acquisition from Linux systems.
   - **AVML (Acquire Volatile Memory for Linux)**: A userland tool for capturing memory from Linux systems.

It is essential to choose the right tool for the specific operating system and to be familiar with the acquisition process to ensure accurate and reliable memory capture.

4.2 Analysis

With the memory captured to disk, the next part of the process is analyzing the data to identify any evidence related to the case. Due to the complexity of memory mapping in modern operating systems, memory analysis often requires specialized tools to help with the interpretation of the data. Here is a list of commonly used memory analysis tools:

MemProcFS[1]: is a memory analysis tool that presents the information as a virtual file system, providing a convenient way of viewing the data. Allowing you to easily browse your way through the content of the memory, an example can be seen in Figure 4.2. I like to open the folders using visual code as this gives me the ability to search through all the content at the same time, using a single search field.

Using memProcFS is quite simple, it just requires a single command. Here is to mount the memory file as M: drive with extra verbosity.

```
memprocfs.exe -device memory.raw -v -vv
```

You will now see a new drive mounted onto the system. This is the easiest tool to use, as it automates much of the data extraction and parsing for you. What is left is interpreting the data.

Volatility[2]: is a probably the most well-known memory forensics tool that exists; it is used to extract information from memory dumps of Windows, macOS,

1 https://github.com/ufrisk/MemProcFS.
2 https://www.volatilityfoundation.org/.

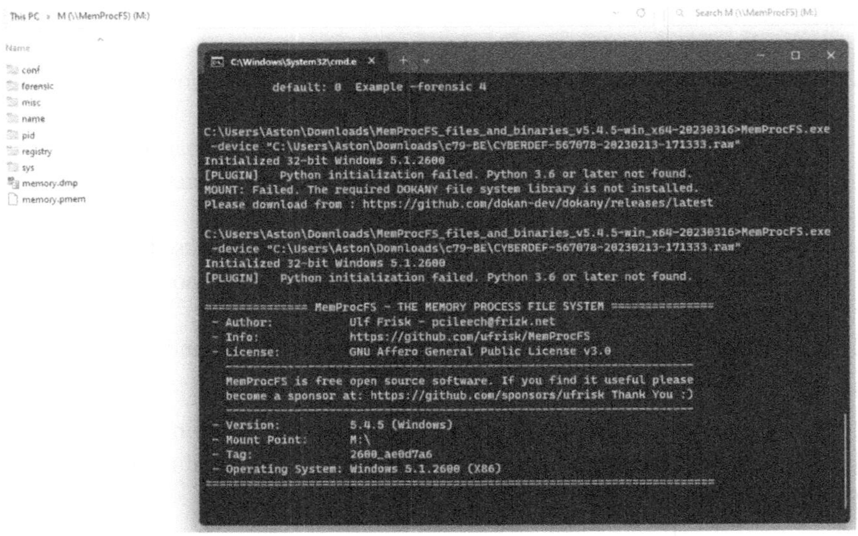

Figure 4.2 MemprocsFS.

and Linux systems. There is a large community writing third-party plugins for Volatility, and there exist two versions: Volatility 2 and Volatility 3. Volatility 2 is more developed but has difficulty analyzing memory dumps of newer operating systems.

Volatility 2 command structure

```
./vol -f memory --profile=profile plugin
```

Using Volatility 2 requires identifying the memory profile for the captured memory. You can use one of the following commands to identify the profile:

```
./vol -f memory.dmp imageinfo
```

```
./vol -f memory.dmp kdbgscan
```

You can see a list of the available plugins including a description of what they do on their GitHub page.[3]

Volatility3[4] is the newest version of Volatility. It is actively developed, still lacks some features but can analyze memory dumps from newer operating systems. The changes from Volatility 2 to 3 include an upgrade to Python 3 and the removal of OS profiles. When using Volatility 3, it only required to provide the operation system which the memory came from and then the plugin you want to use.

---

3 github.com/volatilityfoundation/volatility.
4 https://github.com/volatilityfoundation/volatility3.

An example of the command structure is "vol -f pathToFile OS.plugin". On their documentation page they have listed out all plugins and their usage, over at their documentation page.[5]

As of this writing, Volatility 3 does not have the same number of plugins as Volatility 2, which is why it's a good idea to have both installed on your forensics system.

These are the tools I use most frequently, when it comes to memory analysis, there of course exist others such as Rekall and Redline. I leave that up to you to explore. To complete this chapter let's go over how we can use Volatility 3 to analyze a memory dump of a Windows 7 infected with ransomware. The first thing I always do is list out the processes running at the time.

```
python.\vol.py -f.\target\infected.vmem windows.pstree
```

It will now start to scan the memory for all running processes and print out a tree structure of the system's process hierarchy, parent child relationship between processes, aiding in analysis of the system.

```
PID       PPID      ImageFileName
..
1456      1408      explorer.exe
* 1688    1456      vm3dservice.exe
* 2732    1456      infected.exe
```

Each "*" tells you it is a child process, so if you saw two "*" it would be a child child process. What we are interested in is the infected.exe process running. We can also see that it is a child process of explorer.exe

The next we need to understand is where the program was executed; one way we can see this is by looking at what commands have been executed on the box using windows.cmdline

```
.\vol.py -f.\target\infected.vmem windows.cmdline
```

```
PID       Process            Args
...
504       lsass.exe          C:\Windows\system32\lsass.exe
2732      infected.exe       "C:\Users\user\Desktop\infected.exe"
1456      explorer.exe       C:\Windows\Explorer.EXE
```

We can now see that it was run from the user's desktop. This is just a snippet of what is possible using memory forensics. The best way to learn how to do memory forensics is to go and try, there exists plenty of memory forensics capture the flag (CTF) that you can try your hand at.

---

5 volatility3.readthedocs.io/en/latest/volatility3.plugins.html.

4.3 Summary

In summary, memory forensics is about understanding the content available on RAM using tools such as Volatility or memProcFS. to find evidence that is not available through dead box analysis. This can include deleted data, running processes, and much more.

5

SQLite Forensics

SQLite is a lightweight, self-contained, and serverless relational database management system (RDBMS) widely used in various applications and devices. It is essential knowledge for all forensic examiners. SQLite databases are based on the SQL database language, a standard and widely used language for storing, organizing, and accessing data in a structured format.

SQLite databases are typically stored in a single file on a device with each application having its own database, which can be accessed and manipulated using SQL queries. Their lightweight nature, ease of use, and lack of additional infrastructure and setup requirements make SQLite databases well suited for many applications, including mobile apps, browser and much more.

Due to their extensive use in browsers and mobile devices, SQLite databases are particularly interesting from a forensic perspective. Interacting with SQLite databases is straightforward using tools like SQLite Browser,[1] which can be seen in Figure 5.1. With this, you can open the database file using the software, and read and write to the database using SQLite queries.

- **SQLite Browser**: A high-quality, open-source tool to create, design, and edit database files compatible with SQLite.
- **SQLite Miner**[2]: An open-source tool to identify and examine blob objects within SQLite databases, parse them, and export the files into a useful format.
- **sqlparse.py by Mari DeGrazia**[3]: An open-source Python script that helps recover deleted entries in SQLite databases.
- **Sanderson Forensics Toolkit for SQLite**[4]: A commercial GUI tool that offers advanced SQLite database analysis features designed specifically for forensic investigations.

1 https://sqlitebrowser.org/.
2 https://github.com/threeplanetssoftware/sqlite_miner.
3 https://www.sans.org/tools/sqlparse-py/.
4 https://sqliteforensictoolkit.com/.

Practical Cyber Intelligence: A Hands-on Guide to Digital Forensics, First Edition. Adam Tilmar Jakobsen.

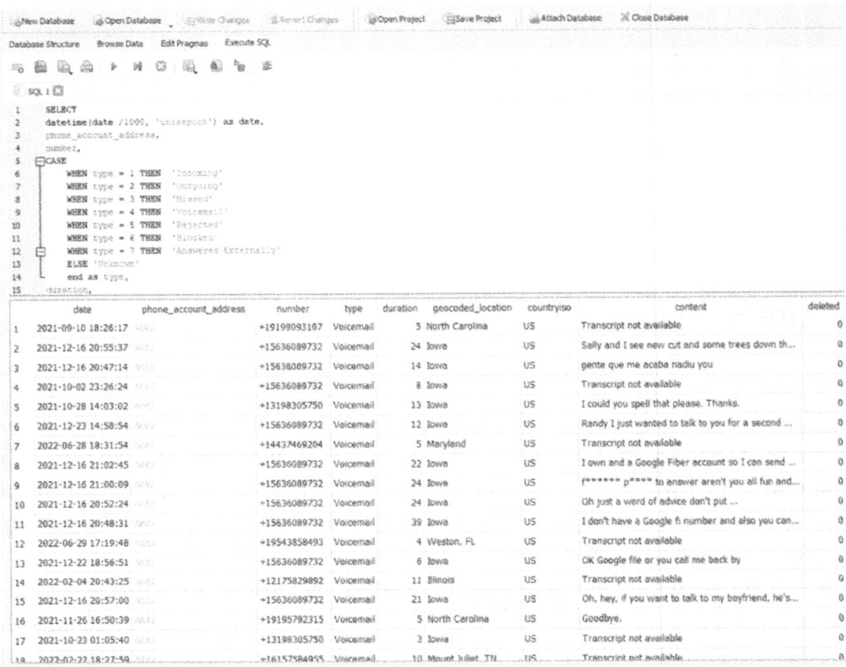

Figure 5.1 SQLite browser.

These tools can help forensic analysts and investigators interact with SQLite databases more efficiently, recover deleted data, and analyze their content for digital forensic purposes.

5.1 Analyzing

Analyzing SQLite databases involves using SQL queries to interact with the data. The basic structure of an SQL query consists of three parts:

1. The action you want to perform (e.g., SELECT, INSERT, UPDATE, DELETE).
2. The columns you want to read or modify, using "*" to select all columns.
3. The table you want to read from or modify.

For example, the following SQL query selects all columns from a table:

```
SELECT * FROM table_name;
```

To learn more about SQL and how to create more complex queries, you can search for "SQL tutorial" online. Numerous free resources are available to help you understand and master SQL. These tutorials will teach you how to construct different types of queries, such as filtering data, joining tables, and aggregating data.

As you become more proficient in SQL, you will be better equipped to analyze SQLite databases in various digital forensics scenarios. Understanding how to construct and execute SQL queries will allow you to extract valuable information from SQLite databases and perform in-depth analyses of the data contained within them. Understanding the context around the data in a database is one of the biggest challenges in data analysis. It often requires extensive testing of the application to determine the circumstances under which the data was saved. This can be a time-consuming and complex task, but it's necessary to accurately interpret the data stored in the database.

5.1.1 Timestamps

Throughout your forensics journey you will see developers encode timestamps in a wide variety of formats. This is why being able to identify and correctly handle the different formats is crucial. Converting these timestamps into a standard format like ISO DateTime will make the data more consistent and easier to comprehend. Below are some common timestamp formats and SQL queries that can be used to convert them into ISO DateTime standards:

UNIX EPOCH (seconds since 1/1/1970)

```
SELECT DATETIME(dateColumn, 'unixepoch') AS ISOdate FROM tableName;
```

UNIX EPOCH (milliseconds since 1/1/1970)

```
SELECT DATETIME(ROUND(dateColumn / 1000), 'unixepoch') AS ISOdate
   FROM tableName;
```

Mac Absolute (seconds since 1/1/2001)

To convert Mac Absolute time to epoch, you need to add the number of seconds from epoch to 1/1/2001 (978307200).

```
SELECT DATETIME(column + 978307200, 'unixepoch') AS ISOdate FROM
   tableName;
```

CHROME time (microseconds since 1/1/1601)

Converting Chrome time to epoch requires dividing the data by 1,000,000.

```
SELECT DATETIME(column / 1000000 + (strftime('%s', '1601-01-01')),
   'UNIXEPOCH') AS ISOdate FROM tableName;
```

Using these queries, you can convert various timestamp formats into the ISO DateTime standard, ensuring the consistency and readability of the data during your SQLite database analysis.

5.1.2 Temporary Files

SQLite uses temporary files for both journals and write-ahead logs (WAL) to ensure data integrity and improve performance.

Journaling is a feature created to protect against writing errors. When a page is about to be written, a backup is created using a temporary file. This allows the database to roll back to the previous state if the write operation fails.

With the introduction of version 3.7, SQLite incorporated the **write-ahead log (WAL)**, which means new changes are instead written to a temporary file, leaving the database untouched until the transaction log is committed to the database. The default value for when committing the log file to the database is around 1000 commits. WAL was developed to enhance the speed of I/O transactions and is not created by default; developers must enable this feature of SQLite in their code. When performing forensics on a database, it's crucial to check the WAL for data to ensure you have the most recent records. The thing is WAL can contain both new and deleted data, and in some cases in an unencrypted state, which makes it valuable to check when performing forensics.

If you ever encounter a "sqlcipher encrypted error" while trying to read a database, this is because the database requires the WAL file to access the data. This can be fixed by exporting the WAL from the disk image and placing it in the same folder as the database. Some database software will then automatically import the WAL into the database file.

To determine if the database is set up for journaling or WAL, open the SQLite database file in a hex viewer and look at the bytes at offsets 18 and 19:

- journaling, the bytes at offset 18 and 19 are 01 01.
- WAL, the value of the bytes at offset 18 and 19 is 02 02.

Understanding these temporary files and their implications is vital for conducting accurate forensic analysis on SQLite databases.

5.1.3 Deleted Content

SQLite stores data in fixed-size pages, and the page size is specified in the file header. These unused pages are stored on the freelist and are first overwritten when a new page is needed. This setup allows forensic analysts to look for deleted data. Searching for deleted data is done by opening the database in a hex editor and looking for information unavailable within the SQLite browser. This process, called data carving, aims to identify deleted data. Recognizing deleted content within an SQL database is valuable, as it can reveal data no longer present due to system removal or intentional evidence destruction. A straightforward method of identifying deleted content is by looking for missing primary ID entries. Once the data has been found, it must be parsed to understand the context around it.

sqlparse.py by Mari DeGrazia is a tool that aids in recovering deleted entries from SQLite databases. Using such tools and techniques can greatly enhance the effectiveness of analyzing SQLite databases.

5.2 Summary

SQLite forensics is an essential aspect of digital investigations due to the widespread use of SQLite databases in various applications across computers and mobile devices. These databases are popular among developers because they are lightweight and easy to interact with using SQL queries. The process of completely deleting information from SQLite databases is relatively difficult, which allows forensic examiners to recover deleted data in many cases. As a result, understanding SQLite databases and the methods for analyzing and recovering data has become a critical skill for digital forensic professionals.

6

Windows Forensics

Windows, being the most widely used operating system in the world, is the reason a significant focus of digital forensics research is aimed at it. Although the operating system does not specifically maintain records for forensic purposes, what it does is generate a wealth of data related to user activities and preferences. This data is used by the system to enhance usability, such as providing quick access to recently opened files or improving network connections. For forensic professionals, this wealth of data provides an opportunity to piece together a timeline of user activities on a Windows device and get insights into a user's behavior. Understanding the Windows operating system and the various data artifacts it produces is an essential skill for any digital forensics practitioner.

6.1 New Technology File System (NTFS)

The New Technology File System (NTFS)[1] provides several advantages over other Table 6.1 like File Allocation Table (FAT) and Extended File Allocation Table (exFAT) including features like:

1. **Metadata**: NTFS stores detailed metadata for each file, including security attributes, access control lists, and owner information.
2. **Advanced file structure**: NTFS supports advanced file structures such as alternate data streams, which allow multiple data streams to be associated with a single file.
3. **Journaling**: NTFS includes a journaling feature that helps ensure the consistency and integrity of the file system in the event of a system crash or power failure.

1 https://en.wikipedia.org/wiki/NTFS.

Table 6.1 File system.

File system	Max file size	Max volume size	Time resolution
Fat	4 GB	32 GB	10 ms since Jan 1, 1980
exFAT	~ volume size	16 TB	10 ms since Jan 1, 1601
NTFS	16 TB	256 TB	100 ns since Jan 1, 1601

4. **Compression**: NTFS provides built-in file compression to save disk space.
5. **Encryption**: NTFS supports the Encrypting File System (EFS), which allows files to be encrypted on the disk for added security.

In digital forensics, understanding NTFS and its features is crucial, as this knowledge can aid in the recovery and analysis of crucial evidence. For instance, unallocated data blocks in NTFS can be examined to recover deleted files and traces of previously stored data.

6.1.1 MFT (Master File Table)

One of the main components of NTFS is the Master File Table (MFT).[2] It can provide valuable information about files and directories on an NTFS volume. Analyzing MFT can help recover metadata: file names, locations, sizes, creation/edit dates, permissions, and security settings. Furthermore, understanding how the MFT stores and manages files, e.g., files smaller than 1024 bytes, have their content stored within MTF; otherwise, there will be a pointer to a cluster on the disk which contains the content. This can be beneficial when attempting to locate or recover specific data.

Tools like MFTECmd[3] and MFTExplorer,[4] both developed by Eric Zimmerman, are incredibly useful for forensic investigators working with NTFS volumes. MFTECmd is a command-line tool that can extract information from an MFT file and output it as a CSV file, while MFTExplorer is a GUI-based tool that offers a more visual and interactive experience.

```
MFTECmd.exe -f ".\$MFT" --csv.
```

By leveraging these tools one can understand the underlying structure and function of the MFT.

2 https://learn.microsoft.com/en-us/windows/win32/fileio/master-file-table.
3 github.com/EricZimmerman/MFTECmd.
4 ericzimmerman.github.io/.

6.1.2 $I30

$I30 files on NTFS are responsible for storing information about files and directories, including their metadata. Each directory has its own $I30 file. With this file, it is possible to find deleted files by examining the slack space within these files.

Two tools can aid in the analysis of $I30 files: INDXRipper[5] and MFTECmd.

1. INDXRipper is a useful tool for extracting and parsing $I30 files. It can create a timeline in CSV format, detailing the contents of the analyzed files. To use INDXRipper, simply point it to the mounted drive and the desired output file, and the tool will handle the rest.

```
.\INDXRipper.exe\.\G: outfile.csv
```

2. Another options is MFTECmd with it versatility allowing it to analysis both $MFT and $I30 files. To use MFTECmd with $I30 files, you will first need to extract the files and then point the program to the extracted files.

Both tools can be used to analyze the data; I recommend trying both to find the tool that performs the best for you.

6.1.3 Journal

Journaling stores a transaction log of all changes made to the system. In the event of a crash or failure, the file system can use these records to roll back any changes and continue from where it left off. These journal files are stored in three files: two in $USNJournal and the third in $LogFile.

One of the most important is the $J file which is used to keep track of high-level changes to files and directories. The amount of historical data stored depends on the system's activity; the typical size is 32 MB and will perform rollover on the oldest data when the size grows over the 32 MB.

```
$Extend\$USNJRNL\$MAX
$Extend\$USNJRNL\$J
```

$LogFile tracks detailed changes to the MFT metadata. The usual size of the $LogFile is around 64 MB, with data typically lasting only hours to a few days. The file is located at the root of the file system.

Eric Zimmerman's tool MFTECmd, shown in Figure 6.1, currently supports $J file; as of the time of writing, but it does not support $LogFile. To use MFTECmd, you need to extract both the $MFT and $J from the system. Then by using the -m flag, this tells the tool to parse both the $MFT and $J. This will allow the tool to populate the parent path column in the output.

5 https://github.com/harelsegev/INDXRipper.

Figure 6.1 MFTCMD.

```
MFTECmd.exe -f '$J' -m '$MFT' --csv "output"
```

With these files you have to create a timeline of the file system event; this can even include deleted files.

6.1.4 Alternate Data Stream Zone Identifier (ADS)

Alternate Data Streams (ADS) and Zone Identifiers provide additional security and metadata capabilities for files. ADS allow multiple data streams to be associated with a single file. ADS are often used to store Zone Identifier information, which is used by the Windows operating system to determine the security zone associated with a file. This information is stored in an alternate data stream attached to the file and is used by the operating system to determine how to handle the file.

For example, if a file was downloaded from the internet, the Zone Identifier information can be used to determine whether the file should be treated as potentially unsafe and subject to additional security checks. This can give us the ability to tell the source of the data, as it will be stored inside the ADS named zone.Identifier. If the zone.Identifier is not present, it most likely came from a FAT format device. The zone.Identifier has six ZoneIDs that tell the type the file came from, which can be seen in Table 6.2.

Table 6.2 Zone identifier.

Zone	Key
NoZone	−1
MyComputer	0
Intranet	1
Trusted	2
Internet	3
Untrusted	4

Files with a Zone 3 attribute are particularly interesting. These files are downloaded from the Internet. The URL source of the file can also be present within the Zone.Identifier. Identifying the source of a file can give valuable information; to retrieve the ADS from files, you can use a simple PowerShell command:

```
Get-ChildItem -Recurse | Get-Content -Stream Zone.Identifier
```

This command will search through all the files in the current directory and subdirectories, and if present display the Zone.Identifier for each file.

6.1.5 Volume Shadow Copy

Volume Shadow Copy, a feature within Windows, allows for point-in-time backups of the system. This includes both system and user files. This feature can be helpful in a variety of situations, such as accidental file deletion or edits. We can use this to analyze the previous state of a computer and possibly recover deleted data. There are multiple tools and methods to analyze shadow copies on a computer, including both graphical user interfaces (GUIs) and command-line options.

Shadow Explorer[6] is a GUI-based tool that allows users to easily locate and open shadow copies, presenting the data in an easy-to-use interface; you can get a view of it in Figure 6.2.

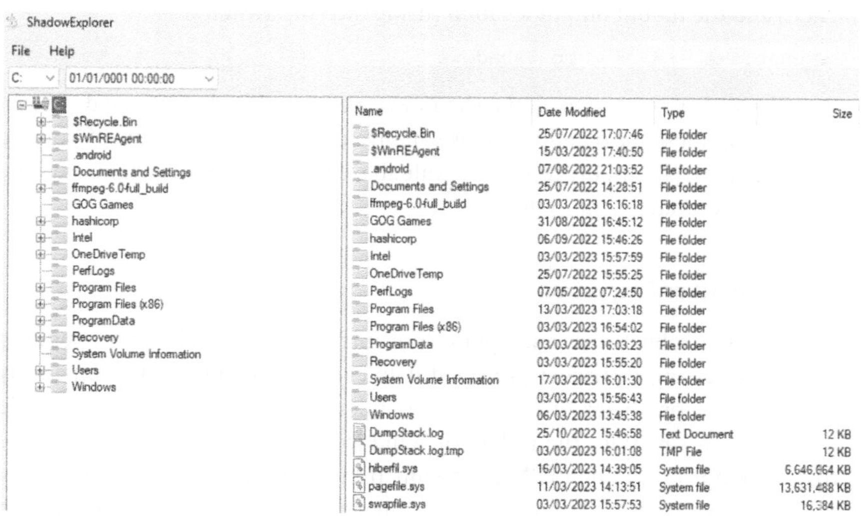

Figure 6.2 Shadow Explorer.

6 https://www.shadowexplorer.com/downloads.html.

You can also use the built-in commands vssadmin[7] and mklink[8] to list shadow copies, create symbolic links, and interact with the shadow copies directly. This method offers the advantages of being scriptable and automatable.

To list the available shadow copies on a specified disk, use the following command (remember to replace # with the drive letter for the drive you want to list the shadow copy for):

```
vssadmin list shadowstorage /on=#:
```

You can identify the location of the file by looking at the "Shadow copy volume." Interacting with the shadow copy requires you to create a symbolic link using the mklink. It requires only two parameters: the target destination (e.g., C:\shadowcopy) and the source (the "Shadow copy volume" path). Make sure you add a trailing backslash to the "Shadow copy volume" path or the link will not work; here is an example:

```
mklink /d C:\shadowcopy \\?\GLOBALROOT\Device\
   HarddiskVoulmeShadowCopy#\
```

You should now be able to browse files stored inside the shadow copy. If a system has multiple shadow copies this process has to be repeated for every single one of them. Eric Zimmerman has also created a tool for interacting with shadow copy called VSCMount.[9] It requires two parameters: the drive (defined by the –dl switch) and the mount output location (using the –mp switch).

```
VSCMount.exe --dl # --mp \shadows
```

It will now have mounted all the shadow copies stored in the defined drive.

Leveraging these tools and methods can give access to the contents of Volume Shadow Copies, potentially recovering valuable data and gaining insights into the history of a computer's file system.

6.1.6 BitLocker Encryption

BitLocker is a robust disk encryption tool integrated into Windows operating systems. Accessing BitLocker-protected data can be a daunting task, especially when the user or owner of the system is unavailable or unwilling to provide the encryption key. With the rollout of Windows 11 and the requirement of the Trusted Platform Module (TPM), the shift from encrypted by default is slowly being rolled out. This will make it more challenging/impossible to access data on

---

7 https://learn.microsoft.com/en-us/windows-server/administration/windows-commands/vssadmin.

8 https://learn.microsoft.com/en-us/windows-server/administration/windows-commands/mklink.

9 https://github.com/EricZimmerman/VSCMount.

Figure 6.3 Bitlocker.

a dead box. However, when dealing with a live system, it's essential to identify if BitLocker is enabled and follow the proper procedure to ensure you have the necessary encrypted key to unlock the encrypted disk. Here the BitLocker recovery key is crucial. It serves as a backup method to unlock encrypted drives without the user's password or PIN. The method of extracting the Bitlocker recovery key:

1. **Identify the device**: Ensure you are dealing with a BitLocker-encrypted device. Look for signs such as the lock icon on the disk in Explorer as shown in Figure 6.3.
2. **Access the Control Panel**: On Windows 10 or 11, open the Control Panel, go to "System and Security," and click on "BitLocker Drive Encryption." On Windows 7 or 8, navigate to the Control Panel, click on "System and Security," and then click on "BitLocker Drive Encryption."
3. **Locate the recovery key**: In the BitLocker settings, you may find the option to back up the recovery key. Select this option to view the key and save it to a secure location. If the key is not readily available, you may need administrator or user credentials to access it.

For a more streamlined approach, you can also use command-line tools to extract the BitLocker recovery key. The following command will retrieve the recovery key for the BitLocker-protected drive (replace "C:" with the appropriate drive letter):

```
manage-bde -protectors -get C:
```

This command can be further streamlined by piping the output to a file on a portable disk. With the recovery key in hand, you are now able to unlock the disk and perform acquisition on the disk.

6.2 Acquisition

Acquisition of a Windows device can be done in multiple ways, including direct disk extraction, imaging through a portable OS, and dealing with encrypted devices. Let's take a closer look at each of these methods and how they can be used in digital forensics.

1. **Direct disk extraction**: If the disk can be removed from the device, you can attach it to a write blocker to prevent any accidental changes to the data. Imaging tools like FTK Imager can be used to create a physical copy of the disk, which can then be analyzed in a forensics lab.
2. **Imaging through a portable OS**: In cases where the disk cannot be removed, or when dealing with devices like laptops with PCIe 4.0 SSDs, booting the system with a portable OS like [CAINE] (https://www.caine-live.net/) can be a viable option. CAINE offers a suite of forensics tools that can be used to acquire data from the device while minimizing the risk of altering the original data.
3. **Dealing with encrypted devices**: For devices with encrypted disks, it is a little different. If the encryption key is not available, one option is to try and use brute force to guess the correct key. However, this can be a time-consuming and resource-intensive process with no guarantee of success; otherwise if you have the recovery key as mentioned before, you can just perform acquisition directly from the disk, when the partition then gets mounted Windows should prompt you for the password; here you can pass the recovery key.

Once the acquisition process is complete, you can move on to analyzing the acquired data. The analysis process typically involves examining the disk image and identifying various Windows artifacts.

6.3 Analysis

Analysis is the examination and investigation of Windows-based systems. The key areas that we will focus on include Windows artifacts such as registry entries, event logs, file systems, browser history, and user profiles. These artifacts can uncover the user activities that have happened on the device.

6.3.1 Registry

The Windows registry is a crucial component of the operating system that stores configuration data for both the system and installed applications. It is organized into a collection of databases known as hives, with each database entry containing a key, value type, value, and last write time (UTC). The most common way to interact with the register is through the register view aka regedit, as shown in Figure 6.4.

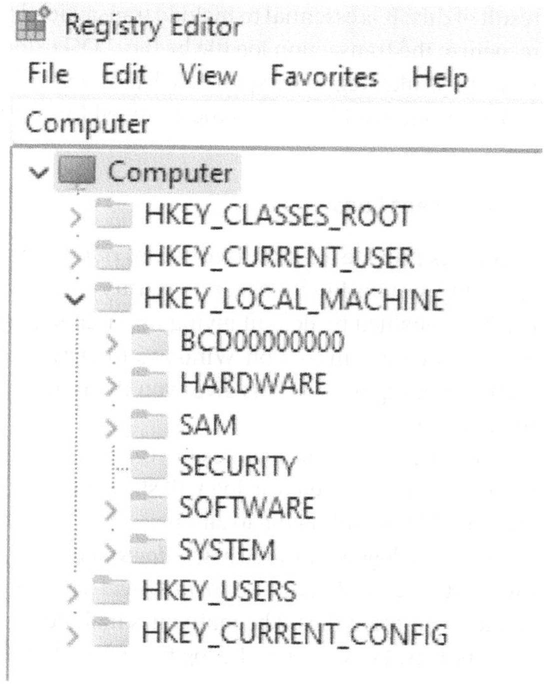

Figure 6.4 Regedit.

System-specific registry databases are located in the *Windows\system32\config* folder:

1. SAM
2. SECURITY
3. SYSTEM
4. SOFTWARE

User-specific registry hives, including NTUser.dat and UsrClass.dat, which are stored in individual user profile directories. When it comes to what tool to use to analyze these registry hive files, Registry Explorer[10] and TZWorks Cfae[11] are highly recommended. These tools allow analysts to examine registry keys and their values with relative ease.

Another important thing to know about the registry data is the transaction log. These files store data that has not yet been written to the registry hives. They work as cache files to help improve the efficiency of the system. This data within the cache is typically flushed at least once per hour or when the system is idle, as a

10 ericzimmerman.github.io/.
11 tzworks.com/download_links.php.

result of this. It is essential to include transaction log files in your analysis. You can recognize the transaction log file by the .LOG extension, e.g., NTUSER.dat.LOG1. Some tools like Registry Explorer will automatically identify if the hive file is dirty and a transaction file needs to be included for you to see the newest information.

6.3.2 Event Logs

Event logs provide a centralized record of information about software, hardware, operating system functions, and security. Starting from Windows Vista, logging has been enabled by default giving us a rich source of information which we can utilize. The built-in tool on Windows to view the log is called event viewer and is shown in Figure 6.5. This gives you the minimum tools required to search and filter on alerts.

By default, the event log files (.evtx) have a size limit of 20 MB. Once this size limit has been reached, the log will start overwriting historical events. Event logs are stored in the following locations:

For XP the logs are located at *windows\system32\config* and for Vista and beyond the location is at *Windows\System32\winevt\Logs*.evtx*. These event log files are stored in different files. The main ones include Security, System, Application, and Custom logs. Let's go over the log files and what information they store:

1. **Security**: Records access control and security settings information based on audit and group policies, updated only by the LSASS process.
2. **System**: Contains events related to Windows services, system components, drivers, resources, etc. (e.g., service stop/start, system reboot).

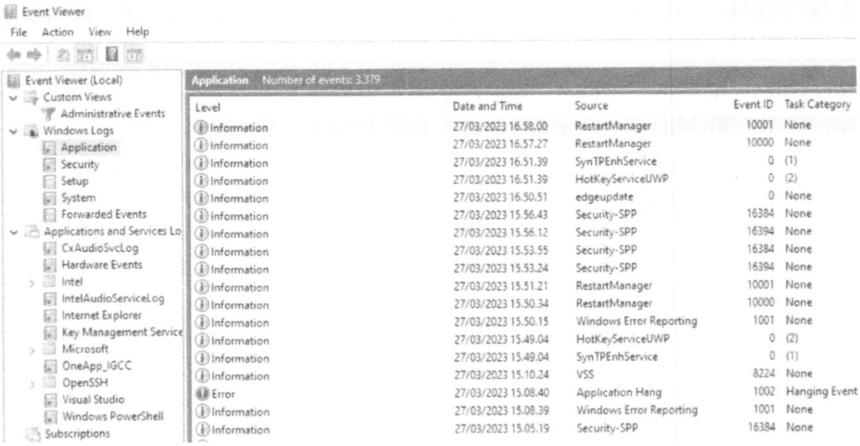

Figure 6.5 Event viewer.

Table 6.3 Event log type.

Event type	Description
Error	Significant problems, such as loss of data or functionality
Warning	Not significant, but could indicate a future problem
Information	Successful operation of an application, driver, or service
Success Audit	Audit event completed successfully
Failure Audit	Audit event not completed successfully

3. **Application**: Software events unrelated to the operating system (e.g., SQL server fails to access a database).
4. **Custom**: Custom application logs, including server logs such as directory service, DNS server, and file replication service.

Logs are also categorized into different event types, based on severity shown in Table 6.3.

To analyze event logs, tools like Event Log Explorer[12] can be used to efficiently analyze the log files. I will later in the chapter specify the logs we care the most about.

6.3.3 Memory Forensics

Windows Memory Forensics is the process of analyzing the contents stored within memory (RAM) to gather information about the system's state and uncover potential evidence during an investigation. Capturing memory can be a crucial step in some cases, as some information, such as encryption keys and currently running processes, only exists within the memory. The capture of memory must happen before the device gets shut down; otherwise, all data will be lost. Some key data available within memory include:

1. Processes, open files, registry keys, and devices
2. Encryption keys and passwords
3. Network connections
4. Configuration parameters
5. Memory-only exploits and rootkits

Before we can analyze any memory we need to dump the content of the memory to disk. To do this requires you to first be an administrator on the device. It should

12 https://eventlogxp.com/.

be noted that any execution program to get hold of memory will also affect the state of memory as it will be loaded into memory. Tools for capturing memory includes the following:

1. Belkasoft Live RAM Capturer[13]
2. Magnet Forensics RAM Capturer[14]
3. VolatileDataCollector[15]

When Windows goes into hibernation, the content of memory gets saved to a file which is stored at %systemDrive%\hiberfile.sys. This is another potential data source for memory content. These files store the current memory state of the computer when it enters hibernation or uses fast startup; the different types can be seen in Table 6.4. Hibernation files need to be decompressed before they can be analyzed using tools such as Volatility imagecopy,[16] hibr2bin,[17] or Arsenal Hibernation Recon.[18]

When analyzing memory, the approach can vary depending on the context of the case. A good starting point is examining the running processes and network connections to understand the system's state at the time of capture. Further investigation can include identifying rogue processes, analyzing process DLLs and handles, reviewing network artifacts, looking for evidence of code injection, checking for signs of rootkits, and dumping suspicious processes and drivers. The go-to analysis tools for memory include Volatility[19] and MemProcFS,[20] shown in Figure 6.6.

The analysis of memory, as many other things, can vary significantly depending on the context of the case. A good starting point is looking at the process that was running and network connections. This will give you a good starting point to understand what happened on the system at the moment of capture.

Table 6.4 Hibernation file size.

Hibernation file type	Default size	Supports
Full	40% of memory	Hibernation, hybrid sleep
Reduced	20% of memory	Fast startup

13 https://belkasoft.com/ram-capturer.
14 https://www.magnetforensics.com/resources/magnet-ram-capture/.
15 https://github.com/gtworek/VolatileDataCollector.
16 https://github.com/volatilityfoundation/volatility/wiki/Command-Reference#imagecopy.
17 https://github.com/MagnetForensics/Hibr2Bin.
18 https://arsenalrecon.com/products/hibernation-recon.
19 https://www.volatilityfoundation.org/.
20 https://github.com/ufrisk/MemProcFS.

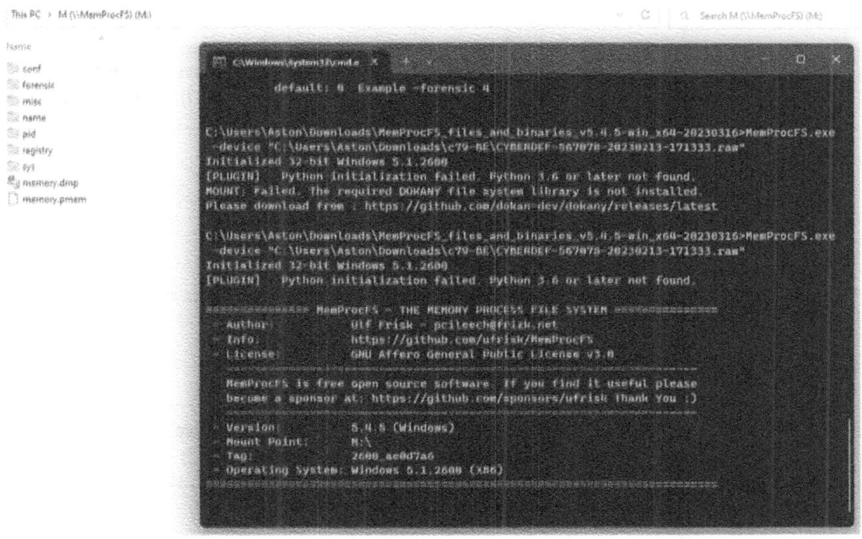

Figure 6.6 MemprocsFS.

Tips and Tricks:

- Identify rogue processes: name, path, parent, command line, start time, and SID.
- Analyze process DDLs and handles
- Network artifacts
- Dump suspicious processes and drivers

In summary, by utilizing specialized tools to analyze memory we can reconstruct what happened in the system at the moment of capture.

6.3.4 Timestamps

File timestamps are essential in digital forensics as they provide valuable information about when specific actions were taken on a file. Timestamp precision varies depending on the file system used. For NTFS, the precision is 100 nanoseconds since January 1, 1601. Timestamps can be affected by various actions, such as file creation, access, editing, renaming, copying, moving, and deletion.

Tables 6.5 and 6.6 show how different user actions affect file timestamps on Windows 10 and 11. Keep in mind that if the modified date is older than the created date, it typically indicates that the file or folder has been copied. This rule does not apply to files downloaded from the internet.

As demonstrated by the table, some changes have been made from Windows 10 to 11, emphasizing the importance of thorough research on the systems being

Table 6.5 File timestamps on Windows 10.

	Create	Access	Edit	Rename	Copy	Local move	Move (CLI)	Move (cut/paste)
Creation	C	NA	NA	NA	A	NA	A	I
Access	C	A	NA	NA	A	NA	A	A
Modified	C	NA	A	NA	I	NA	I	I
Metadata	C	NA	A	A	A	A	I	I

C, created; A, altered; I, inherited; NA, no change.

Table 6.6 File timestamps on Windows 11.

	Create	Access	Edit	Rename	Copy	Local move	Move (CLI)	Move (cut/paste)
Creation	C	NA	NA	NA	A	NA	A	I
Access	C	A	NA	A	A	A	A	A
Modified	C	NA	A	NA	I	NA	I	I
Metadata	C	NA	A	A	I	A	A	A

C, created; A, altered; I, inherited; NA, no change.

investigated to ensure a complete understanding of each component. Special thanks to sans.org for providing this information.

6.3.5 Creation of Timeline of Activity

Timeline analysis is crucial in digital forensics as it allows investigators to understand the sequence of events that occurred on a system. Several tools can be used to create a timeline, such as a combination of Plaso and Volatility3. An example of a timeline can be viewed in Figure 6.7.

6.3.5.1 Plaso

Plaso is a Python-based tool that generates timelines from raw and E01 disk images. To install Plaso on Ubuntu, follow these steps:

1. Add the repository to your system:

```
sudo add-apt-repository ppa:gift/stable
```

2. Update and install Plaso-tools:

```
sudo apt-get update
sudo apt-get install plaso-tools
```

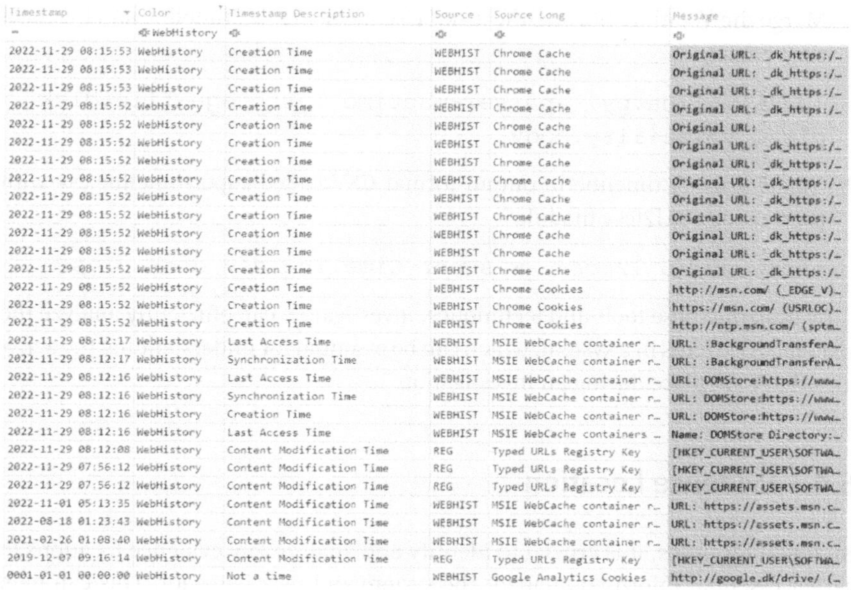

Timestamp	Color	Timestamp Description	Source	Source Long	Message
–	WebHistory				
2022-11-29 08:15:53	WebHistory	Creation Time	WEBHIST	Chrome Cache	Original URL: _dk_https:/…
2022-11-29 08:15:53	WebHistory	Creation Time	WEBHIST	Chrome Cache	Original URL: _dk_https:/…
2022-11-29 08:15:53	WebHistory	Creation Time	WEBHIST	Chrome Cache	Original URL: _dk_https:/…
2022-11-29 08:15:52	WebHistory	Creation Time	WEBHIST	Chrome Cache	Original URL: _dk_https:/…
2022-11-29 08:15:52	WebHistory	Creation Time	WEBHIST	Chrome Cache	Original URL:
2022-11-29 08:15:52	WebHistory	Creation Time	WEBHIST	Chrome Cache	Original URL: _dk_https:/…
2022-11-29 08:15:52	WebHistory	Creation Time	WEBHIST	Chrome Cache	Original URL: _dk_https:/…
2022-11-29 08:15:52	WebHistory	Creation Time	WEBHIST	Chrome Cache	Original URL: _dk_https:/…
2022-11-29 08:15:52	WebHistory	Creation Time	WEBHIST	Chrome Cache	Original URL: _dk_https:/…
2022-11-29 08:15:52	WebHistory	Creation Time	WEBHIST	Chrome Cache	Original URL: _dk_https:/…
2022-11-29 08:15:52	WebHistory	Creation Time	WEBHIST	Chrome Cache	Original URL: _dk_https:/…
2022-11-29 08:15:52	WebHistory	Creation Time	WEBHIST	Chrome Cache	Original URL: _dk_https:/…
2022-11-29 08:15:52	WebHistory	Creation Time	WEBHIST	Chrome Cache	Original URL: _dk_https:/…
2022-11-29 08:15:52	WebHistory	Creation Time	WEBHIST	Chrome Cookies	http://msn.com/ (_EDGE_V)…
2022-11-29 08:15:52	WebHistory	Creation Time	WEBHIST	Chrome Cookies	https://msn.com/ (USRLOC)…
2022-11-29 08:15:52	WebHistory	Creation Time	WEBHIST	Chrome Cookies	http://ntp.msn.com/ (sptm…
2022-11-29 08:12:17	WebHistory	Last Access Time	WEBHIST	MSIE WebCache container r…	URL: :BackgroundTransferA…
2022-11-29 08:12:17	WebHistory	Synchronization Time	WEBHIST	MSIE WebCache container r…	URL: :BackgroundTransferA…
2022-11-29 08:12:16	WebHistory	Last Access Time	WEBHIST	MSIE WebCache container r…	URL: DOMStore:https://www…
2022-11-29 08:12:16	WebHistory	Synchronization Time	WEBHIST	MSIE WebCache container r…	URL: DOMStore:https://www…
2022-11-29 08:12:16	WebHistory	Creation Time	WEBHIST	MSIE WebCache container r…	URL: DOMStore:https://www…
2022-11-29 08:12:16	WebHistory	Last Access Time	WEBHIST	MSIE WebCache containers …	Name: DOMStore Directory:…
2022-11-29 08:12:08	WebHistory	Content Modification Time	REG	Typed URLs Registry Key	[HKEY_CURRENT_USER\SOFTWA…
2022-11-29 07:56:12	WebHistory	Content Modification Time	REG	Typed URLs Registry Key	[HKEY_CURRENT_USER\SOFTWA…
2022-11-29 07:56:12	WebHistory	Content Modification Time	REG	Typed URLs Registry Key	[HKEY_CURRENT_USER\SOFTWA…
2022-11-01 05:13:35	WebHistory	Content Modification Time	WEBHIST	MSIE WebCache container r…	URL: https://assets.msn.c…
2022-08-18 01:23:43	WebHistory	Content Modification Time	WEBHIST	MSIE WebCache container r…	URL: https://essets.msn.c…
2021-02-26 01:08:40	WebHistory	Content Modification Time	WEBHIST	MSIE WebCache container r…	URL: https://assets.msn.c…
2019-12-07 09:16:14	WebHistory	Content Modification Time	REG	Typed URLs Registry Key	[HKEY_CURRENT_USER\SOFTWA…
0001-01-01 00:00:00	WebHistory	Not a time	WEBHIST	Google Analytics Cookies	http://google.dk/drive/ (…

Figure 6.7 Windows timeline.

3. Create a timeline Plaso file from a raw disk image:

```
log2timeline.py --storage-file disk.plaso image.raw
```

4. Convert the file to CSV:

```
psort.py -o dynamic -w registrar.csv timeline.plaso
```

   Alternatively, you can use the psteal command to achieve the same result in a single step:

```
psteal.py --source image.e01 -w timeline.csv
```

6.3.5.2 Volatility 3 Timeline

Volatility 3 can be used to create a timeline of events within a memory file.

1. Create a timeline file from the memory:

```
vol -f memory.raw timeliner --create-bodyfile
```

2. The output needs to be modified before it can be used with Plaso. This can be done with a standard text editor or a script.

6.3.5.3 Creating a Super Timeline

Creating a super timeline involves merging the Plaso and Volatility files into a single CSV file for analysis.

1. Merge the Volatility file into the disk.plaso file using log2timeline and the mactime parser:

   ```
   log2timeline.py --parser=mactime --storage-file=disk.
   plaso volatility.body
   ```

2. Create a super timeline in output format CSV called super-timeline.csv with psort using the l2tcsv module:

   ```
   psort.py -o l2tcsv -w super-timeline.csv disk.plaso
   ```

By utilizing these tools and techniques, investigators can efficiently analyze the sequence of events in a system, which can be essential for understanding the activities that took place during an investigation.

6.4 Evidence Location

In digital forensics, it is crucial to identify and analyze key evidence locations to gather essential information about the system and user behavior. This can help build a comprehensive understanding of the case and support the investigation.

By utilizing these evidence locations, investigators can efficiently analyze the sequence of events on a system, which can be essential for understanding the activities that took place during an investigation.

6.4.1 System Information

Here are some locations that can be used to gather information about the system:

- OS version (Timestamp is unixepoch in seconds):

  ```
  SOFTWARE\Microsoft\Windows NT\CurrentVersion
  ```

- Computer name:

  ```
  'SYSTEM\CurrentControlSet\Control\Computername\Computername'
  ```

- Time zone infomation:

  ```
  SYSTEM\CurrentControlSet\Control\TimeZoneInformation
  ```

- NTFS last access time on/off (value = 0x1 meant it disables):

  ```
  SYSTEM\CurrentControlSet\Control\Filesystem
  ```

- Network interfaces:

  ```
  SYSTEM\CurrentControlSet\Services\TcpIPp\Parameters\Interfaces
  SOFTWARE\Microsoft\Windows NT\CurrentVersion\NetworkCards
  ```

- Shutdown (hex-encoded windows 64-bit time):

```
SYSTEM\CurrentControlSet\Control\Windows
```

- Volume info (Stores the serial number for each drive and the volume drive letter):

```
SYSTEM\mounteddevices
```

- Installed software (app id from Windows store or software name):

```
SOFTWARE\Microsoft\Windows\CurrentVersion\Uninstall
```

- Network interfaces:

```
SYSTEM\CurrentControlSet\Services\Tcpip\Parameters\Interface
```

- Defender settings:

```
Software\Microsoft\Windows Defender
```

6.4.1.1 Time Zone Information

Identify the system time zone. It is critically important because some log files and register keys are set in the system time zone, and others in UTC. Hence it is critically important to know the difference between system time and UTC.

Very useful when you need to correlate events across multiple devices and you need to make sure that you view the time in the same format and time zone across all devices.

```
SYSTEM\CurrentControlSet\Coontrol\TimeZoneInformation
```

6.4.1.2 Network Interfaces

Contains a list of every available network interface and their last known configurations. The two keys are connected via the interface GUID value.

```
SYSTEM\CurrentControlSet\Services\TcpIPp\Parameters\Interfaces
```

NetworkCards key can provide more detail on the interface.

```
SOFTWARE\Microsoft\Windows NT\CurrentVersion\NetworkCards
```

List network interfaces of the machine. Allows you to determine if the machine has a static IP or uses DHCP; this also stores the DHCP server address and the default gateway for each network interface.

It does not store all network interfaces when Windows records network interface is not known. When an interface is recorded it includes the first and last network connections. The datetime is stored in local time using the Windows system 128-bit format. It also lists any networks that have been connected via VPN.

It is possible to use the SSID of the WIFI to physically locate a person, using https://wigle.net/ to Geolocate the WIFI signal.

```
SYSTEM\CurrentCOntrolSet\Services\Tcpip\Parameters\Interfaces
```

6.4.2 Account Usage

Information about accounts and authentication events can be found in these locations:

- SAM accounts:

  ```
  SAM\Domain\account\Users
  ```

- Security events:

  ```
  Window\System32\winevt\logs\Security.evtx
  ```

- Remote desktop protocol (RDP):

  ```
  %userprofile%\appdata\local\Microsoft\Terminal server client\
     cache
  ```

- User Access Logging:

  ```
  C:\Windows\System32\LogFiles\Sum'
  ```

6.4.2.1 SAM Accounts

List the local account on the system and information such as:

- Last login
- Last failed login
- Logon count
- Password policy
- Password change

```
SAM\Domain\account\Users
```

Store information on Account creation time, last login time, and last password change, all are stored in UTC. The tool used to analyze the SAM data is *SamInsider*

Tips and Tricks

- User with NT-hash starting with *31DCFE0D16AE931B7* the user has a blank password.
- An Internet user name with no successful logins and an invalid login count at 0 is a strong indicator for being a Microsoft account.

6.4.2.2 Security Events

The event within security.evtx related to authentication

```
Windows\System32\winevt\logs\Security.evtx
```

Security event

The event within security.evtx related to authentication

```
Window\System32\winevt\logs\Security.evtx
```

Logon event types

Give information about the nature of the account authentication, Tables 6.7 and 6.8

Table 6.9 determine which account has been used for the authentication attempt.

Table 6.7 Logon events (4624).

Code	Description
2	Logon via console
3	Network Logon
4	Batch Logon
5	Windows Service Logon
7	Credentials used to unlock screen
8	Network logon sending credentials (cleartext)
9	Different credentials used than logged on user
10	Remote interactive logon (RDP)
11	Cached credentials used to logon
12	Cached remote interactive (similar to Type 10)
13	Cached unlock (similar to Type 7)

Table 6.8 Authentication events.

Code	Description
4776	Successful/failed account authentication Event ID Codes (Kerberos protocol)
4768	Ticket Granting Ticket was granted (successful logon)
4769	Service Ticket requested (access to server resource)
4771	Pre-authentication failed (failed logon)

Table 6.9 Success and failed logon events.

Code	Description
4624	Successful logon
4625	Failed logon
4634	4647 – Successful logoff
4648	Logon using explicit credentials (Runas)
4672	Account logon with superuser rights (Administrator)
4720	An account was created

6.4.2.3 Dead Box Password Cracking

Having both SAM and SYSTEM hive files you can export account hashes by using Mimikatz.[21]

Dump NT hashes

```
lsadump::sam /system:system /sam:sam
```

Password cracking using hashcat[22]

```
hashcat -m 1000 -a 3 hash.txt
```

6.4.2.4 User Access Logging

Windows Server 2012 and up tracks user logins in a database file, at the specified location. It tracks the username, IP address, and role on the local system; the information is stored for up to three years.

The file is an Extensible Storage Engine (SES) with the extension mdb Current.mdb is the current year's active copy. You will also find three files with GUID which are backup files of the current year, the last and two years prior.

```
C:\Windows\System32\LogFiles\Sum
```

6.4.3 User Activity

User activity on a device can provide crucial information for digital forensics investigations. By examining specific locations, you can learn more about user behavior and potentially identify important evidence. Here are some locations that describe specific user activity on the device:

- Search history:

  ```
  'ntuser.dat\software\microsoft\windows\CurrentVersion\Explorer\
      wordwheelQuery'
  ```

21 https://github.com/ParrotSec/mimikatz.
22 https://hashcat.net/hashcat/.

- Typed path:

```
'ntuser.dat\software\microsoft\windows\CurrentVersion\Explorer\
    TypedPaths'
```

- Windows common dialog box:

```
'NTUser.dat\software\Microsoft\windows\currentVersion\Explorer\
    ComDlg32\LastVistedPidlMru'
```

- XP search:

```
'NTUSER.dat\software\microsoft\search\assistant\ACMRU\#'
```

- Search database:

```
'\Programdata\microsoft\search\data\application\windows\windows
    .edb'
```

- Thumbnails:

```
'%Userprofile%\AppData\Local\Microsoft\Windows\Explorer'
```

- Remote desktop protocol (RDP):

```
Cache: '%userprofile%\appdata\local\Microsoft\Terminal server
    client\cache'
Logs: '%system root%\system32\winevt\logs\security.evtx'
```

By analyzing these locations, investigators can gain insights into user behavior, preferences, and activities. This can help in determining the sequence of events in a system and potentially uncovering crucial evidence related to the case.

6.4.3.1 Search History

User keyword searched in the start menubar shown in Figure 6.8, added in win7+. The keywords are added in Unicode and listed in an MRU list, with position *0* being the newest.

```
ntuser.dat\software\microsoft\windows\CurrentVersion\Explorer\
    wordwheelQuery
```

6.4.3.2 Typed Path

The paths are typed into the Explorer address bar. Windows uses it to perform auto-complete shown in Figure 6.9, allowing you to search for previously opened directories.

```
ntuser.dat\software\microsoft\windows\CurrentVersion\Explorer\
    TypedPaths
```

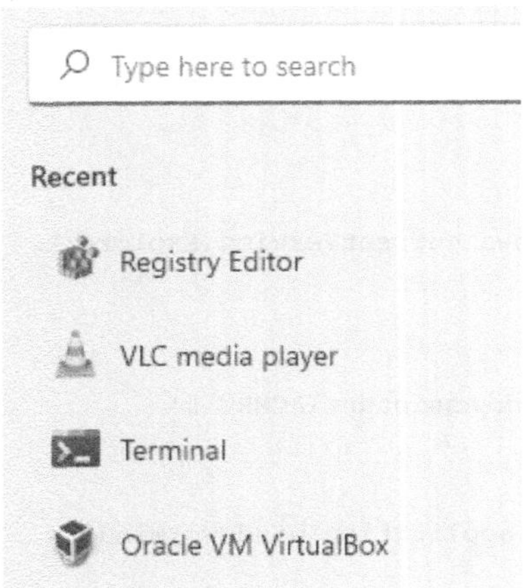

Figure 6.8 Search bar.

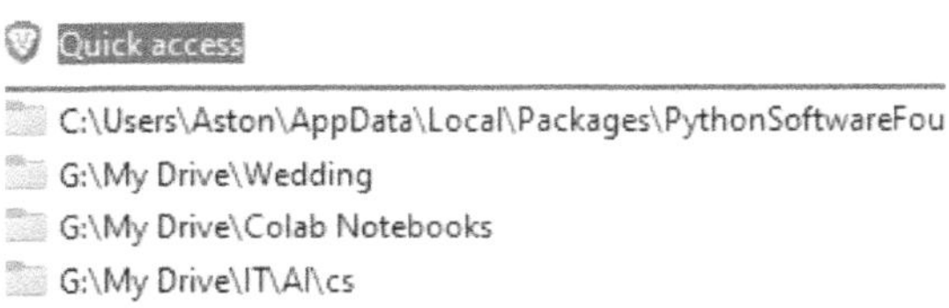

Figure 6.9 Typed path.

6.4.3.3 LastVisitedMRU (Windows common dialog box)

Tracks the last folder an application has opened or saved a file in using the Windows dialog box shown in Figure 6.10.

Any other method of opening or saving a file is not saved in this key. If you see a GUID instead of an executable name it is a standard Windows application.

```
LastVisitedMRU: NTUser.dat\software\Microsoft\windows\
    currentVersion\Explorer\ComDlg32\LastVistedPidlMru
```

Figure 6.10 Dialog box.

6.4.3.4 XP Search

XP search assistant will remember user search terms for filename, computer, and words inside files.

Interpretation

1. 5001 = search internet
2. 5603 = all or part of a document name
3. 5604 = word or phrase in a file
4. 5647 = printers, computers, or people

```
NTUSER.dat\software\microsoft\search\assistant\ACMRU\#
```

6.4.3.5 Thumbnails

Windows operation system creates thumbnails of pictures, office documents, and folders. The goal is to speed up the displaying of the preview of pictures using Windows Explorer.

Within Windows, the file that stores all the thumbnails is called the thumb cache. The name of the files is thumbcache_xxx.db, with *xxx* being the maximum size of the thumbnails stored within the database file. These database files are located at

```
'%Userprofile%\AppData\Local\Microsoft\Windows\Explorer'
```

Each user has their own database, allowing us to prove that specific users have been to a folder containing the pictures. The way you view the thumbnails inside the thumbcache is done by using thumbcache viewer[23] The problem this the thumbcache database is that it does not store the original path of the images. There is some potential for mapping the thumb cache to a path by using the *Windows.edb* files located at

```
\Programdata\microsoft\search\data\application\windows\windows.edb
```

Mapping of thumbnails can be done using *thumbcache viewer*; there is no guarantee that it will successfully map all the thumbnails to a file. Though it is not possible to identify the path of the original files it is still a valuable tool to identify what pictures have existed on the system. As it will also store thumbnails for deleted pictures, it can also be used to prove the existence of deleted pictures.

6.4.3.6 Remote Desktop Protocol (RDP)

It is used to cache part of the screen that does not change frequently to help with performance; each tile is saved as *64x64* bitmap, within appdata.

```
Cache: '%userprofile%\appdata\local\Microsoft\Terminal server
    client\cache'
```

23 https://thumbcacheviewer.github.io/.

Table 6.10 RDP event logs.

Event ID	Description
4778	Session connected/reconnected
4779	Session disconnected

To extract the bitmap tiles from the cache files bmc-tools[24] can be used; a downside is that it is unable to reassemble the bitmap tiles to create a full picture. The upside is that the tool is very simple to use; it requires only two parameters, a source directory and a destination directory.

```
python bmc-tools.py -s cache_dir -d output
```

The specified output directory is now full of 64x64 bitmap tiles, which you can try to reassemble by hand to create the original picture.

The security event Log tracks the usage of remote desktop protocol for logins to the device. Another benefit of the RDP log is that it will log the origin hostname of the connection; no matter how many nodes they go through, the event id we care about is displayed in Table 6.10.

```
Logs: '%system root%\system32\winevt\logs\security.evtx'
```

6.4.4 File or Folder Opening

Different locations and methods are used by the operating system to track files or folders that have been opened. These locations can provide valuable information during digital forensic investigations.

1. **Recent files**:

   ```
   NTUSER.DAT\Software\Microsoft\Windows\CurrentVersion\Explorer\
       RecentDocs
   ```

2. **Shortcut (.LNK) files**:

   ```
   \%USERPROFILE\AppData\Roaming\Microsoft\Windows\Recent
   ```

3. **Office recent files**:

   ```
   NTUSER.DAT\Software\Microsoft\Office\<version>\<program>
   ```

24 https://github.com/ANSSI-FR/bmc-tools.

4. **Shellbag**:

```
USRCLASS.DAT\Local Settings\Software\Microsoft\Windows\Shell
    \Bags
USRCLASS.DAT\Local Settings\Software\Microsoft\Windows\Shell
    \BagMRU
```

5. **IE History**:

```
\%appdata\local\microsoft\windows\webcache\WebCacheV*.dat
```

6. **Open/Save MRU**:

```
NTUSER.DAT\Software\Microsoft\Windows\CurrentVersion\Explorer\
    ComDlg32\OpenSavePIDlMRU
```

By analyzing these locations, investigators can obtain information on user behavior and activities, such as files and folders opened, timestamps, and other related data. This information can be helpful in determining the sequence of events in a system and potentially uncovering crucial evidence related to the case.

6.4.4.1 Recent Files

The Registry Key will track the last files and folders opened and is used to populate data in the "Recent" menus of the Start menu. It uses the MRU list, so the order by files is opened.

RecentDocs This key will track the overall order of the last 150 files or folders opened. The MRU list is ordered when the file was opened. Recentdocs is structured with a subfolder for each file extension opened. The last entry and Edit time of the key will be the time and location the last file with the specific extension was opened.

.??? File Extensions This subkey stores the last files with a specific extension that was opened. MRU list will keep track of the order in which each file was opened. The last entry and Edit time of this key will be the time when and location where the last file of a specific extension was opened. Can hold up to 10 records.

Folder This subkey stores the last folders that were opened. The MRU list will keep track of the order in which each folder was opened. The last entry and Edit time of this key will be the time and location of the last folder opened.

```
NTUSER.DAT\Software\Microsoft\Windows\CurrentVersion\Explorer\
    RecentDocs
```

6.4.4.2 Shortcut (.LNK) Files

lnk files are also called shell link. These .lnk files are automatically created by Windows, starting with Windows 8 in the recent folder when opening files or folders either locally or remotely. Each user has their own recent folder. The limit of .lnk files that can exist is 149. These .lnk files can also be used to identify files open on USB devices. Any non-executable will generate two .lnk files, one for the target file and one for the parent folder of the target file. With Windows 10, when a folder is created, the .lnk files for both the parent and grandparent folders will also be created. Shortcut files are not only limited to files and folders; they also record the URL when clicking on a link in an application.

LNK files are typically stored in the following locations, as shown in Figure 6.11:

Standard LNK files:

```
%USERPROFILE%\AppData\Roaming\Microsoft\Windows\Recent\
```

Office documents LNK files:

```
%USERPROFILE%\AppData\Roaming\Microsoft\Office\Recent\
```

One thing to note about .lnk files their uniqueness is based on the file name, which means if two files with the same name but in different locations are opened,

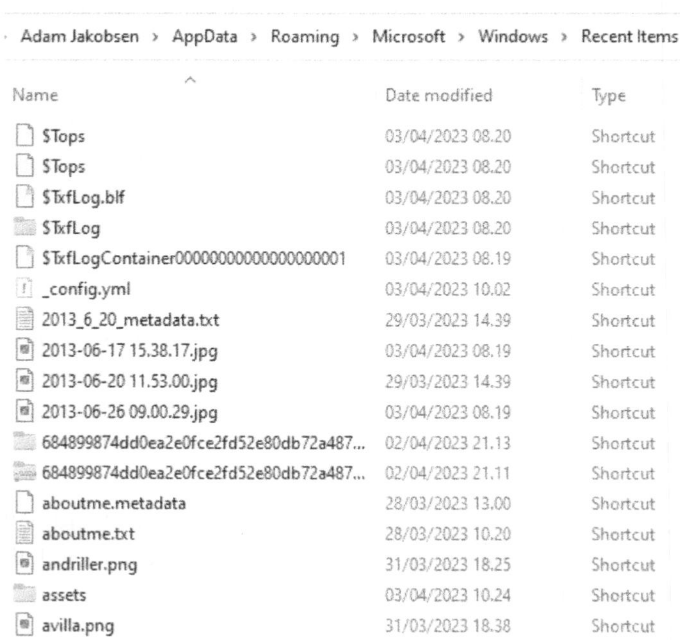

Figure 6.11 LNK files.

only one shortcut file will be created. When it comes to the timestamp of the .lnk files the creation timestamp is the first time a file with the given name was opened, and the Edit date is the last time a file with that name was opened. The information inside the .lnk only points to one file, which is the last file that was opened, allowing us to identify the first and last times a file with a given name was opened.

Data stored in LNK files includes:

1. Timestamps:
   (a) Created: Time when the target file was first opened
   (b) Modified: Time when the target file was last opened
2. Size of the target file
3. Volume information, such as name, type, and volume GUID
4. Fixed, removable, or network target
5. Original path and location of the target file

The examination of LNK files can be done using the following tools:

1. LEcmd by Eric Zimmerman
2. LP by TZWorks.net

These tools can help you analyze the contents of LNK files and gather valuable information about the files or URLs accessed by the user. Manual parsing of lnk files is beyond the scope of this book; those interested should look at the Microsoft documentation for shell link.[25]

6.4.4.3 Office Recent Files

Tracks what files in MS Office programs have recently been opened. The first task is to find the corresponding version that is installed on the system.

Office versions:

- 16.0 = Office 365 (2016)
- 15.0 = Office 2013
- 14.0 = Office 2010
- 11.0 = Office 2003
- 12.0 = Office 2007
- 10.0 = Office XP

Depending on the version installed, the next step is to find what recent files have been opened using Office, which can be found in one of two places:

Pre-Office 365:

```
NTUSER.DAT\Software\Microsoft\Office\<version>\<program>\
```

25 https://learn.microsoft.com/en-us/openspecs/windows_protocols/ms-shllink/16cb4ca1-9339-4d0c-a68d-bf1d6cc0f943.

Location for Office 365:

```
NTUSER.DAT\Software\Microsoft\Office\<version>\<program>\UserMRU
    \<LiveID_# or ADAL_#> \<FileMRU placeMRU>
```

The reading location key stores useful information such as the last cursor location for files, the full file path, and the datetime for when the file was last closed.

For example, Office 365 reading location:

```
NTUSER.dat\SOFTWARE\Microsoft\Office\16.0\Word\Reading Locations
```

6.4.4.4 Shellbag

Shellbags are a part of Windows registry found within NTUser.dat and USRClass.dat registry hives, and each user on the system has their own shellbags. The purpose of the shellbag is to record folders accessed by the user and viewing preferences of Windows Explorer (e.g., window size, icon, position) and creating a representation of folders, network locations, libraries, and virtual folders the user has visited, with their preferences. The advantage of shellbags is that they persist even after the directories have been removed. Shellbags can provide valuable information about deleted folders and the contents of external drives that were previously connected to the system. Below in Figure 6.12 you can see a view of the directory shellbag recorded on my computer. Over half of the drives listed in the shellbag were attached when I captured this and lists all folders that existed

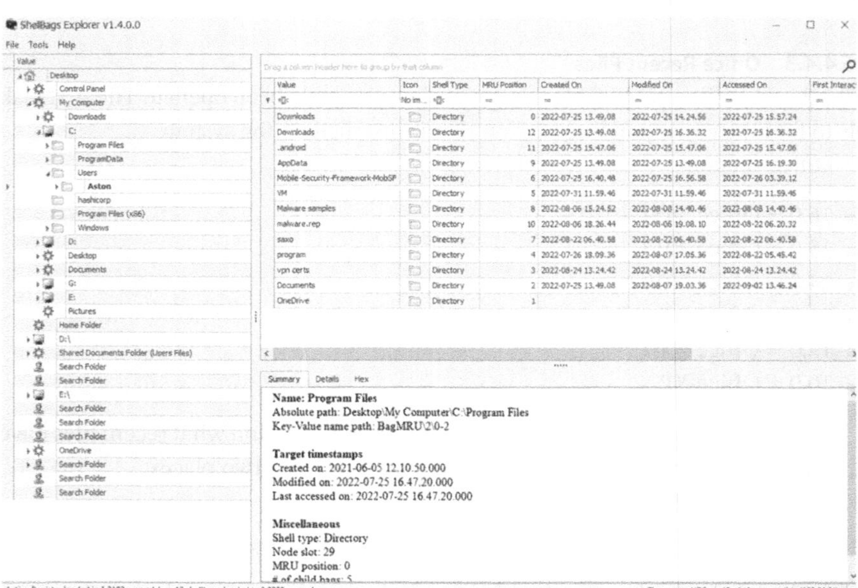

Figure 6.12 Shellbag Explorer.

within the drive. This is a powerful tool that not only shows deleted files but also what files existed within external drives.

It can be used to identify the access time of folders and pinpoint deleted folders. When it comes to parsing the data the tools by Eric Zimmerman can be used ShellbagExplorer and SBEcmd.[26]

Most of the data for shellbags is stored in the UsrClass:

USRCLASS.dat stores the vast majority of shellbag data, which includes local, network, and removable directories. With usrclass.dat located at:

```
%userprofile%\AppData\Local\Microsoft\Windows\
```

Location for the shellbag data within USERCLASS.DAT:

```
USRCLASS.DAT\Local Settings\Software\Microsoft\Windows\Shell\Bags
USRCLASS.DAT\Local Settings\Software\Microsoft\Windows\Shell\BagMRU
```

NTUSER.dat (stores additional network folders):

```
NTUSER.DAT\Software\Microsoft\Windowshell\BagMRU
NTUSER.DAT\Software\Microsoft\Windowshell\Bags
```

The "Bags" key stores folder preference data, such as window size and layout, while "BagMRU" stores the directory structure of folders accessed using Explorer. Each BagMRU key contains three subkeys:

1. **MRUListEx**: Stores the order in which subfolders were accessed. The data is stored in a 79-byte array, with every 4-byte value indicating folder access, with the most recently accessed listed first.
2. **NodeSlot**: Points to the "Bags" key, which stores the data for that folder.
3. **NodeSlots**: Only found in the BagMRU key and is updated upon new shellbag creation.

The registry structure mirrors the tree structure of Explorer. To identify the folder name, you must open the parent key and look at the "Data value" for the target node.

By examining the folder as shown in Figure 6.13 within the MRUListEx, it is possible to determine when the directory was accessed. The Last Write Time stored within the registry can be used to identify the first or last update time of the folder, applicable for all BagMRU keys. Additionally, you can identify the file system by the inode number for FAT32, the sequence number is null, while for NTFS, the sequence number is filled.

6.4.4.5 Open/Save MRU

Tracks files that have been opened and saved using the Windows shell dialog box. This is done by file extension and records the last open file by extension. The star

26 https://ericzimmerman.github.io.

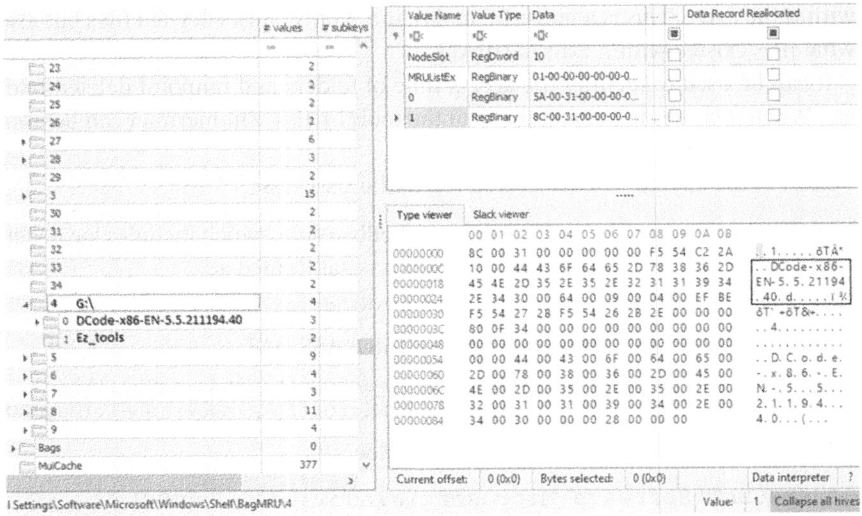

Figure 6.13 Bag MRU.

(*) key tracks the most recent files of any extension input in an Open/Save dialog. The .??? subkey stores specific extension info from the Open/Save dialog box.

XP:

```
NTUSER.DAT\Software\Microsoft\Windows\CurrentVersion\Explorer\
    ComDlg32\OpenSaveMRU
```

Win7/8/10:

```
NTUSER.DAT\Software\Microsoft\Windows\CurrentVersion\Explorer\
    ComDlg32\OpenSavePIDlMRU
```

Also tracks files opened by specific extensions. It tracks the last file and folder opened and is used to populate data in recent menus of the Start menu.

6.4.5 Program and File Execution

Windows systems store a wealth of information about program and file execution in various locations, such as registry keys and database files. Some of the key artifacts include:

1. **UserAssist**: Lists GUI-based programs executed by a user, including the run count, application name, last run time, and focus time.
2. **MUICache**: Identifies GUI applications run by users, but without timestamps.
3. **Windows 10 Timeline**: Records recently used applications and files in a timeline accessible via the "win+tab" key.

4. **BAM & DAM**: Tracks the path of both GUI and non-GUI executed files and their last execution times on Windows 10.
5. **Amcache.hve**: Tracks installed applications on the system, including the full path, SHA1 hash, and first-run time.
6. **Jump List**: Records recent files opened and tasks performed by applications, allowing for analysis of frequency and timestamps.
7. **Last-visited MRU**: Tracks file extensions used with specific applications and the directories of the accessed files.
8. **RecentApp**: Records user execution of GUI-based applications and files recently opened by those applications.
9. **Prefetch**: Enhances performance by caching required files and resources, providing information about the execution of PE files.
10. **LastVisitedMRU**: Tracks the specific executable used by an application to open files documented in the OpenSaveMRU key.
11. **Taskbar Feature Usage**: Records user interaction with the taskbar, tracking GUI applications only.
12. **CapabilityAccessManager**: Monitors application usage of microphones, cameras, and other settings.
13. **RUN Box Execution**: Records the execution of programs or commands through the RUN box (Win+R).

6.4.5.1 UserAssist

UserAssist stores data about GUI-based programs executed by specific users and their run counts. The information is organized by application GUID. The good thing is Microsoft has created a list of folder GUIDs.[27] The key includes the following information:

6.4.5.2 MUICache

MUICache identifies GUI applications run by users but does not provide timestamps for when the application was executed. The registry key for MUICache is:

```
USRCLASS.dat\Software\Microsoft\Windows\Shell\MuiCache
```

You can use Nirsoft UserAssistView to analyze this information.

6.4.5.3 Windows 10 Timeline

Windows 10 Timeline records recently used applications and files. This data is stored in an SQLite database located at:

```
C:\Users\AppData\Local\ConnectedDevicesPlatform\<GUID>\
    ActivitiesCache.db
```

You can use an SQLite browser to analyze this data.

27 https://learn.microsoft.com/en-gb/windows/win32/shell/knownfolderid.

6.4.5.4 BAM and DAM

Windows Background Activity Moderator (BAM) and Desktop Activity Moderator (DAM) are used for application throttling and utilization to save battery power. They track the path of both GUI and non-GUI executed files and the last execution time of the file. This only exists on Windows 10.

```
BAM registry key: SYSTEM\CurrentControlSet\Services\bam\
    UserSettings\<SID>
DAM registry key: SYSTEM\CurrentControlSet\Services\dam\
    UserSettings\<SID>
```

6.4.5.5 Amcache.hve

Amcache.hve tracks installed applications on the system. It includes an entry for every executable run on the system. Amcache can be used to identify systems where malware has been executed because it stores the SHA1 hash of the executable. It stores information such as the full path, SHA1 hash, $StandardInfo, and last edit time (first run time).

The location of the Amcache.hve is at C:\Windows\AppCompat\Programs\Amcache.hve. The key that stores the desired data is:

```
amcache.hve\File\<Volume GUID>\#
```

To analyze this artifact, you can use the amcacheParser or SBEcmd[28] tools developed by Eric Zimmerman.

6.4.5.6 Jump List

Jump Lists are a feature in Windows that allows users to quickly access frequently and recently used items by right-clicking an application in the taskbar as shown in Figure 6.14. This feature was introduced in Windows 7 and includes not only recent files but also recent tasks. It not only tracks program execution but also what files have been used with the application.

The data jump list is based on data stored in the AutomaticDestinations folder using the naming convention AppID.AutomaticDestinations-ms where every file corresponds to a specific application version defined by the application ID. [EZJumpList](https://dfir.to/EZJumpList) have a list of the most common applications and their application id.

AutomaticDestinations:

```
%USERPROFILE%\AppData\Roaming\Microsoft\Windows\Recent\
    AutomaticDestinations
```

The other source is CustomDestinations. This is an optional feature developers can enable for their application; what is recorded here is up to the

28 https://ericzimmerman.github.io/.

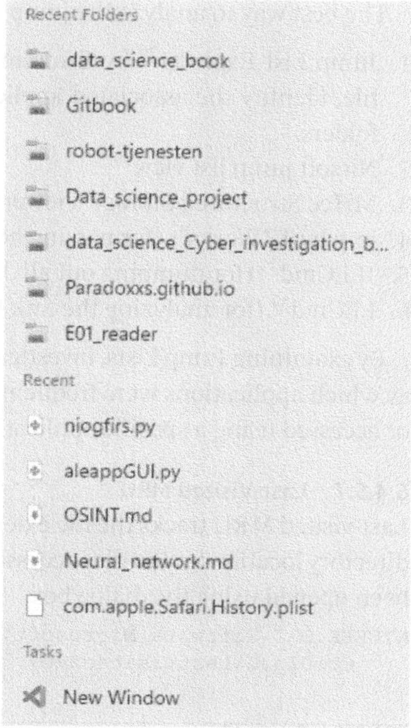

Figure 6.14 Recent open.

developer. They follow the same naming convention as AutomaticDestination with {AppID}.CustomDestinations-ms, e.g., Firefox custom entries track newly opened tabs, even if the user was using private browsing mode.

CustomDestinations:

```
%USERPROFILE%\AppData\Roaming\Microsoft\Windows\Recent\
    CustomDestinations
```

These jump list files are OLE databases with multiple streams each containing a .lnk file. As stated before deleting from a database is difficult; this allows us to recover deleted data. It is possible to extract the lnk files with a tools like JLECmd and then analyze them using LeCMD to extract the data; an even easier way is to use Jump List Explorer which does everything for you in a nice GUI interface. It is also possible to judge the frequency for which an application has been used by the size of the jump list file. The timestamp of the jump list files can be used to identify the first and last times the application was executed.

- First time of execution of the application, Creation Time = First-time item added to the AppID file.
- Last time of execution of application w/file open, Edit Time = Last time item added to the AppID file.

The best way to analyze the jump list files is by using one of the tools below:

1. Jump List Explorer[29] by Eric Zimmerman: This tool can open any Jump List file, identify the associated application, and display recently opened files and folders.
2. Nirsoft jump list view[30]
3. MiTec Structured Storage Viewer[31] (for AutomaticDestination)
4. jmp by TZWorks[32] (for parsing both automatic and custom files)
5. JLECmd[33] (for dumping out all .lnk files)
6. LECmd[34] (for analyzing the .lnk files)

By examining Jump Lists, investigators can gain insights into user behavior, such as which applications were frequently used and which files were recently opened or accessed using a specific application.

6.4.5.7 Last-Visited MRU

Last-visited MRU tracks the file extensions used with specific applications and the directory location for the files accessed by that application. It records files that have been opened using the dialog box.

```
NTUSER.DAT\Software\Microsoft\Windows\CurrentVersion\Explorer\
    ComDlg32\LastVisitedMRU
```

6.4.5.8 RecentApp

RecentApp tracks user execution of GUI-based applications and files recently opened by those applications. The registry key locations are:

Registry key locations: Keys: RecentApp GUID

- APPID = name of application
- LastAccessedTime = last execution time in UTC
- LunchCount = count for how many times the application has been executed

```
ntuser.dat\Software\microsoft\windows\CurrentVersion\Search\
    RecentApps
```

Recent item key: RecentItem GUID (the file the application opens)

- Path of file or destination
- LastAccessTime

```
ntuser.dat\Software\microsoft\windows\CurrentVersion\Search\
    RecentApps\<APP GUID>\RecentItems
```

---

29 https://ericzimmerman.github.io/.
30 https://www.nirsoft.net/utils/jump_lists_view.html.
31 https://www.mitec.cz/ssv.html.
32 https://tzworks.com/prototype_page.php?proto_id=20.
33 https://github.com/EricZimmerman/JLECmd.
34 https://github.com/EricZimmerman/LECmd.

6.4.5.9 Prefetch

Prefetch is used to increase the performance of the execution of PE files by caching the first 10 seconds of the required files and resources into memory. The cache manager takes all the files and directories used by an executable and maps them into a .pf file. Allows Prefetch to track both the execution of PE files and any files the executable has interacted with; this will also include the dynamic link library (DLL) that was loaded, which can potentially be very useful in malware cases. There are two Prefetch files with the same name but two different hash values at the end; this can indicate that the file was executed from two different locations or with different parameters. Forensic examiners can use Prefetch to prove application execution.

Is the Prefetch folder empty? This is an indicator that Prefetch is disabled on the system. To verify this it is possible to use the register key at the following location:

```
SYSTEM\Controlset001\Control\Session Manager\Memory management\
    PrefetchParameters\
```

Each .pf will include the first and last times of execution, the number of times it was run, and the file path.

- Win8+, there are up to 1024 files .pf files, with each storing the last 8 times the file was executed.
- Created date – first executed
- Modified date – last executed

```
Window\prefetch\*.pf
Window\prefetch\layout.ini
```

To analyze Prefetch files, you can use tools such as:

- PEcmd,[35] Prefetch Explorer cmd
- pf[36] from TZworks.net

6.4.5.10 LastVisitedMRU

LastVisitedMRU tracks the specific executable used by an application to open the files documented in the OpenSaveMRU key. The registry key location is:

```
NTUser.dat\software\Microsoft\windows\currentVersion\Explorer\
    ComDlg32\LastVisitedPidlMRU
```

6.4.5.11 Taskbar Feature Usage

Taskbar feature usage tracks how users interact with the taskbar. It only tracks GUI applications and does not store timestamps.

35 https://github.com/EricZimmerman/PECmd.
36 https://www.tzworks.com/prototype_page.php?proto_id=1.

- AppLaunch track data for pinned application only (shows knowledge of the application)
- AppSwitched track count of application focus (user interaction with application)

```
NTUSER\Software\Microsoft\Windows\CurrentVersion\Explorer\
    FeatureUsage
```

6.4.5.12 CapabilityAccessManager

CapabilityAccessManager tracks application usage of microphones, cameras, and other application-specific settings. The registry key locations are:

```
NTUSER\Software\Microsoft\Windows\CurrentVersion\
    CapabilityAccessManager\ConsentStore
SOFTWARE\Microsoft\Windows\CurrentVersion\CapabilityAccessManager\
    ConsentStore
```

6.4.5.13 RUN Box Execution

RUN Box Execution tracks the execution of programs or commands through the RUN box (Win+R), shown in Figure 6.15. The keys are ordered by when the command was executed.

The registry key location is:

```
NTuser.dat\Software\microsoft\windows\CurrentVersion\Explorer\
    RunMRU
```

6.4.6 External Device/USB Usage

You might see a lot of places talk about how Windows stores the device serial number. This is not always true; the number can also be a Windows-assigned identification number. This identification is uniquely generated based on multiple factors such as the USB used, the port it was plugged into, and if the Windows version has changed since the last time. And it could have nothing to do with the manufacturer's serial number.

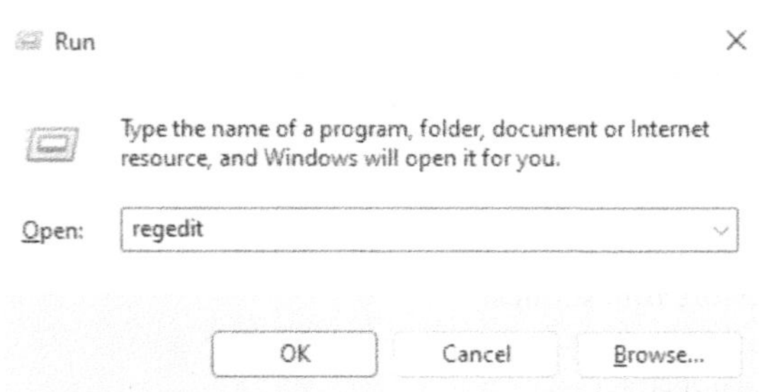

Figure 6.15 Run dialog box.

In other cases, the value stored in the register is the serial ID of the controller which can be shared across multiple disks from the same provider. The factor in play that it comes down to if the computer uses the disk serial number or the controller? is the response speed of the disk; if the disk is too slow to return the serial, it will use the controller serial number instead of the disk.

This means we cannot use this information to identify a specific USB or tell if there are any missing devices. You can read more about the topic in the paper "The Truth About USB Device Serial Numbers."[37]

6.4.6.1 USB Device Types

1. Mass Storage Class (MSC), also referred to as USB Mass Storage.
2. Picture Transfer Protocol (PTP)
3. Media Transfer Protocol (MTP), a newer edition of PTP

1. **USBSTOR**: Tracks USB devices plugged into the machine and identifies by the serial number
2. **Device Connection Time**: Determines the first and last times a USB device was connected to a Windows machine, using the setupapi log file and registry.
3. **PnP Events**: Logs Plug and Play driver installations, which are not enabled by default, and records device information and connection status.
4. **Drive Letter and Volume Name**: Identifies the last drive letter and volume name for a USB device, which can be correlated with other data for analysis.
5. **Volume Identification Number**: Discovers the identification number of the file system on a USB device, allowing for data correlation across LNK files and the RecentDocs key.
6. **MTP Device**: MTP devices might create LNK files depending on the app and file type, pointing back to the MTP source device or the WPDNSE folder on the machine.
7. **User USB Device**: Determines the unique USB devices plugged in by a user, using the device identification number.
8. **Removable Devices Logs**: Logs USB events, such as driver installations and access attempts, if enabled.

Examining these artifacts can help investigators uncover information about user activities involving USB devices, providing insights into potential data transfers, unauthorized access, and more.

6.4.6.2 Plugged in USB

Tracks USB devices plugged into the machine and identifies the following information about the USBs: Serial number vendor, and product, Volume GUID.

37 https://www.sans.org/blog/the-truth-about-usb-device-serial-numbers/.

Devices that do not have a serial number get assigned a unique Windows-assigned identification number which can be identified by having an "&" in the third character in their serial number; the windows identifier is only unique to the system.

Another thing to note, because of the scheduled task "Plug and Play Cleanup," many of the evidence will only store up to 30 days of activity.

The serial number is identified here, can be corrected with the other information about the USB:

```
HKEY\_LOCAL\_MACHINE\SYSTEM\CurrentControlSet\Enum\USBSTOR
```

Find the vendor and product id by using the serial number to find the correct entry at:

```
HKEY\_LOCAL\_MACHINE\SYSTEM\CurrentControlSet\Enum\USB\vid_###&
    pid_###\{Serial number}
```

The vendor and product ID can be looked up online at sites like https://the-sz.com/products/usbid/index.php.

Find the correct "Windows portable Devices" entry is done by looking for the serial number in the key name, which will contain the serial number and the device GUID. The data will have the friend name aka volume name of the USB. The key last write time is when the USB was last connected to the device:

```
SOFTWARE\Microsoft\Windows Portable Devices\Devices
```

To find the Volume GUID and Drive letter, use the serial number or device GUID inside the "Device data" field to find the correct entries; there should be two entries for each device: one for the drive letter and another for the volume serial GUID:

```
SYSTEM\MountedDevices
```

Knowing the Volume Name and drive letter can be correlated to shortcut files (LNK) and RecentDocs.

- The Shortcut File (LNK) can contain the drive letter and volume name.
- RecentDocs Registry Key, in most cases, will contain the volume name when the USB device is opened via Explorer.

6.4.6.3 Setupapi

Setupapi is the plug-and-play log file, containing the first connected time. You can locate the device of interest by searching for the Windows-assigned identification number and looking at the first entry. The log file is set to the local time zone.

```
C:\Windows\inf\setupapi.dev.log
```

6.4.6.4 Plug-and-Play Cleanup

"Plug-and-play cleanup" will remove this information. The system hive contains the first, last, and removal times. It cannot be viewed on a live machine; only forensics tools can be used to view this information.

- 0064 = First Install (Win7-10)
- 0066 = Last Connected (Win8-10)
- 0067 = Removal (safe eject or pull)

```
System\CurrentControlSet\Enum\USBSTOR\<Vendor_Product_Version>\
    <USBSerial#<\Properties\<83da6326-97a6-4088-9453-a19231573b29>
    \####
```

6.4.6.5 PnP Events

Plug and play driver installation. This is not enabled by default. The log files can be used to identify the device type and Windows-assigned identification number, but it will only show the first time a device was plugged in. All the events are located in the security log.

Event id:

- 20001 – Plug and Play driver install attempted
- 4663 – Attempt to access removable storage object
- 6416 – New external device was recognized on the system

Key data:

- Timestamp
- Device information
- Serial number
- Status (0 = no errors)

Event log:

```
%system root%\System32\winevt\logs\System.evtx
```

6.4.6.6 MTP Device

Might create LNK files depending on the app and file type. Some MTP LNK files will not point back to the MTP source device but instead to the WPDNSE folder on the machine only.

```
%userprofile%\appdata\local\temp\wpdnse\textbackslash\<GUID>
```

6.4.6.7 User USB Device

Unique USB device plugged in by the user. The device "GUID" can be used to identify the user that plugged in the device. Look for the same "GUID" in _SYSTEM\MountedDevices.

"Last write time" of this key will correspond to the last time the device was plugged into the device by the user.

```
NTUSER.dat\software\Microsoft\Windows\CurrentVersion\Explorer\
    MountPoints2
```

6.4.6.8 Removable Devices Logs

Using event logs to detect USB events; needs to be enabled before any logs get written.

Events id:

- 2001 (system log) – Plug and Play driver install attempted
- 4663 (Security log) – Attempt to access removable storage object
- 4656 (Security) – Failure to access removable storage object
- 6416 (Security) – A new external device was recognized on the system

```
windows\system32\winevt\logs
```

6.4.7 Network Activity Artifacts

Analyzing network activity artifacts can provide valuable information about user behavior, network connections, and possible unauthorized access or data transfers. By examining these artifacts, investigators can uncover information about the networks a computer has connected to, user activities involving network shares, and potential unauthorized access or data transfers. This information can be crucial for understanding user behavior, tracking device location, and identifying security breaches.

6.4.7.1 Network Mapping

Will list any network shares that have been mapped by the user.

```
NTUSER.dat\software\Microsoft\Windows\CurrentVersion\Explorer\
    MountPoints2
```

6.4.7.2 Network History

Track the networks the computer has been connected to, both wired and wireless, which are located at three different keys. They record the domain/intranet name, the SSID, and the gateway MAC address for each network. Can be used to identify intranets and networks that the computer has been connected to. Allowing one to determine the last time the computer have been connected to the network.

```
SOFTWARE\Microsoft\Windows NT\CurrentVersion\NetworkList\Nla\Cache
SOFTWARE\Microsoft\Windows NT\CurrentVersion\NetworkList\
    Signatures\Managed
```

Contains the WIFI connection with:

- DNSSuffix – Domain
- Firstnetwork – SSID
- DefaultGatewayMac – MAC address
- ProfileGuid – Used in the\NetworkList\Profiles

```
SOFTWARE\Microsoft\Windows NT\CurrentVersion\NetworkList\
    Signatures\Unmanaged
```

6.4.7.3 Network Profiles Key

Identify the type of network the computer was connected to, and store the SSID of the previous wireless network and the first and last connected to the network. Time is recorded in computer local time using HEX encoding.

- Nametype value 0×47 = wireless
- Nametype value 0×06 = wired
- Nametype value 0×F3 = Broadband (3g)
- Nametype value 0×17 = VPN

```
SOFTWARE\Microsoft\Windows NT\CurrentVersion\NetworkList\
Profiles
```

6.4.7.4 IP Address

Track the IP address the machine was assigned to, for each network interface.

```
SYSTEM\currentcontrolset\services\tcpip\parameters\
interfaces\<GUID>
```

6.4.8 Commands

Command artifacts provide information about the commands executed on a device, offering insights into user activities and possible malicious actions. Analyzing these command artifacts can help investigators uncover user actions, identify potential security risks, and detect malicious activities.

6.4.8.1 Powershell History

History of the PowerShell commands executed by the user. The default size is 4096 commands.

```
%appdata%\roaming\Microsoft\Windows\Powershell\PSReadLine\
    consoleHost_History.txt
```

6.4.8.2 WMI

```
Get-WMIObject -Namespace root\Subscription -Class _ _EventFilter
Get-WMIObject -Namespace root\Subscription -Class _ _EventConsumer
Get-WMIObject -Namespace root\Subscription -Class
    _ _FliterToConsumerBinding
```

6.4.8.3 WMI Database

Objects.data = object managed by WMI Index.btr = binary tree index, index files imported into objects.data Mapping[1-3].map = correlates data in objects.data and index.btr

```
%systemroot%\system32\wbem\repository
```

6.4.8.4 Command Line Event Log

Remember, for this to be recorded, you need to activate the correct policy. For CMD logging, you can find the policy inside "Computer Configuration\Administrative Templates\System\Audit Process Creation\Include command line in process creation events"(Set to enabled).

Event ID:4688, A new process has been created.

Look at the field "New Process Name"

```
Windows\System32\winevt\logs\Security
```

Event ID:4103-4104

1. 4103, Microsoft-Windows-PowerShell: look at "Command Path"
2. 4104, Execute a Remote Command: Look at the following fields "Account name," "Account domain," "client address," "Client port,"

```
Windows\System32\winevt\logs\Powershell\operational
```

6.4.8.5 WMI Event Log

WMI-activity/operational From event ID: 5847 to 5861

```
Windows\System32\winevt\logs\Security
Windows\System32\winevt\logs\Powershell\operational
```

6.4.9 Browser Usage Artifacts

Browser usage artifacts provide insights into a user's online activities, including visited websites, downloaded files, and stored cookies. By examining these artifacts, investigators can gain a better understanding of a user's online behavior, identify potential security risks, and uncover malicious activities.

1. **Account Records**: Records the number of times a site has been visited for different browsers such as Internet Explorer, Firefox, and Chrome.
2. **Cookies**: Gives insights into websites visited and user activity. Cookie storage locations differ for Internet Explorer, Firefox, and Chrome.
3. **History**: Records of websites visited, with storage locations varying for Internet Explorer, Firefox, and Chrome.

4. **Cache**: Cached web page components to speed up site loading times. Cache storage locations differ for Internet Explorer, Edge, Firefox, and Chrome.
5. **Browser Download Manager**: Provides information on downloaded files and accessed applications on the system. Storage locations differ for Firefox and Internet Explorer.
6. **Session Restore**: Crash recovery data stored in different locations for Internet Explorer, Firefox, and Chrome.
7. **Browser Passwords**: Stores user passwords for different browsers like Chrome and Edge.
8. **Supercookies**: Local stored objects (LSO) or flash cookies stored in a specific location on the user's computer.

6.4.9.1 Account Records

Records the number of times a site has been visited for different browsers such as Internet Explorer, Firefox, and Chrome.

Internet Explorer

```
IE8-9: %USERPROFILE%\AppData\Roaming\Microsoft\Windows\
    IEDownloadHistory\index.dat
IE10-11: %USERPROFILE%\AppData\Local\Microsoft\Windows\WebCache\
    WebCacheV\*.dat
```

Firefox

```
%USERPROFILE%\AppData\Roaming\Mozilla\Firefox\Profiles.default\
    places.sqlite
```

Chrome

```
Win7/8/10: %USERPROFILE%\AppData\Local\Google\Chrome\User Data\
    Default\History
```

6.4.9.2 Cookies

Cookies give insight into websites visited and activity.

Internet Explorer

```
IE6-8: %USERPROFILE%\AppData\Roaming\Microsoft\Windows\Cookies
IE10: %USERPROFILE%\AppData\Roaming\Microsoft\Windows\Cookies
IE11: %USERPROFILE%\AppData\Local\Microsoft\Windows\INetCookies
```

Firefox

```
XP: %USERPROFILE%\Application Data\Mozilla\Firefox\Profiles.
    default\cookies.sqlite
Win7/8/10: %USERPROFILE%\AppData\Roaming\Mozilla\Firefox\Profiles.
    default\cookies.sqlite
```

Chrome

```
XP: %USERPROFILE%\Local Settings\ApplicationData\Google\Chrome\
    User Data\Default\Local Storage
Win7/8/10: %USERPROFILE%\AppData\Local\Google\Chrome\User Data\
    Default\Local Storage
```

6.4.9.3 History

Records of websites visited.

Internet Explorer

```
IE6-7: %USERPROFILE%\Local Settings\History\History.IE5
IE8-9: %USERPROFILE%\AppData\Local\Microsoft\Windows\History\
    History.IE5
IE10, 11, Edge: %USERPROFILE%\AppData\Local\Microsoft\Windows\
    WebCache\ WebCacheV\*.dat
```

Firefox

```
XP: %USERPROFILE%\Application Data\Mozilla\Firefox\Profiles.
    default\places.sqlite
Win7/8/10: %USERPROFILE%\AppData\Roaming\Mozilla\Firefox\
    Profiles.default\places.sqlite
```

Chrome

```
XP: %USERPROFILE%\Local Settings\Application Data\Google\Chrome\
    User Data\Default\History
Win7/8/10: %USERPROFILE%\AppData\Local\Google\Chrome\ User Data\
    Default\History
```

6.4.9.4 Cache

Cache for web page components to speed up site load time.

6.4.9.5 Internet Explorer

```
IE8-9: %USERPROFILE%\AppData\Local\Microsoft\Windows\Temporary
    Internet Files\Content.IE5
IE10: %USERPROFILE%\AppData\Local\Microsoft\Windows\Temporary
    Internet Files\Content.IE5
IE11: %USERPROFILE%\AppData\Local\Microsoft\Windows\INetCache\IE
```

Edge

```
%USERPROFILE%\AppData\Local\Packages\microsoft
```

Firefox

```
XP: %USERPROFILE%\Local Settings\ApplicationData\Mozilla\Firefox\
    Profiles.default\Cache
Win7/8/10: %USERPROFILE%\AppData\Local\Mozilla\Firefox\Profiles.
    default\Cache
```

Chrome

```
XP: %USERPROFILE%\Local Settings\Application Data\Google\Chrome\
    User Data\Default\Cache\data\_ and f\_
Win7/8/10: %USERPROFILE%\AppData\Local\Google\Chrome\User Data\
    Default\Cache\- data\_ and f\_
```

6.4.9.6 Browser Download Manager

A little-known fact about IE History is that the information stored in the history files is not just related to Internet browsing. The history also records local and remote (via network shares) file access, giving us an excellent means for determining which files and applications were accessed on the system, day by day.

Firefox

```
XP: %USERPROFILE%\Application Data\Mozilla\Firefox\Profiles.
    default\downloads.sqlite

Win7/8/10: %USERPROFILE%\AppData\Roaming\Mozilla\Firefox\Profiles.
    default\downloads.sqlite
```

Internet Explorer

```
IE6-7: %USERPROFILE%\LocalSettings\History\History.IE5

IE8-9: %USERPROFILE%\AppData\Local\Microsoft\WindowsHistory\
    History.IE5

IE10-11: %USERPROFILE%\AppData\Local\Microsoft\Windows\WebCache\
    WebCacheV\*.dat
```

6.4.9.7 Session Restore

Crash recovery

```
IE Win7+: %USERPROFILE%\AppData\Local\Microsoft\Internet Explorer\
    Recovery
Firefox Win7+: %USERPROFILE%\AppData\Roaming\
 Mozilla\ Firefox\Profiles.default\sessionstore.js
Chrome Win7/8/10: %USERPROFILE%\AppData\Local\Google\Chrome\User
    Data\Default\Files = Current Session, Current Tabs, Last
    Session, Last Tabs
```

6.4.9.8 Browser Password

```
Chrome Win7+: C:\Users\\$username\AppData\Local\Google\Chrome\User
    Data\Default
Edge Win7+: \%userprofile\appdata\local\Microsoft\Edge\ User Data\
    Default\Login Data
```

6.4.9.9 Supercookies

Local stored objects (LSO) or flash cookies are stored in a specific location on the user's computer.

```
%appdata%\Roaming\macromedia\Flashplayer\#sharedObjects\
    <randomprofileid>
```

6.4.10 Mail

Outlook is a popular mail application used in enterprise environments. Key artifacts related to Outlook include mail archives, offline folder files, and unread mail.

6.4.10.1 Mail Archives

Enabled by default, mail archives can store up to 50 GB of emails and calendar data in .pst files. The archive location for Outlook 2010 and earlier is

```
\%userprofile\appdata\local\microsoft\outlook
```

6.4.10.2 Offline Folder Files

These files, with the .ost extension, enable offline mail access using the "cached exchange mode." By default, they store the last 12 months of mail and can hold up to 50 GB. The Outlook offline folder location is at:

```
%USERPROFILE%\AppData\Local\Microsoft\Outlook for Windows 7/8/10.
```

To access .pst and .ost files, consider using PST viewer[38] or OST viewer[39] from Nucleus Technologies.

6.4.10.3 Unread Mail

The unread mail registry key HKCU\Software\Microsoft\Windows\Current Version\UnreadMail displays the combined number of unread items for all accounts, for mail applications that expose their unread count, such as Outlook, Outlook Express, or Windows Live Messenger. The DateTime is stored in little-Endian Hexadecimal formats.

When analyzing these artifacts, investigators can provide valuable insights into a user's email activities, communications, and potential security risks or malicious behavior. Note that for private email, users typically rely on cloud-based services like Gmail.

This section only covers the location for Outlook, as it is the only mail application I have seen used in enterprises. When it comes to private, it is mostly cloud-based email applications like Gmail, which is not stored on the device.

---

38 https://www.nucleustechnologies.com/pst-viewer.html.
39 https://www.nucleustechnologies.com/ost-viewer.html.

6.4.11 Persistence

Persistence artifacts are the locations and methods that can be used by programs to remain active between system boots. Analyzing these artifacts can help identify potentially malicious programs or processes that are set to run automatically.

6.4.11.1 Auto Start Programs

Programs can be set to start automatically at boot using the following registry locations:

```
NTUSER.dat\Software\Microsoft\Windows\CurrentVersion\Run
NTUSER.dat\Software\Microsoft\Windows\CurrentVersion\RunOnce
SOFTWARE\Microsoft\Windows\CurrentVersion\RunOnce
SOFTWARE\Microsoft\Windows\CurrentVersion\Policies\Explorer\Run
SOFTWARE\Microsoft\Windows\CurrentVersion\Run
```

Programs can also be set to run at startup using the following file path:

```
{Startup folder}: \%userprofile\AppData\Roaming\Microsoft\Windows
    \Start menu\Programs\Startup
{Startup registry Explorer}: SOFTWARE\Microsoft\Windows\
    CurrentVersion\Policies\Explorer
{Startup registry userinit}: SOFTWARE\Microsoft\Windows NT\
    CurrentVersion\ Winlogon\Userinit
```

6.4.11.2 Scheduled Tasks

Tasks set to run at specific times or intervals can be identified using the following registry locations and log files:

Registry:

```
Software\Microsoft\Windows NT\CurrentVersion\Schedule\TaskCache\

    Tasks
Software\Microsoft\Windows NT\CurrentVersion\Schedule\TaskCache\
    Tree
```

Logs: Event IDs of interest:

- 106
- 141
- 200
- 4698

```
Windows\System32\winevt\logs\security.evtx
Windows\System32\winevt\logs\task scheduler.evtx
```

The location for scheduled tasks jobs.

```
\Windows\System32\Tasks
```

6.4.11.3 Service

Analyze logs for suspicious service events using the following Event IDs:

System:

- 7034 – Service crashed unexpectedly
- 7035 – Service sent a Start/Stop control
- 7036 – Service started or stopped
- 7040 – Start type changed (Boot — On Request — Disabled)
- 7045 – A service was installed on the system (Win2008R2+)

Security:

- 4697 – A service was installed on the system

Log file locations:

```
Windows\System32\winevt\logs\System.evtx
Windows\System32\winevt\logs\Security.evtx
```

Services located at SYSTEM\CurrentControlSet\Services that have a 0x2 flag start at boot:

6.4.12 Evidence Destruction

The following locations and methods can be used to detect attempts at evidence destruction on a device:

6.4.12.1 Log Clearing

Event logs that are created when logs are cleared can be an indication of evidence tampering. Look for the following Event IDs in the specified log locations: Event IDs:

- Security: 1102
- System: 104

Log locations:

```
\item Windows\System32\Winevt\logs\Security
\item Windows\System32\Winevt\logs\System
```

6.4.12.2 File Deletion Detection Using $J

The $J file is a journal file that records activity on the file system. You can analyze this file to detect file deletion events. MTFECmd can be used to parse the file.

The $J file is located at /$Extend/$UsnJrnl/J$

To create a CSV file of both $J and $MFT, we can use MFTECmd with the following arguments:

```
MFTECmd.exe -f "D:\Edu\$J" -m "D:\Edu\$MFT" --csv.
```

The **entry number** can be used to identify if the unallocated data of the file has been overwritten and determine if it is possible to recover the data. Use the following command to analyze the entry number:

```
MFTECmd.exe -f "D:\Edu\$MFT" --de #EntryNumber
```

By examining these locations and using the provided tools, you can detect attempts at evidence destruction on a device and gather valuable information for further investigation.

6.5 Summary

Summary of Windows Forensics:

The Windows operating system remains the most prevalent OS in use, making it an essential area of focus in digital forensics. Due to its widespread use and relatively lax security settings in its default configuration, Windows systems often provide a wealth of information for forensic investigators.

Windows systems track an extensive amount of user behavior data, which can be invaluable when building a profile of the system's usage. Key areas of interest in Windows forensics include:

1. User accounts and login activity
2. Registry analysis
3. File system analysis (including $MFT and $J files)
4. Browser usage (history, cookies, cache, downloads, etc.)
5. Email (primarily Outlook) data, including mail archives and unread mail
6. Persistence mechanisms (auto-start programs, scheduled tasks, etc.)
7. Evidence of destruction (log clearing and file deletion detection)

By examining these areas and utilizing the appropriate tools and techniques, forensic investigators can gather valuable information about the system and its users, aiding in their overall analysis and investigation.

7

macOS Forensics

The macOS operating system developed by Apple and is a modified version of the Unix system, which means it shares some similarities with Linux. As such, some skills and techniques used in Linux forensics can be applied to macOS forensics like any other computer system. In this overview, we'll go through some key areas of interest in macOS forensics and the tools and techniques used to extract evidence from the device.

7.1 File System

Let's start with the file system, macOS uses APFS (Apple File System) which is a file system developed by Apple to be used on their devices. This includes Macintosh computers, iPhones, and iPads. It was first introduced in macOS 10.13 (High Sierra). APFS was created to replace the older HFS+ file system used in the previous generation. It is designed for handling modern storage technologies like solid-state drives (SSDs) and flash storage. APFS also uses a 64-bit architecture and supports full encryption, both hardware-accelerated and software-based encryption, depending upon the device the file system is implemented on.

With APFS, Apple Extended Attributes were also introduced. These attributes extend the metadata of files. Extended Attributes are responsible for timestamps of files and can include information such as file flags, access control lists (ACLs), and Finder tags. When analyzing macOS systems, it is crucial to use tools that can parse and understand Apple Extended Attributes or you might be missing important information.

Another feature of APFS is called "Time Machine"[1] which is a utility tool used for creating backups. The first step to utilizing the feature of "Time Machine," is that the users must activate it and choose a local or remote disk to store the

1 https://support.apple.com/en-us/HT201250.

Practical Cyber Intelligence: A Hands-on Guide to Digital Forensics, First Edition. Adam Tilmar Jakobsen.

backup file on. Time Machine then creates incremental backups, allowing users to restore their system to a specific point in time.

Some tools that can be used for analyzing APFS volumes and Extended Attributes include:

- **APFS-fuse:** An open-source project that allows you to mount APFS volumes on non-macOS systems. This can be helpful for forensic investigators who need to analyze macOS data on other platforms.
- **Autopsy:** A widely used open-source digital forensics platform that supports analysis of APFS volumes and Extended Attributes with the help of plugins.

Using the appropriate tools ensures that valuable insights from the APFS file system and Extended Attributes are not overlooked in the analysis process.

Let's also take a look at how the different file systems handle file timestamps. Understanding how different actions affect the timestamp of files on macOS file systems is essential in forensic analysis, to know when files were last touched. Below in Tables 7.1 and 7.2 is a summary of how various actions affect the timestamps for both HFS+ and APFS file systems.

This is for GUI interaction only:
C = Created A = Altered, I = Inherited, NA = No change

It's important to note that these timestamp changes are based on GUI interactions in macOS. When interacting with files through the command line, the

Table 7.1 HFS+.

Action	Creation	Execute	Edit	Copy (new)	Local file move
Creation	C	NA	NA	A	NA
Access	C	A	A	A	NA
Modified	C	NA	A	NA	NA

Table 7.2 APFS.

Action	Creation	Execute	Edit	Copy (new)	Local file move
Creation	C	NA	NA	NA	NA
Access	C	A	A	A	NA
Modified	C	NA	A	NA	NA
Metadata	C	NA	A	A	NA

results might differ. As a forensic investigator, understanding these timestamp behaviors can help accurately reconstruct the timeline of events and user actions on the system.

7.1.1 Native File Types

macOS comes with a native file type which is essential to be familiar with. These file types can be unfamiliar to you especially if you're coming from a Windows environment. Here are some of the most common macOS file types you should know about:

- **Mach-O**: The Mach object file format (Mach-O) is the native executable format for binaries in macOS. At a low level, Mach-O files consist of three parts or regions: the header, load commands, and data.
- **Bundle**: Bundles are self-contained application files that include everything needed to run the application. When transferred to a Windows machine, they appear as folders containing multiple files.
- **Plist**: Plist, or Property List files, are used to store information about properties and configurations for the system or applications. They come in one of two formats: XML using UTF-8 encoding, or binary. To read XML Plist files, you can use any text editor. To convert a binary Plist to XML, you can use the `plutil` command:

```
plutil -convert xml1 /path/to/propertylist.plist
```

Learn to be familiar with these file types. It will allow you to more effectively at conducting forensic investigations.

7.2 Security

Apple is one of the leading companies in securing their devices with encryption introduced back in 2003 with Filevault[2] and later in 2011 Apple introduced Filevault2, which was a redesign of the first iteration. This allowed the entire disk to be encrypted. Let's go through some of the security features that you will see when facing a modern macOS:

- **T2 Security Chip**[3]: A dedicated hardware chip for handling encryption keys and the encryption and decryption of data. With the T2 chip, you will not be able to extract any data without the password, and there is a limit on the number of

2 https://en.wikipedia.org/wiki/FileVault.
3 https://en.wikipedia.org/wiki/Apple_T2.

attempts. Currently, the maximum number of tries is 118. The T2 chip enhances the security of the device by adding a dedicated component to handle security features, ensuring that the data never leaves the chip and remains separate from the operating system. The T2 chip provides the following features:
  - Automatic SSD encryption, which also includes unallocated space.
  - Secure boot, which only allows verified operating systems trusted by Apple to run.
  - Disabling booting from an external drive.
- **FileVault**: FileVault is a full-disk encryption feature that can only be decrypted with the user login password or a recovery key, which is created when FileVault is first activated. FileVault ensures that the data on the device is protected even if the device is lost or stolen. These security features make macOS a robust and secure operating system for users. When conducting forensic investigations on macOS devices, it's essential to be aware of these security measures and how they may impact the data extraction process, which is why it is important to either get the password from the user or if found live and unlocked to do the acquisition immediately.

7.3 Acquisition

For older macOS systems without full-disk encryption, creating a forensic image is straightforward. You can either use the built-in command *dd* to create the image. Let's go through the process of creating a full-disk acquisition using *dd*:

- Boot the target device into Recovery Mode → connect an external drive to the target device → take an image with `dd` and choose the external drive as the destination.
- Boot the target device into Target Disk Mode → connect it to the Mac → take an image with `dd` which is run from the analysis Mac.

This is the dd command to run for creating the disk image:

```
dd if=/dev/DISK of=image.dd bs=512
```

With full-disk encryption and other hardware settings that have existed over time, there are some exceptions and challenges that you should be aware of before acquiring data from a macOS system:

- **Fusion Drives**[4]: Fusion Drives are a hybrid drive technology developed by Apple and were part of production from 2012 to 2020. These drives combine an

4 https://en.wikipedia.org/wiki/Fusion_Drive.

HDD and an SSD storage device within the same device. The operating system automatically manages the drive by storing the most frequently accessed data on the SSD. Acquisition of these types of drives must be done logically, as performing physical imaging will only acquire the HDD partition.

- **T2 Chipset with Full-Disk Encryption**[5]: On devices with the T2 Security Chip and full-disk encryption enabled, you will need to have the user's login password or recovery key to access the encrypted data. Physical imaging is no longer possible in these cases due to the added security measures. Instead, you may need to use specialized forensic tools or techniques to acquire physical copies of these devices. Another approach is doing a logical or live system acquisition. Be prepared for more complex and time-consuming acquisition processes on devices with advanced security features like the T2 Security Chip.

7.3.1 Memory

Dumping memory on macOS can be difficult depending upon the age of the device on macOS systems with Intel architecture up to around 2020, you can use the osxpmem[6] tool from Google, However, please note that osxpmem is archived and do not supported the newer macOS systems with Apple Silicon architecture; in these cases commercial tools are required.

To dump memory from a macOS system using osxpmem, follow these steps:

1. Download osxpmem from the GitHub repository.
2. Extract the osxpmem archive and navigate to the extracted folder.
3. Dump the memory in raw format by running the following command:

```
/osxpmem.app/osxpmem --format raw -o /tmp/dump_mem
```

After dumping the memory using osxpmem, the analysis of the dump memory can be done using Volatility3, by simply using the Mac plugins shown in the Memory Forensics chapter.

7.3.1.1 Hibernation and RAM

When macOS goes to sleep, the system stores the data that is currently within RAM and is dumped to this /var/vm/sleepimage file on the disk. Extracting information from these files can be problematic, with the introduction of macOS version 10.7 and later the content of these files is now encrypted by default, making them difficult to recover data from.

5 https://support.apple.com/en-us/HT208344.
6 https://github.com/google/rekall/releases/download/v1.5.1/osxpmem-2.1.post4.zip.

7.4 Analysis

Let's look at what is necessary when it comes to analyzing macOS. First I recommend using another Mac device to analyze the disk image. This is due to the many proprietary systems explained above such as the file system and the native files. There are of course commercial tools available that collect and parse the data for you no matter the system you are on. However, if you do not have access to these applications, I recommend using a Mac as your forensic workstation. Luckily there are two free tools that will parse images from Mac devices. The one I recommend using is[7]; the other is[8], which is no longer maintained and should not be used.

The good thing about macOS is that most of the files you will analyze are Plist and text files, which do not require any special tools to be parsed. And macOS is based on the Unix system; it has many of the same artifacts, but they are stored in different places.

7.5 Evidence Location

These are some of the key locations where forensic investigators can gather valuable information about the macOS system and its users.

7.5.1 System Configuration

Information about the system itself:

- Time zone: /etc/localtime
- System installation date: /var/log/install.log
- OS installation time (Look at the file Edit time): /var/db/.AppleSetupDone
- Software installation history: /Library/Receipts/InstallHistory.plist
- System logs: /private/var/log/asl/*.asl

7.5.2 User Accounts and Activity

macOS stores user account information and login activity in various locations. Key areas to examine include:

- User's home directory: /Users/username/
- Directory containing the user preferences for applications:
- Users password (hash+salted): /var/db/dslocal/nodes/Default/users/*

7 https://github.com/ydkhatri/mac_apt.
8 https://github.com/Yelp/osxcollector.

- Terminal command history: /users/{username}/.bash_history
- Includes information about the last user logging in: /Library/Preferences/-com.apple.loginwindow.plist
- Notification database: /user/username/com.apple.notificationcenter/db2/db
- Application logs: /users/{username}/Library/Logs and /Library/Logs

7.5.2.1 Keychain

The `%%users.homedir%%/Library/Keychains/*` holds user keychain files.

It is possible to dump the decrypted password using the `security` command, which requires you to have the user password.

```
security dump-keychain -d
```

7.5.2.2 Notes

User-generated notes can be found in the following SQLite database */Library/Group/Containers/group.com.apple.notes/NoteStore.sqlite*. To read the notes, you can use the simple query:

```
select ZDATA from ZICNOTEDATA
```

7.5.2.3 Recent Items

What were the user's recently opened applications and files can be viewed here `Users/{username}/Library/Preferences/com.apple.recent spiopsxmltex73items.plist`. And what recently opened files by a specific application are stored here `Users/{username}/Library/Preferences/ *LSSharedFilespiopsxmltex74List.plist`

7.5.3 System Logs

macOS system logs can provide valuable information about system events and user activities. Some important logs to analyze include:

- General system log containing information about system events.: /var/log/system.log
- Authentication-related log that records user login attempts and other authentication events.: /var/log/authd.log
- Wireless networking log that can provide information about connected Wi-Fi networks.: /var/log/wifi.log
- Wireless connection: /Library/Preferences/SystemConfiguration/com.apple.airport.preferences.plist
- Stores the Bluetooth preference and historically paired devices: /Library/Preferences/com.apple.Bluetooth.plist

7.5.4 Browser Usage

macOS users typically use Safari as their web browser. Analyzing browser history, cookies, cache, and downloads can provide important information about user activity. Browser data is typically stored in the user's home directory: */Library/Safari/*

7.5.5 Email

macOS users often use Apple's Mail app or other email clients. Analyzing mail data, including mail archives and unread mail, can provide valuable information. Key location for Apple's Mail app is: */Library/Mail/* Here you will find mailboxes, messages, and account settings.

7.5.6 Persistence Mechanisms

macOS has various persistence mechanisms, such as startup items, login items, and LaunchDaemons, which can be used by programs to persist between boots. Investigating these areas can reveal potentially malicious software or other unwanted behavior:

- Startup items: /Library/StartupItems/
- Login items: /Library/Preferences/loginwindow.plist
- LaunchDaemons: /Library/LaunchDaemons/
- Cron jobs: /private/var/at/tabs
- Periodic (Similar to cron jobs): /private/etc/periodic/

7.5.6.1 Login Item

A common method for software to automatically be executed when a user logs on:

```
System preferences => users and groups => login items
```

7.5.6.2 Launch Items (Agents and Daemons)

Launch items are a way to persist non-application binaries like software updates and background processes. There are two types: Daemons and agents.

Daemons are non-interactive and run before the user logs in.

Agents launch on user login and interact with the user session.

To become a launch item, the malware needs to create a property list (plist) in a specific location. This file will describe what is being launched with Launchd Key:

- program or program arguments
- value: path
- key: RunAtLoad
- values: boolean

tells the system to launch the item.

Agents and Daemons:

- /System/Library/Launchagents
- /Library/LaunchAgents
- /System/Library/LaunchDaemons

7.5.6.3 Log In/Log Out Hooks

By creating a login or logout hook, a script or command will be executed when a user logs in or out of the system. The hooks are stored inside a plist, which is located here: "/Library/Preferences/com.apple.loginwindow.plist". The key pair to look for is either LoginHook or LogoutHook.

7.5.6.4 Dynamic Libraries (dylib)

Instead of loading the whole program at runtime into memory, to speed up the execution of the application, dynamic libraries allow the program to only load what is necessary at the moment and load the other parts at runtime when needed. When it comes to malware, it will try to piggyback off another process for persistence by injecting DYLD_INSERT_LIBRARIES into a process plist.

Detection: Scan all launch items and applications and check the relevant property list for DYLD_INSERT_LIBRARIES key/value pair. The tool used to analyze dylib is Dylib Hijack Scanner.[9]

7.5.6.5 At Tasks

At tasks are used to schedule tasks to execute at a defined time. The task that has been created on the system is located here: /private/var/at/jobs

7.5.6.6 Event Monitor Rules

The event monitor binary emond at /sbin/emond will load any rules from the /etc/emond.d/rules directory. The rule files are in the plist format and define the name, event type, and action to take.

7.5.6.7 Re-opened Applications

Allow the user to start up applications that were shut down during the log-out process. The application that will be open again is stored in the following plist. /Library/Preferences/ByHost/com.apple.loginwindow.<UUID>.plist

7.5.7 Evidence of Destruction

Examining traces of log clearing, file deletion, and other attempts to destroy evidence can be crucial in a forensic investigation. File recovery tools like TestDisk and PhotoRec can be used to attempt recovery of deleted files.

---

9 https://objective-see.org/products/dhs.html.

By examining these areas and utilizing appropriate tools and techniques, forensic investigators can gather valuable information about the macOS system and its users, aiding in their overall analysis and investigation.

7.6 Summary

macOS forensics research is still behind that of Windows. This makes it a good starting point for researchers as there are still a lot of things that are unknown about macOS because of Apple's usage of proprietary technology and a closed-source approach to development. Another factor is the security features launched by Apple, such as their T2 security chip, forcing full-disk encryption on the device, requiring us to have the password of the device to perform any acquisition.

macOS forensics is less advanced than its Windows counterpart, largely due to Apple's proprietary technology and closed-source development approach. As a result, there are still many aspects of macOS that remain unexplored, presenting unique challenges and opportunities for forensic researchers. In recent years, Apple has introduced advanced security features such as the T2 security chip, which enforces full-disk encryption on devices. This added security layer requires investigators to possess the device password to perform any data acquisition, further complicating the forensic process.

Despite these challenges, macOS forensics remains an important area of study, especially considering the growing popularity of Apple devices. Forensic investigators must develop specialized knowledge and expertise in macOS systems to effectively analyze and gather evidence. Key areas of investigation include:

1. **User Accounts and Login Activity:** Examine system log files in /var/log/ and user-specific files in /Users/{username}/.
2. **File System Analysis:** Analyze metadata, deleted files, and file paths in HFS+ or APFS file systems.
3. **System Logs:** Review important logs such as /var/log/system.log, /var/log/authd.log, and /var/log/wifi.log.
4. **Persistence Mechanisms:** Check startup items, login items, and LaunchDaemons in directories such as /Library/StartupItems/, /Library/Preferences/loginwindow.plist, and /Library/LaunchDaemons/.
5. **Evidence of Destruction:** Examine traces of log clearing and file deletion, using tools like TestDisk and PhotoRec for file recovery.

By staying up to date with the latest developments and techniques in macOS forensics, and understanding the nuances of Apple's file systems and evidence locations, investigators can effectively handle cases involving Apple devices.

8

Linux Forensics

Linux, an open-source operating system, has gained popularity in recent years as it has become more user-friendly and provides greater control over the system. Because of the open-source nature of Linux, there exist numerous distributions, but this guide will focus on Debian.[1] While different distributions have some variations in package management and configuration or log file locations, their forensic analysis processes are very similar.

When comparing Windows and Linux forensics, the acquisition process is the same, using tools like FTK Imager to create a physical copy of the disk. The main difference lies in the locations of the evidence. Although Windows has a centralized registry system for user and configuration activities, Linux stores configuration information in individual files at different locations.

One of the considerations when dealing with Linux systems is that, in many of the cases, the users have better technical skills compared to the average user, making them potentially more adept at hiding their tracks and using encryption. However, even skilled users occasionally overlook security measures, or simply human laziness leaving the system insecure allowing us to extract information from the system.

To effectively analyze a Linux system, you should familiarize yourself with the nuances of the operating system, including key evidence locations and the unique challenges presented by different distributions.

8.1 File System

Linux file systems are responsible for managing the storage and organization of files on a Linux system. Several common file systems are used in Linux, including ext4, Btrfs, and XFS. Each file system has its unique features and capabilities,

1 https://www.debian.org/index.da.html.

Practical Cyber Intelligence: A Hands-on Guide to Digital Forensics, First Edition. Adam Tilmar Jakobsen.

but all are designed for efficient and reliable data storage and retrieval on Linux systems.

- **ext4**[2]: The Fourth Extended File System succeeds ext3 and offers improved performance, support for larger file sizes and volumes, and additional features like multiblock allocation and delayed allocation.
- **Btrfs**[3]: The B-tree file system is a newer Linux file system that provides advanced features such as snapshotting, device removal, and online defragmentation. It is scalable and flexible, making it suitable for large-scale enterprise environments.
- **XFS**[4]: The Extended File System is known for its high performance and scalability and is often used in high-performance computing environments.

Understanding the differences and capabilities of each file system is crucial for forensic investigators when analyzing a Linux file system. By being familiar with the nuances of each file system, investigators can more effectively locate and analyze deleted evidence on the device.

Linux follows a specific hierarchy for storing system data in various locations. This hierarchy is called the Linux Filesystem Hierarchy Standard (FHS), which organizes the files into a structured directory. I will not go into details about all the nodes in the tree; the most important folders are:

- **/ (Root)**: The top-level directory that contains all other directories and files.
- **/etc**: Stores system-wide configuration files and scripts, like passwd, fstab, and system initialization scripts.
- **/home**: Contains individual user home directories, where users store their files and settings.
- **/media**: A directory for mounting removable media, such as USB drives and CDs.
- **/root**: The home directory for the root user, which is separate from the regular user's /home directory.
- **/var**: Holds variable data files, such as logs, mail, print spools, and caches, which are expected to change over time.

Understanding this hierarchy is essential to locate and analyze evidence stored in various directories throughout the system.

8.1.1 File System Timestamps

Table 8.1 illustrates how various actions, such as file creation, access, Edit, copying, and local moving, impact the different timestamps (creation, access, and Edit)

2 https://en.wikipedia.org/wiki/Ext4.
3 https://en.wikipedia.org/wiki/Btrfs.
4 https://en.wikipedia.org/wiki/XFS.

Table 8.1 File system timestamp.

Action	Creation	Access	Modified	Copy (new)	Move
Creation	C	NA	C	A	A
Access	C	A	NA	A	NA
Modified	C	NA	A	A	NA

C = Created, A = Altered, NA = No change.

on files in a Linux file system. Understanding these timestamp changes is crucial for digital forensic investigators, as it can help them track user activity and identify potential evidence during an investigation. The analysis in Table 8.1 is on the file timestamp that was performed on Ubuntu 22.04.

8.2 Security

Because Linux distributions can vary much, they might have full-disk encryption enabled by default, and it all depends on the specific distribution. If you encounter a live Linux device, it is important to determine the Linux distribution and research if it has encryption enabled by default; to get the distribution name, open the terminal and enter the following command: *uname -a*, and it will print the full information about the distribution. Another option is to use the command.

```
sudo dmsetup status
```

This will print out if any of the partitions use LUKS encryption. The output looks something like this.

```
ubuntu-home: 0 195305472 linear
ubuntu-swap_1: 0 8364032 linear
sda4_crypt: 0 624637944 crypt
ubuntu-root: 0 48824320 linear
```

The Disk Utility application in Ubuntu will also show the encryption layer and the configuration in a graphical manner. Also, be sure to check for any running encryption applications, such as *Veracrypt*.[5] You can identify which processes are running on the system using the command: `ps -aux` as shown in Figure 8.1.

In the above image, the Veracrypt process is running on a Linux system, indicating that the system might be using Veracrypt for encryption. Identifying an encrypted disk or partition is crucial in a digital forensic acquisition process, as it

5 https://www.veracrypt.fr/code/VeraCrypt/.

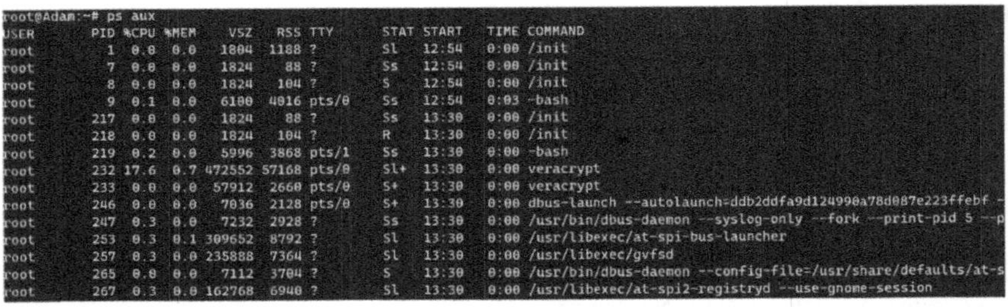

```
root@Adam:~# ps aux
USER       PID %CPU %MEM    VSZ   RSS TTY      STAT START   TIME COMMAND
root         1  0.0  0.0   1804  1188 ?        Sl   12:54   0:00 /init
root         7  0.0  0.0   1824    88 ?        Ss   12:54   0:00 /init
root         8  0.0  0.0   1824   104 ?        S    12:54   0:00 /init
root         9  0.1  0.0   6100  4016 pts/0    Ss   12:54   0:03 -bash
root       217  0.0  0.0   1824    88 ?        Ss   13:30   0:00 /init
root       218  0.0  0.0   1824   104 ?        R    13:30   0:00 /init
root       219  0.2  0.0   5996  3868 pts/1    Ss   13:30   0:00 -bash
root       232 17.6  0.7 472552 57168 pts/0    Sl+  13:30   0:00 veracrypt
root       233  0.0  0.0  57912  2660 pts/0    S+   13:30   0:00 veracrypt
root       246  0.0  0.0   7036  2128 pts/0    S+   13:30   0:00 dbus-launch --autolaunch=ddb2ddfa9d124990a78d087e223ffebf -
root       247  0.3  0.0   7232  2928 ?        Ss   13:30   0:00 /usr/bin/dbus-daemon --syslog-only --fork --print-pid 5 --p
root       253  0.3  0.1 309652  8792 ?        Sl   13:30   0:00 /usr/libexec/at-spi-bus-launcher
root       257  0.3  0.0 235888  7364 ?        Sl   13:30   0:00 /usr/libexec/gvfsd
root       265  0.0  0.0   7112  3704 ?        S    13:30   0:00 /usr/bin/dbus-daemon --config-file=/usr/share/defaults/at-s
root       267  0.3  0.0 162768  6940 ?        Sl   13:30   0:00 /usr/libexec/at-spi2-registryd --use-gnome-session
```

Figure 8.1 PS veracrypt.

can help investigators prepare for potential challenges and what precautions need to be taken. Remember to always exercise caution when handling live systems with encryption enabled, as improper handling can result in the loss of valuable evidence or worse make data recovery impossible.

8.3 Acquisition

Performing disk acquisition in a Linux system is the same as in Windows if the disk is not encrypted.

8.3.1 Dump Memory

When dealing with a live-running Linux system, it can in some cases be necessary to capture the system's memory. With memory, it can contain valuable information that might not be available elsewhere. When it comes to performing memory dump of Linux devices Microsoft has developed an open-source tool called avml[6] (Acquire Volatile Memory for Linux), which is available over at Microsoft Github. This tool will enable you to dump the memory of any Linux machine using a single command:

```
avml output.lime
```

Tools can even capture the memory in compressed format by simply adding the –compress flag to the command. After running, create a memory dump. You will have a LiME (Linux Memory Extractor) formatted memory dump of the system, which can be analyzed using the Volatility framework. Analyzing the memory dump will have information on the processes running, open network connections, user sessions, and other crucial information, all that happened at the time of capture.

6 github.com/microsoft/avml.

8.4 Analysis

Analyzing a Linux system involves understanding the distribution in question as it affects the location of forensic evidence. The easiest way to identify the distribution on a dead box is by examining the `/etc/os-release` file. In this section, I will focus on dead box analysis evidence locations for both Debian and Red Hat distributions.

8.4.1 chroot

chroot allows you to interact with the image directory as if it were the system's directory. This requires the forensic image to be mounted onto your system. Assuming you have an `E01` image, the first step is to mount the evidence file with `ewfmount`:

```
ewfmount image.e01./phy
```

Next, mount the partition using the partition offset:

```
sudo mount -o ro,loop,offset=(partitionoffset) phy/ewf1 /log
```

You can now change the root to the mounted directory with `chroot`:

```
sudo chroot /log
```

The system is now essentially logged into the system you are performing forensics analysis. This allows you to run any command as if it were logged into the device. I found this a useful technique as some information can only be retrieved using terminal commands.

8.5 Evidence Location

Let's go into detail about the different evidence that exists on a Linux device.

8.5.1 System Info

Let's start by looking at collecting information about the system.

8.5.1.1 System Version

Identify the distribution:

```
/etc/os-release
```

8.5.1.2 Computer Name

The hostname of the computer:

```
/etc/hostname
```

8.5.1.3 Localtime Settings

The data is stored in binary format, which can be read using the zdump command on Linux:

```
/etc/localtime
```

8.5.1.4 Boot Logs

Stores the information about boot time:

```
/var/log/boot.log
```

8.5.1.5 Kernel Logs

Information about kernel logs:

```
/var/log/kern.log
```

8.5.1.6 Apt Install Repository Sources

```
/etc/apt/sources.list.d/
/etc/apt/sources.list
```

8.5.1.7 Hosts File

Local system DNS table:

```
/etc/hosts
```

8.5.1.8 Root UUID

```
/var/log/dmesg
```

8.5.1.9 Services

Keep track of services running in the background:

```
/var/log/daemon.log
```

8.5.1.10 Syslogs

Syslogs track pretty much everything happening on the system. If you do not see any syslog files on the system, it probably means that it is not installed or the service has not been started.

- **Debian**: /var/log/syslog
- **RedHat**[7]: /var/log/messages

8.5.1.11 Background Processes

Record events generated by background processes and services. The three first fields are the most important ones:

- device-spec, label
- mount-point, where the content can be accessed after the mounting
- fs-type, filesystem type

```
/var/log/daemon.log
```

8.5.1.12 Disk Partitions

List all available disk partitions on the system.

```
/etc/fstab
```

8.5.2 User Activity

What evidence exists on Linux that describes user activity on the system.

8.5.2.1 Accounts and Groups

These two files will list users on the system, including their rights, permissions, hashed passwords, and more.

```
/etc/passwd
/etc/shadow
```

8.5.2.2 Group Information

List what groups exist in the system:

```
/etc/group
```

8.5.2.3 Command History

Tracks user bash command history activity. It only gets written to the file once the user has logged off the system and does not store the timestamps of the commands.

```
/home/{user}/.bash_history
```

---

7 https://www.redhat.com/en.

8.5.2.4 Authentication

Information about user authentication, including:

- Login times of users
- Sudo activity
- Session length

`utmp` stores full information about the current status of the system, with information such as boot time, user log-in and logout, and system events:

```
/var/log/utmp
```

To see more historical information of data within `utmp`, look at wtmp. It can be read using the "last -f btmp" command, the location of btmp file can be found here.

```
/var/log/wtmp
```

- auth.log and secure are also available with information about login and authentication processes, such as the usage of sudo:
- **Debian**: /var/log/auth.log
- **Redhat**: /var/log/secure

8.5.2.5 Last Login

Contains information at the last login performed on the server

```
/var/log/lastlog
```

8.5.2.6 Failed Logon Attempts

List all failed login attempts:

```
/var/log/faillog
```

Another source is the `btmp` logs which also keep track of failed login attempts. It can be read using the "last -f" command, location of btmp file.

```
/var/log/btmp
```

8.5.2.7 Installation of Software

Track the installation of system and software packages using package manager:

- **dpkg**: `/var/log/dpkg.log`
- **apt**: `/var/log/apt/history.log`
- **Redhat**: `/var/log/yum.log`

8.5.2.8 File Edit

Having the ability to find all files that have been modified in the last 5 days requires you to have the ability to perform commands on the system either directly or using chroot

```
find / -mtime -o -ctime -5
```

8.5.3 Network

Information related to network activity

8.5.3.1 Interfaces

Configuration files for network setup

```
/etc/network/interfaces
```

8.5.3.2 DNS Configuration

These files store the information related to DNS resolution, which can be used to identify DNS poisoning.

```
  \item \textbf{Host DNS files}: \texttt{/etc/hosts}
  \item \textbf{DNS configuration}: \texttt{/etc/resolv.conf}
```

8.5.3.3 Wi-Fi SSID

Stores the SSID (service set identifier) to which the system will automatically connect.

```
/etc/wpa_supplicant/*.conf
```

8.5.4 File Execution and Information

Describes the locations that hold artifacts about the execution of programs and files.

8.5.4.1 Cronjobs

Execution of files through scheduled jobs, what jobs are scheduled can be found here `/etc/cron.*`

You can also run the following command on the box and it will list what scheduled tasks exist.

```
crontab -l
```

8.5.4.2 Processes

What is currently running on the machine, is useful if you need to quickly identify if an instance of `veracrypt` is running before shutting down the system.

Lists the currently running processes, this will give the most details about the processes.

```
ps aux
```

Will create a tree-like structure of how the different processes relate to each other.

```
pstree
```

8.5.4.3 SGID

Find user ID files

```
find / -perm -6000 -type f
```

8.5.4.4 SUID

Find SUID files owned by root and check entries

```
find / -perm -4000 -user root -type f
```

8.5.5 External Drive

Artifacts that can be used to identify external devices.

8.5.5.1 Dmesg

Dmesg[8] contains messages that identify external hardware drivers. The information in dmesg is also viewable in messages. When it comes to timestamps, beware that dmesg messages are based on the Hardware clock, while the `/var/log/messages` content is based on the System clock, and they are not synchronized.

```
/var/log/dmesg
```

8.5.5.2 USB Log

The log files contain information about the USB devices that have been connected. If you do not see any syslog files on the system, it probably means that it is not installed or the service has not been started.

- **Debian**: `/var/log/syslog*`
- **RedHat**: `/var/log/messages*`

---

8 https://en.wikipedia.org/wiki/Dmesg.

8.5.6 Persistence

Locations where applications or malware can achieve persistence between boots.

8.5.6.1 Cron Jobs

Cron jobs[9] are scheduled jobs that allow scripts, commands, binaries, etc. to be executed within a defined interval.

```
/etc/cron.*
/etc/crontab
```

8.5.6.2 SSH Key Authentication

The public key stored inside */<user>/.ssh/authorized_keys* allows anyone with access to the corresponding private key to SSH into the machine without using the password.

8.6 Summary

Linux, an open-source operating system, offers various distributions that handle tasks differently. Predominantly found in server environments, Linux users typically possess a higher level of technical knowledge. As a result, they may attempt to hide or delete evidence of their actions or engage in activities beyond those of an average user.

Important evidence locations in Linux:

1. **System Information**: /etc/os-release, /etc/hostname
2. **User Activity:** /etc/passwd, /etc/shadow, /home/user/.bash_history
3. **Authentication Logs:** /var/log/auth.log, /var/log/secure, /var/log/last log
4. **Network Configuration:** /etc/network/interfaces, /etc/resolv.conf
5. **File Execution & Application Usage:** /etc/cron.*, /home/user/.config/, /home/user/.local/share
6. **External Devices:** /var/log/dmesg, /var/log/syslog*, /var/log/messages*
7. **Persistence Mechanisms:** /etc/crontab, /user/.ssh/authorized_keys

Remember that Linux distributions can have small variations, making the evidence location discussed above might not be applicable to your case.

9 https://en.wikipedia.org/wiki/Cron.

9
iOS

This section covers mobile devices created by Apple, which utilize the iOS operating system. Based on Unix, iOS is similar to Apple macOS but specifically designed for mobile devices. It includes a range of security features, such as encryption, secure boot, and more to protect user data. Since Apple devices do not support SD cards, all the data is stored on the internal NAND flash drive. The most common data formats you will see when analyzing iOS devices are SQLite and Plist.

9.1 File System

Modern iOS employs the Apple File System (APFS), a modern and efficient file system that was introduced in iOS 10.3.[1] APFS is designed to leverage the latest storage technologies, such as solid-state drives (SSD) and flash storage, and is optimized for SSDs with low latency in mind. APFS has become the de facto file system for iOS, tvOS, and watchOS. Security features include full disk encryption and file-based encryption.

The iOS file system is organized in a hierarchical structure, with directories and files arranged in a tree-like pattern, similar to Linux, with ("/") being the root directory. Here are some of the key directories within the iOS file system includes:

- **/Library**: This directory contains system-wide resources, such as fonts, preferences, and configuration files.
- **/Applications**: This directory holds the built-in applications that come preinstalled on iOS devices.
- **/private/var**: This directory is used for storing variable data, such as caches, temporary files, and user-specific settings. It also contains the **/private/var/mobile** directory, where user data and third-party applications are stored.

1 https://en.wikipedia.org/wiki/IOS_10.

Practical Cyber Intelligence: A Hands-on Guide to Digital Forensics, First Edition. Adam Tilmar Jakobsen.

9.2 Security

iOS devices incorporate a robust array of security features designed to safeguard the device against unauthorized access and protect the confidentiality of the user's data. These features are critical in maintaining user privacy and ensuring the device remains resilient to various forms of cyberattacks.

At the heart of iOS security is AES[2] 256-bit encryption for full disk encryption, making brute-force attacks, attempting to systematically guess the encryption key, highly impractical. In addition to AES 256-bit encryption, iOS devices also incorporate a dedicated hardware component known as the Secure Enclave. This separate coprocessor is responsible for managing cryptographic operations, secure boot, and biometric authentication processes such as Touch ID or Face ID. By isolating sensitive data and operations, the potential for unauthorized access or tampering is significantly reduced.

With the combination of full disk encryption and the Secure Enclave, physically acquiring data from an iOS device is no longer a feasible option, without specialized tools. Which limit the method of extracting data from iOS to logical acquisition.

Furthermore, Apple's iOS security extends beyond encryption. The operating system also employs a range of application security mechanisms. such as app sandboxing, code signing, and app review processes. These measures work in tandem to ensure that only trusted applications get installed on iOS devices and are restricted from accessing sensitive system data or interfering with other apps on the device.

9.2.1 Keychain

Keychain serves as the password management system for Apple devices. It is used to store sensitive information such as passwords, payment data, and more. Limited access to the keychain can be achieved either by using the phone or through iCloud. This will include accounts and Wi-Fi passwords but not the encryption key used by application keys; to access these keys, full access to the phone is required, typically though jailbreak the phone. With full access, tools like Keychain-Dumper[3] can be used to extract all passwords and keys stored on the device. This is particularly relevant for secure chat applications, whose databases are often encrypted.

A note about keychain and how the availability of the keys depends on the attribute the developer has given them in code. If the device is in the Before First Unlock (BFU) state, it is only possible to extract keys with the

---

2 https://en.wikipedia.org/wiki/Advanced_Encryption_Standard.

3 https://github.com/ptoomey3/Keychain-Dumper.

kSecAttrAccessibleAlways[4] attribute; this tag makes key always available, even in BFU states. With After First Unlock, the *kSecAttrAccessibleAfterFirstUnlock*[5] attribute determines if the key can be extracted or not. Last the *keychain-2.db* database stores what keys are saved within the keychain. If iCloud synchronization is enabled, it will show passwords stored from other devices as well. You can find the database at: */private/var/keychains/keychain-2.db*. To display what keychains are stored on the device, use the following query:

```
select distinct agrp from genp union select distinct agrp from
   inet union select distinct agrp from cert union select distinct
   agrp from keys
```

9.3 Applications

To secure the device, Apple has designed in such a way that application runs inside a sandboxed environment; this ensures that the application is containerized thereby minimizing interaction with the underlying OS.

It is possible to install a large variety of apps from the App Store.[6] Apple stores applications with the *.ipa* file extension, which compresses data into a single file. This *.ipa* archive format can be opened allowing you to extract the application components. These IPA files do not live on the device, as they are immediately unpacked into private/var/mobile/Containers/Data/Application/<app id>/<appName>.app. Then by compressing the folder, you get the ipa file. The data generated by the user for the specific application is stored inside <appName>.app/document; other locations where data can be stored include:

- */private/var/mobile/Containers/Shared/AppGroup/<app id>*
- */private/var/mobile/share/appgroup.*

The way to identify the application ID of applications is by consulting the *applicationstate.db*[7] database which contains information about all applications installed on the device.

One last thing to note about iOS applications is when an application gets updated. Developers sometimes change the storage file or database used. When this happens, the old database is not deleted; it may still exist on the device. This means that the tool used checks for old databases that could contain historical data.

---

4 https://developer.apple.com/documentation/security/ksecattraccessiblealways.
5 https://developer.apple.com/documentation/security/ksecattraccessibleafterfirstunlock.
6 https://www.apple.com/app-store/.
7 /private/var/mobile/Library/FrontBoard/applicationstate.db.

9.4 Acquisition

The most straightforward method for acquiring data from iOS devices is by utilizing the built-in iTunes backup function. You can learn more about it on the Apple website.[8] The recommended free tool to assist in creating of backup is iBackupBot[9] and image can be shown in Figure 9.1. For iBackupBot to recognize your iOS device, you must launch iTunes on the computer and ensure your device is unlocked and connected to iTunes.

When Apple prompts you to encrypt the backup, always select **yes** as it will store additional data in the backup compared to an unencrypted backup. The amount of data extracted is limited. With any other device, the deeper the access, the more data you will acquire. This is why you would always aim for full access using either jailbreaking techniques or other methods to gain root access.

9.4.1 Jailbreaking

A more advanced method of acquiring data is by using jailbreaking. This can be used to gain full access to the phone by exploiting a flaw in the device to gain access.

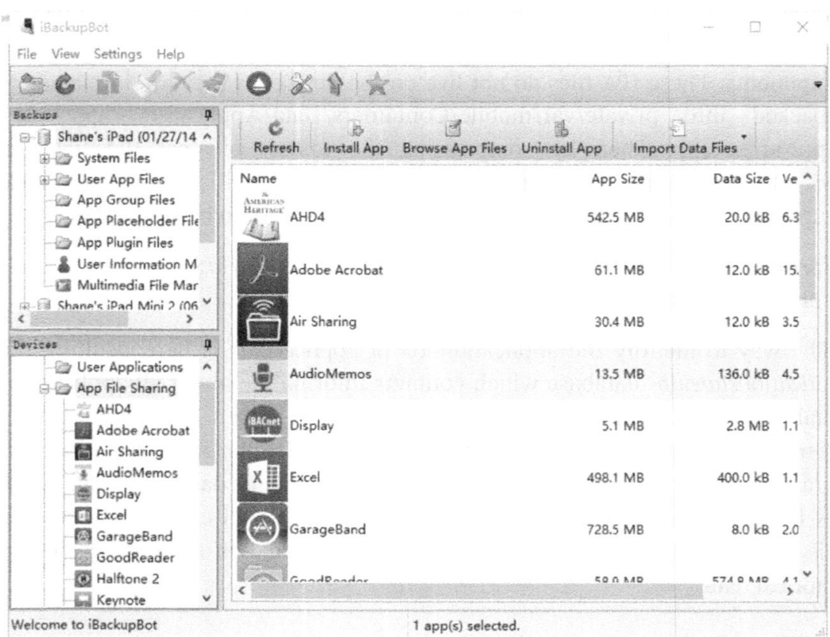

Figure 9.1 iBackupBot.

8 https://support.apple.com/en-gb/HT203977.
9 https://www.icopybot.com/itunes-backup-manager.htm.

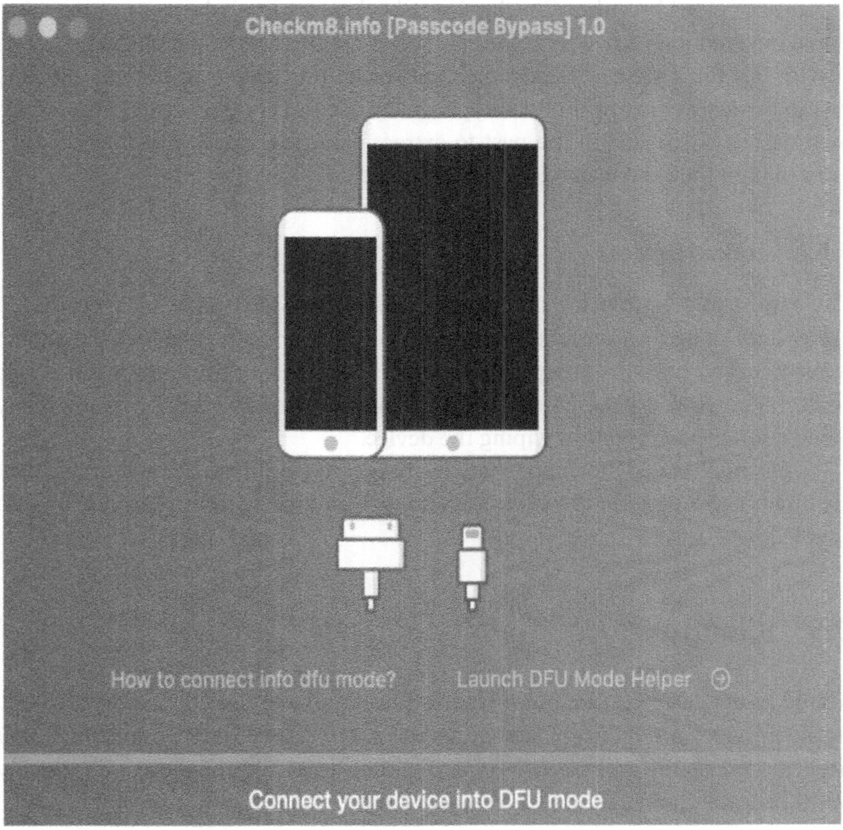

Figure 9.2 Crackm8.

There are two methods for older phones due to a chip vulnerability. The first one is Checkm8,[10] and an image of the software can be seen in Figure 9.2; it is an exploit discovered by axi0mX, which only runs in RAM, making it a non-permanent jailbreak. It is available for a small fee, ranging from 25 to 65 USD, depending on the version. However, the problem is that it only supports up to the iPhone X, which is a five-year-old device.

The other option is Checkra1n, which is the first public jailbreak leveraging the checkm8 exploit. It is made publicly available, allowing everyone to acquire a full file. Checkra1n[11] leaves a permanent trace on the phone but is available to everyone. At the moment of writing, it supports iPhone 5s to iPhone X with iOS version 12 and onwards. It is recommended to try it if you come across a

10 https://checkm8.info/.
11 https://checkra.in/.

device supported by either Checkm8 or Checkra1n, simply because of the additional information gained by getting full file system access to the phone.

With full file system, it is possible to access to the device's keychain, allowing you to extract the application encryption key used to encrypt the database. This method has been used in the past to extract data from applications like Signal, even though their database is encrypted.

9.4.2 Locked Devices

The easiest way to unlock a phone is by using the code. This is why you should always try asking the user for the code, as it might be one way to unlock the phone; otherwise, you have to attempt to either guess the code or brute-force the device code. Trying to guess the password on a locked device can be risky, as too many failed attempts can result in wiping the device.

It's essential to use the appropriate technique to maximize the amount of data acquired, depending on the device's condition and the security features that are enabled.

9.5 iCloud

iCloud is not iOS-specific, but a significant amount of user data is saved here. Apple provides 5 GB of free storage to users. To acquire data from iCloud, you need the username and password combination to access the data, and possibly multi-factor authentication (MFA) if it's enabled.

9.6 Analysis

After extraction, it must be analyzed. Fortunately, several open-source tools exist that can speed up the process of parsing the data; this includes tools such as ILEAPP[12] shown in Figure 9.3, ArtEx2,[13] and APOLLO.[14] All these tools can parse and present some of the data obtained, making it easier for forensic analysts to quickly examine the information on the device and get a general idea of what the phone has been used for.

It is important to note that no single tool should be relied on, as none can parse all the applications that exists. An example of this is apps with a low user base will most likely not be automatically parsed. In such cases, it is up to the analyst to

12 https://github.com/abrignoni/iLEAPP.
13 https://www.doubleblak.com/ArtEx/
14 https://github.com/mac4n6/APOLLO.

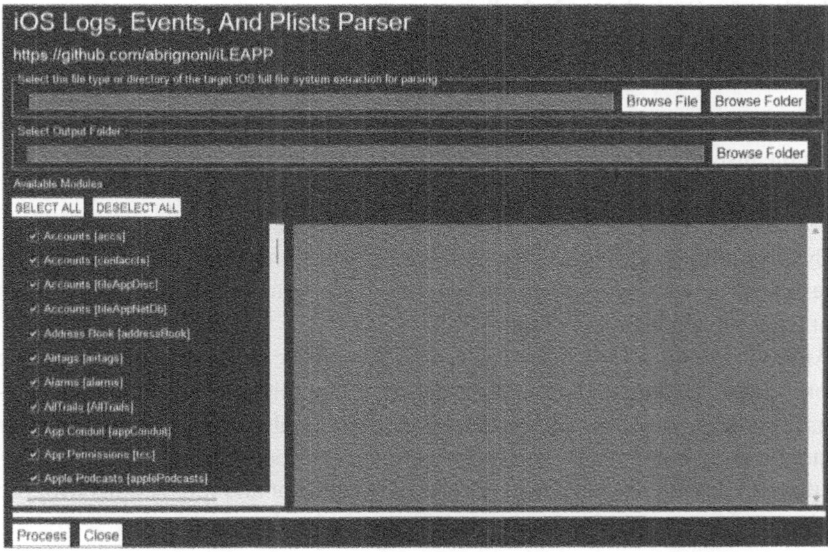

Figure 9.3 ILEAPP.

understand the structure of the data stored within the application and the context surrounding the information. This is why being able to manually go through the data of applications is a critical skill for any analyst; this often requires being able to understand SQLite databases, and some applications have deployed encryption mechanisms in place to protect user data where jailbreaking the device is the only way of gaining access to the encryption key that is used by the application. In some cases, the application might have to be reverse-engineered to understand the context of the data. The process of analysis application can involve the following:

- Understanding the app's data structure and relationships between various data elements
- Identifying relevant timestamps, user actions, or other events recorded by the app
- Correlating app data with other device data, such as location data, call logs, or messages

9.6.1 KnowledgeC

KnowledgeC contains information about how the user interacts with the device, such as:

- Application usage, installation, and activity
- Power status (charging or not charging)

- Lock status (locked or unlocked)
- Battery usage statistics
- Audio status (volume level, mute status)

The file is a combination of both system and user artifacts that may be, offering valuable insights into user behavior. To find the KnowledgeC is stored at:

- /private/var/mobile/Library/CoreDuet/Knowledge

By examining KnowledgeC, one can gain a better understanding of how users interact with their devices. With this data, it is possible to build a timeline of events that have happened on the phone.

Analyzing data from iOS devices can be a complex process, and utilizing the appropriate tools and methods is essential for a comprehensive examination. Analysts must be prepared to manually investigate app databases and understand their structure to ensure that no crucial information is overlooked. KnowledgeC, in particular, can provide valuable insights into user behavior and interactions with the device.

9.7 Evidence of Location

This section focuses on evidence that is available without full file system access. The reason for this is that most people do not have the tools available to achieve root access. This overview will cover the primary locations for evidence that exists on an iOS device. However, it is crucial to remember that new versions of iOS may introduce changes to these files and the value they provide.

9.7.1 Device Info

Location of evidence that can be used to gather information about the device.

9.7.1.1 General Device Info

This Plist holds IMEI, Phone Number, Network Carrier, ICCIDs, IMSIs, etc.

```
/private/var/wireless/Library/Preferences/com.apple.commcenter.
    plist}
/private/var/wireless/Library/Preferences/com.apple.commcenter.
    device_specific_no-Backup.plist
```

9.7.1.2 Operating System Version

```
/private/var/installd/Library/MobileInstallation/LastBuildInfo.
    plist
```

9.7.1.3 Last Boot Time

```
/private/var/mobile/Library/Preferences/com.apple.aggregated.plist
```

9.7.2 User Settings

Describe the user settings the person has had on the device.

9.7.2.1 Homescreen Icon Layout

The layout of application icons on the home screen.

```
/private/var/mobile/Library/SpringBoard/IconState.plist
```

9.7.2.2 Cloud Sync Settings

```
/private/var/mobile/Library/Preferences/com.apple.assistant.
    backedup.plist
/private/var/mobile/Library/Preferences/com.apple.CoreDuet.plist
```

9.7.2.3 iCloud Offline Cache

```
/private/var/mobile/Library/DataAccess/iCloud-[iCloud email
    account name]/OfflineCache/[number]
```

9.7.2.4 Blocked Dialers

List the numbers blocked by the user

```
/private/var/mobile/Library/Preferences/com.apple.cmfsyncagent.plist
```

9.7.3 Account and Password

The available artifacts can be used to identify information about the linked accounts.

9.7.3.1 Account Information

Contains information about what accounts have been linked to the devices.

```
/private/var/mobile/Library/Accounts/Accounts3.sqlite
```

The following SQL query can be used to extract accounts from the database.

```
SELECT
Z_PK,
ZACCOUNTTYPE,
ZPARENTACCOUNT,
DATETIME(ZDATE+978307200,'UNIXEPOCH','UTC') AS 'ZDATE TIMESTAMP',
ZACCOUNTDESCRIPTION,
ZIDENTIFIER,
ZOWNINGBUNDLEID,
ZUSERNAME
FROM ZACCOUNT
```

9.7.3.2 Account Information Used to Set Up Apps

```
/private/var/mobile/Library/DataAccess/
```

9.7.3.3 iCloud Email Account Information

```
/private/var/mobile/Library/DataAccess/iCloud-[iCloud email
    account name]/.mboxCache.plist
```

9.7.4 Communication

Artifacts about user communications.

9.7.4.1 Call Log

Stores the historical logs of calls that have happened on the device.

```
/private/var/mobile/Library/CallHistoryDB/CallHistory.storedata
```

```
select
ZADDRESS as number,
ZNAME as name,
case ZANSWERED
    when 0 then 'No'
    when 1 then 'Yes'
end,
case ZCALLTYPE
    when 0 then 'Third-Party App'
    when 1 then 'Phone'
    when 8 then 'FaceTime Video'
    when 16 then 'FaceTime Audio'
    else ZCALLTYPE
end as type,
case ZORIGINATED
    when 0 then 'Incoming'
    when 1 then 'Outgoing'
end,
datetime(ZDATE+978307200,'unixepoch') as date,
strftime('%H:%M:%S',ZDURATION, 'unixepoch'),
upper(ZISO_COUNTRY_CODE) as duration,
ZLOCATION as location
from ZCALLRECORD
```

9.7.4.2 SMS, iMessage, and FaceTime

Stores the SMS messages that have been sent and received by the phone

```
/private/var/mobile/Library/SMS/sms.db}
```

```
select
text,
datetime((date / 1000000000) + 978307200, 'unixepoch', 'localtime')
    AS "message date",
DATETIME((DATE_DELIVERED/ 1000000000)+978307200,'UNIXEPOCH',
    'LOCALTIME') AS "date delivered",
```

```
DATETIME((DATE_READ/ 1000000000)+978307200,'UNIXEPOCH','LOCALTIME')
    AS "date read",
SERVICE,
ACCOUNT,
IS_DELIVERED,
IS_FROM_ME
FROM MESSAGE
```

Another database is "query_predictions.db"; this database contains iMessage.

```
/private/var/mobile/Library/Suggestions/query_predictions.db
```

```
select
    datetime(creationTimestamp, "UNIXEPOCH") as date,
    content,
    isSent,
    conversationId,
from messages
```

MMS/iMessage attachments files are stored on the file system; it is possible to link the messages with the corresponding attachment by joining multiple tables together found inside sms.db.

```
/private/var/mobile/Library/SMS/Attachments/
```

```
select
text,
datetime((date / 1000000000) + 978307200, 'unixepoch', 'localtime')
    AS "message date",
DATETIME((DATE_DELIVERED/ 1000000000)+978307200,'UNIXEPOCH',
    'LOCALTIME') AS "date delivered",
DATETIME((DATE_READ/ 1000000000)+978307200,'UNIXEPOCH','LOCALTIME')
    AS "date read",
SERVICE,
ACCOUNT,
IS_DELIVERED,
IS_FROM_ME,
attachment.filename,
attachment.mime_type

from message

inner JOIN message_attachment_join on message.ROWID =
    message_attachment_join.message_id
inner join attachment on message_attachment_join.attachment_id =
    attachment.ROWID
```

9.7.4.3 Voicemail

Voicemail artifacts include the voicemail audio files, the database containing metadata, and the plist file containing voicemail settings.

- **Voicemail Audio Files:** */private/var/mobile/Library/Voicemail/*

- **Voicemail Database:** */private/var/mobile/Library/Voicemail/voicemail.db*
- **Voicemail Settings:** */private/var/mobile/Library/Preferences/com.apple.voicemail.imap.client.plist*

9.7.5 Application Usage

Describes the location of application usage artifacts.

9.7.5.1 TCC.db

List application permission and the time when the permission was granted, which can be used to approximate the installation time of the application.

```
/private/var/mobile/Library/TCC/TCC.db
```

9.7.5.2 Application Snapshots

Snapshots are taken on iOS devices when an application is minimized or interrupted by another activity. The images are stored in either .ktx or .png format, depending on the iOS version. The two tables can be linked together by *rowid* and *record_id*.

```
/mobile/Containers/Data/Application/<app UUID>/Library/Cache/
    Snapshots/<bundle id>
```

9.7.5.3 Contacts

The two tables of interest here are *ABPerson*, which contains metadata such as first name, last name, and much more. The other table is *ABMultiValue*, where the contact information such as phone number and email is stored.

```
/private/var/mobile/Library/AddressBook/AddressBook.sqlitedb
```

SQLite query to extract data:

```
select
First,
Last,
value
from ABPerson
inner join ABMultiValue on ABPerson.ROWID = ABMultiValue.record_id
```

9.7.5.4 Contact Images

The image data is stored as *blob* inside the database, similar to the previous, and is linked to the contact person by *ABPerson.RowId* to *record_id*.

```
/private/var/mobile/Library/AddressBook/AddressBookImages.sqlitedb
```

9.7.5.5 Calendar

What we care about is the CalendarItem.

```
/private/var/mobile/Library/Calendar/Calendar.sqlitedb
```

SQLite query:

```
SELECT
rowid,
summary,
description,
datetime(start_date +978307200,'unixepoch') as  start_date,
datetime (end_date +978307200, 'unixepoch') as end_date
FROM CalendarItem;
```

9.7.5.6 Notes

The notes that the user has created in Apple Notes.

```
/private/var/mobile/Library/Notes/notes.sqlite
```

```
Select
znote.Z_PK,
znote.ZGUID as 'GUID',
zaccount.ZNAME as 'Account',
zstore.ZNAME as 'Name',
zstore.ZEXTERNALIDENTIFIER as' ID',
znote.ZAUTHOR as 'Author',
znote.ZTITLE as 'Title',
znote.ZSUMMARY as 'Summary',
znotebody.ZCONTENT as 'Content',
znoteattachment.ZCONTENTID as 'contentID',
znoteattachment.ZFILENAME as 'Filename',
znoteattachment.ZMIMETYPE as 'mimetype',
datetime('2001-01-01', znote.ZCREATIONDATE || ' seconds') as
    'creationdate',
datetime('2001-01-01', znote.ZEditDATE || ' seconds') as 'Editdate'
from znote
join znotebody on znote.ZBODY = ZNOTEBODY.Z_PK
join zstore on znote.ZSTORE = zstore.Z_PK
join zaccount on zstore.ZACCOUNT = ZACCOUNT.Z_PK
left join znoteattachment on znoteattachment."ZNOTE"  = znote.Z_PK
order by creation date desc
```

9.7.5.7 Health Data

Health data, such as steps taken, heart rate, and sleep data, is stored on iOS devices. This information can provide insights into a user's habits and routines.

```
/private/var/mobile/Containers/Data/Application/<Health App GUID>/
    Documents/healthdb_secure.sqlite
```

9.7.6 Device Backup

Examining a device backup can provide a snapshot of the device's data at the time of the backup, which might be useful if more recent data has been deleted or overwritten.

9.7.6.1 iTunes Backup

```
/Users/[username]/Library/Application Support/MobileSync/Backup/
```

9.7.7 Third-Party Apps

Third-party apps can store valuable data, such as chat history, location data, and user activity. It is essential to examine the data stored by each app installed on the device.

9.7.7.1 App-Specific Data

```
/private/var/mobile/Containers/Data/Application/<App GUID>/
```

9.7.7.2 App-Specific Cache

```
/private/var/mobile/Containers/Data/Application/<App GUID>/
    Library/Caches/
```

9.7.8 Multimedia

Information related to multiple media usage.

9.7.8.1 User Created/Saved Photos

Photos that are either user-created or have been saved by the user.

```
/private/var/mobile/Media/DCIM/100APPLE
```

9.7.8.2 Picture Thumbnails Databases

```
/private/var/mobile/Media/PhotoData/Thumbnails/*.ithmb
```

9.7.8.3 Photo Albums Metadata

The data is stored as binary plist.

```
/private/var/mobile/Media/PhotoData/AlbumsMetadata/
```

9.7.8.4 Photos and Videos Database

Contains information about the photos that are stored on the device, which can be used to link photos to applications and much more. Going into details about this is out of scope; I recommend that you take a look at SQLite blog post,[15] which goes into details about the database.

```
/private/var/mobile/Media/PhotoData/Photos.sqlite
```

9.7.9 Browser Activity

Describes the user browser activity on the device, especially when it comes to Safari. Users have the option to install other browsers on their phones, which is why you need to examine every browser that is installed on the device, as they could all contain information. I have chosen to focus on Safari as it is the most used on iOS devices. Safari only stores the last 30 days of user activity. This does not mean everything is lost. Remember to check the free pages of the databases, as they might still contain deleted data that can be recovered using a Hex editor. Most of the data for Safari is stored inside the Bookmarks.db and History.db files, as they contain the most relevant internet activity, which can be extracted using the backup function.

9.7.9.1 History

Stores what sites the user has visited using Safari, including the number of times they have visited it.

```
/private/var/mobile/Library/Safari/History.db
```

9.7.9.2 Safari Bookmarks

The sites the user has bookmarked in Safari.

```
/private/var/mobile/Library/Safari/Bookmarks.db
```

9.7.9.3 Safari Cookies

Can be used to identify websites that the user has visited and possibly some user information.

```
/private/var/mobile/Containers/Data/Application/<App_guid>/
    Library/Cookies/Cookies.binarycookies
```

9.7.9.4 Safari Download History

```
/private/var/mobile/Containers/Data/Application/<App_guid>/
    Library/Safari/Downloads/Downloads.plist
```

15 https://theforensicscooter.com/2022/02/21/photos-sqlite-update/.

9.7.9.5 Safari Tabs Screenshots

Snapshot of Safari tabs stored as PNG or KTX format.

```
/private/var/mobile/Containers/Data/Application/<App_guid>/
    Library/Safari/Thumbnails/
```

9.7.10 Location

The artifacts can be used to identify where the device has been located. The locations below are just some of them; remember that third-party applications can also hold plenty of location data, such as running applications.

9.7.10.1 Apple Maps History

From iOS 8 to 11, and iOS 13 and onwards, the storage location for maps history is located at _GeoHistory.mapsdata. With iOS 12, the data was stored in iCloud, and with iOS 13, it became an optional thing.

```
/private/var/mobile/Containers/Data/Application/<Apple_Maps_GUID>/
    Library/Maps/GeoHistory.mapsdata
```

9.7.10.2 Application Traces and GeoFence Information

```
/private/var/root/Library/Caches/locationd/consolidated.db
```

9.7.10.3 Cache_encryptedB

Stores both Wi-Fi and routined.

```
/private/var/root/Library/Caches/locationd/cache\_encryptedB.db
```

SQL query for getting the location data from the database:

```
SELECT
DATETIME(TIMESTAMP+978307200,'UNIXEPOCH','LOCALTIME') AS TIMESTAMP,
MAC,
CHANNEL,
LATITUDE,
LONGITUDE
FROM WIFILOCATION
ORDER BY TIMESTAMP
```

And query for routined:

```
SELECT
DATETIME(TIMESTAMP+978307200,'UNIXEPOCH','LOCALTIME') AS TIMESTAMP,
LATITUDE,
LONGITUDE,
ALTITUDE,
HORIZONTALACCURACY,
VERTICALACCURACY
FROM LOCATION
```

9.7.11 Cellular Location

The 'lockCache_encryptedA.db' contains the cellular location of the phone.

```
/private/var/root/Library/Caches/locationd/cache\_encryptedA.db
```

```
SELECT
DATETIME(TIMESTAMP+978307200,'UNIXEPOCH','LOCALTIME') AS
TIMESTAMP,
LATITUDE,
LONGITUDE,
MCC,
MNC,
TAC,
CI,
UARFCN
FROM LTECELLLOCATION
```

9.7.12 Network Connection

Describes the network settings of the devices, including the settings and network connections.

9.7.12.1 Wi-Fi

When examining, make sure you look for key artifacts like SSID, BSSID, timestamps, and password requirements. These findings may help you place a suspect in a location at a specific time by using services such as wigle[16] to geolocate the WI-FI SSID.

```
/private/var/preferences/SystemConfiguration/com.apple.wifi.plist
```

9.7.12.2 Seen Bluetooth Devices

This stores Bluetooth devices the device has seen.

```
/private/var/containers/Shared/SystemGroup/<app_id>/Library/
    Database/com.apple.MobileBluetooth.ledevices.other.db
```

9.7.12.3 Paired Bluetooth Devices

This binary plist logs paired devices and the last time they were detected.

```
/private/var/containers/Shared/SystemGroup/Library/Preferences/
    com.apple.MobileBluetooth.devices.plist
```

---

16 https://wigle.net/.

9.7.12.4 iTunes Prefs Computer Connections

Lists what computer the phone has been connected to.

```
/private/var/mobile/Media/iTunes\_Control/iTunes/iTunesPrefs
```

9.7.13 Evidence Destruction

Examine creation timestamps of (sms.db, callhistory.storedata, addressBook.sqlitedb, voicemail.db, notes.sqlitedb); it will be the same as the first time the device gets booted up. .obliterated file exists (not always present).

9.7.13.1 Restore Information

```
/private/var/root/Library/Preferences/com.apple.MobileBackup.plist
```

9.8 Summary

iPhone forensics involves the recovery and analysis of data from iPhones, which can include data extraction from internal storage, cloud backups, or third-party applications. This discussion offers a basic overview of iPhone forensics, highlighting the iBackup method, and emphasizes the need for full file system access to obtain more comprehensive data. Such access can be achieved through jailbreaking older devices or using specialized exploits for newer models that are not publicly available.

Similar to MacOS, iPhones utilize proprietary technology for their file systems and native files, with an emphasis on security. The following are some potential evidence that can be found in various specific locations on an iPhone, which are detailed below:

1. **SMS and Call logs**: SMS messages and call logs are stored in the 'sms.db' SQLite database file located in /private/var/mobile/Library/SMS/.
2. **Contacts**: Contact information is stored in the 'AddressBook.sqlitedb' file located in /private/var/mobile/Library/AddressBook/.
3. **Photos and videos**: Media files are typically stored in the /private/var/mobile/Media/DCIM/ directory, organized into folders.
4. **Browser history**: Safari browsing history can be found in the 'History.db' SQLite database file located in /private/var/mobile/Library/Safari/.
5. **Location data**: Location data is stored in various SQLite database files, such as 'cache_encryptedA.db' and 'cache_encryptedB.db', located in /private/var/mobile/Library/Caches/locationd/.
6. **Notes**: Notes created using the Notes app are stored in the 'notes.sqlite' file located in /private/var/mobile/Library/Notes/.

7. **Installed apps**: Application data, including preferences and user-generated content, is stored within each app's sandbox directory, located in /private/var/mobile/Containers/Data/Application/.

By extracting and analyzing the data from these specific locations, forensic investigators can gather valuable information about user activities and potential evidence relevant to their investigations.

10

Android

Android is the mobile operating system developed by Google and used on a wide range of devices, such as smartphones, tablets, and cars. It is based on the Linux kernel and uses a modified SELinux[1] distribution designed specifically for touch-screen devices.

One of the key features of Android is its open-source[2] nature, which means that the code for Android is available and can be modified to fit your needs. Because of this, the version of Android that exists on a device can vary significantly, as it can be modified by the manufacturers. This is why you will see various versions of Android across different devices. They will of course share some commonalities which we will discuss here.

10.1 File Systems

Let's start with the Android file system which uses a Linux-based file system to manage and organize the files including the data on the device. The specific file system used by Android depends on the version of Android and the manufacturer of the device. The most common file system used by employed on Android is EXT4.

10.2 Security

Android includes several built-in security features to help protect the device and its data from unauthorized access and tampering. Some of the key security features of Android include:

1 https://selinuxproject.org/page/Main_Page.
2 https://source.android.com.

Practical Cyber Intelligence: A Hands-on Guide to Digital Forensics, First Edition. Adam Tilmar Jakobsen.

- **Full-disk encryption**: Encrypts all of the data on the device's storage using a strong encryption algorithm. This makes it difficult for anyone who does not have the encryption key to access the data on the device.
- **Secure boot**: Ensures that the device only runs trusted software. The boot process verifies the integrity of the device's firmware and operating system, preventing the device from booting if any unauthorized edits are detected.
- **Secure startup**: An optional feature, it requires the user to select a passcode to boot up the device. This keeps people from gaining access to the data without the passcode.
- **Application sandbox**: Prevent apps from accessing data and resources they are not privileged to, e.g., other application user data.

These security features make Android devices more resilient against unauthorized access and tampering, protecting user data and the integrity of the device's operating system.

10.3 Application

Applications are small programs that the devices can run. These apps are installed from the Google Play Store. They use the APK file format, which is an archive file package based on the JAR file format. These archives can be unzipped and contain the compiled Java or Kotlin code. Because of how the application code is compiled, it is possible to reverse the processes, making it easier to understand the application's functions, as it is possible to view the source code of the application. When it comes to user-generated data, it is stored within the */data/data/<bundle identifiers>* directory. Most apps' bundle ID names are easy to identify, but that is not always the case. An easy way to determine an app's ID is to go to the Google Play Store using the browser: *play.google.com/store/apps/details?id={bundle id}*, and replace the bundle id with the one of interest and it should open the app play store page. When it comes to the format in which applications use to store the data, the common formats include SQLite databases, XML, and JSON.

10.4 Acquisition

Acquiring data from Android devices involves multiple methods, and the amount of data obtained depends on the level of access to the phone. Here are some common methods used for Android forensic acquisition:

- **Logical acquisition**: This method involves collecting data that is readily accessible on the device, such as contacts, call logs, messages, photos, and app data. Logical acquisition can be done using built-in tools, such as ADB (Android Debug Bridge) or third-party forensic tools.

- **Physical acquisition**: This method involves collecting data directly from the device's storage, bypassing the Android operating system. Physical acquisition can be done using JTAG, ISP, or chip-off techniques. However, these methods may require specialized hardware and software, as well as a high level of expertise.
- **Cloud acquisition**: Android devices can be synced with various cloud services, such as Google Drive, Google Photos, and Google Account. Acquiring data from these cloud services can provide additional information that may not be present on the device itself. This can be done using third-party forensic tools or manual techniques.

In addition to the internal storage, Android devices often have SD cards that can store a significant amount of information. It's essential to acquire data from the SD card outside of the phone, as the device might not be aware of all the data on the card. Moreover, the SD card might not be encrypted unless the user selects the "Use as Internal Storage" option, which isn't available for all Android models.

10.4.1 Android Debug Bridge (ADB)

Android Debug Bridge (ADB) is a command-line tool used to communicate with Android devices. It enables developers and users to send commands to the device, such as installing and debugging apps and accessing the device's internal files and data.

ADB is included as part of the Android Software Development Kit (SDK) and platform tools, which can be downloaded here.[3] This tool is typically used by developers to test and debug their Android apps, while users can use it to access internal files and data or perform advanced troubleshooting tasks.

To use ADB, first enable "USB debugging" on the Android device by enabling "Developer options" in the device's settings and activating "USB debugging." Once USB debugging is enabled, connect the device to your computer using a USB cable and agree to trust the computer shown in Figure 10.1.

Now, you can use ADB to send commands to the device and interact with the phone using the terminal. Using the command "adb devices" which can be seen in Figure 10.2 allows you to see connected devices to the computer and if they are authenticated to interact with the phone.

In our case, ADB enables extracting data from an Android device using just a few commands. However, because ADB interacts with the device on the user level, it is not possible to extract all data from the device. Folders such as the "/user data"

3 https://developer.android.com/studio/releases/platform-tools.

Figure 10.1 Android adb trust.

partition and "/data" folder, which hold system and application data, are mostly off-limits. Nonetheless, we can still obtain plenty of data. The two crucial commands for acquisition to remember are "*pull*" and "*backup*", as they both enable data acquisition from the device.

Create a full backup of the device data and save it as "backup.ab":

```
adb backup -apk -obb -shared -all -system -f backup.ab
```

The backup command creates a backup file using the *ab* archive format, which must be converted into a more common format before opening. This is done using the following command on a Linux device:

```
( printf "\x1f\x8b\x08\x00\x00\x00\x00\x00"; tail -c +25 backup.
   ab ) | tar xfvz -
```

Figure 10.2 adb authentication.

Once the "ab" file is unpacked, it should look something like in Figure 10.3.

Here, there are two folders: "apps" and "shared". The "apps" folder contains application-specific data, while the "shared" folder contains data shared across devices, such as pictures and downloaded files.

Figure 10.3 Android backup folder.

To create a backup of a single application, use the following command:

```
adb backup -f backup com.mypackage.myapp
```

The "*pull*" command retrieves data from the device's storage and outputs it to the current directory on the host device. When running the pull command on Linux, you can redirect stderr to null to prevent permission-denied errors from stopping the data retrieval processes.

```
adb pull /storage/self/primary/ . 2>/dev/null
```

10.4.1.1 ADB Server

The ADB server allows the creation of an ADB server on an open port, so other machines can connect and interact with the device. This feature enables setting up a server where multiple phones can connect for data extraction, freeing up resources on the host machine for other purposes such as analysis.

Start server:

```
adb -a nodaemon server
```

Connect to the server from the client machine:

```
adb -H <HOST_IP> -p 5037 shell
```

10.4.1.2 Extract APK from Android

When it comes to analyzing applications on Android, you need to get hold of the APK file. This can be done by extracting the application's APK file from the Android device; unlike iOS it does not require root access. The first step is to identify the path of the desired APK to be pulled off the device.

```
adb shell pm list packages -f | grep com.mypackage
```

The APK files can exist in one of two possible locations:

- /data/app/com.mypackage.apk
- /data/app/com.mypackage.android-e38UOwqgguuYZNtIfJt0qw==/base.apk

Once the path has been identified, the next step is to pull the APK off the phone using the "pull" command from one of two possible locations.

```
pull /data/app/com.mypackage.android-e38UOwqgguuYZNtIfJt0qw==/
    base.apk
```

You should now have the APK at hand ready for further analysis; this can be done with tools such as Jadx[4] and more automated tools like mobsfscan,[5] it will automatically scan the application to find security vulnerabilities.

10.4.2 Forensics Tools

Luckily for us are the forensics tools that can help with the process of acquiring data from Android devices.

10.4.2.1 Avilla

Avilla[6] is a free mobile forensics tool that can be used to extract data from Android devices using ADB; an image of the Avilla can be seen in Figure 10.4. It automates many processes, such as application downgrade and parsing of common chat applications, and provides many more features. Avilla is an excellent tool if you don't have the budget for commercial software.

10.4.3 Downgrading Applications

Downgrading applications is a technique that can be used to extract additional data. This method can be employed when previous versions of an application, e.g., had the allowBackup flag set to true in the manifest file. This signal to Android that the userdata stored is allowed to be extracted using the backup feature. This technique is commonly used to extract data from critical applications during

4 https://github.com/skylot/jadx.
5 https://github.com/MobSF/mobsfscan.
6 https://github.com/AvillaDaniel/AvillaForensics.

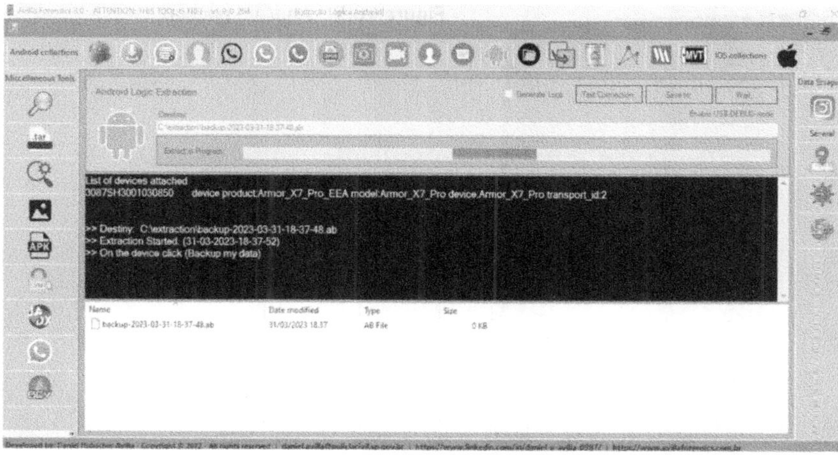

Figure 10.4 Avilla.

investigations. The most challenging part of this method is obtaining the APK file of the desired application version. Here are two places for downloading the APK, and it is possible that the desired version can be found here:

APKMirror (https://www.apkmirror.com/)
APKPure (https://apkpure.com/)

It should be noted that downgrading an application on Android version 12 and beyond can result in database damage and should first be used when you have tried the traditional way of extracting data. When it comes to performing the downgrading, the following command can be used for this purpose:

```
shell pm install -r -d my.package.apk
```

The -r flag tells Android to try and retain data and the second flag -d signals for downgrading. You can now perform acquisition again and you should now have additional data.

10.4.3.1 Rooting

Rooting is the process that grants the user privileged control of the device; this is also known as root access. The goal of rooting is to overcome the limitations that the manufacturer has put on the device. Caution should be exercised when rooting, as it can result in the loss of all user data. For this reason, make sure to acquire all available data from the device before attempting to root it. One approach to rooting the device is entering Download Mode. To enter Download Mode, a specific cable or key combination might be required, an example of Download Mode can be seen in Figure 10.5. Each model has a unique key combination that needs

Figure 10.5 Android backup.

to be pressed. The most common key combination is pressing the power button and both the volume up and down buttons simultaneously during reboot; this will on most devices enter the Download Mode.

Once in Download Mode, users can flash the ROM of the device, which can be used to create a full logical image of the file system. It's noteworthy that flashing the ROM leaves traces on the device, and this action is tracked and displayed when the device re-enters Download Mode, listing the number of flash attempts on the screen.

Pairing the correct ROM with the device model is key, if done incorrectly can brick the phone. If you'd like to try your luck doing it yourself, I recommend looking at the application Magisk.[7] Magisk guides through the rooting process. When it comes to searching for matching boot images, I recommend using desktop.firmware.mobi[8]; this resource has proven to be reliable in the past. On

7 https://magiskmanager.com.
8 https://desktop.firmware.mobi.

completing the processes you should now have root access to the device. This is a very light overview of the process, and depending upon the make and model an image may or may not be available.

10.5 Analysis

When it comes to analysis Android as with so many other types of devices, manual parsing all the information is a very time-consuming process. To speed up this analysis process of devices, people have created open-source programs that perform some of the analysis. One such tool is ALEAPP,[9] which can help you parse and present some of the information from an Android dump; image of ALEAPP can be seen in Figure 10.6.

It is important to note that no tool will parse all the data that exists within an Android device, nor should any evidence should not be trusted blindly. This is why any evidence found should be verified manually, and for applications that are not parsed, it is up to the analyst to understand the structure of the database tables within the application and the context around the data to get a clear understanding of what has happened.

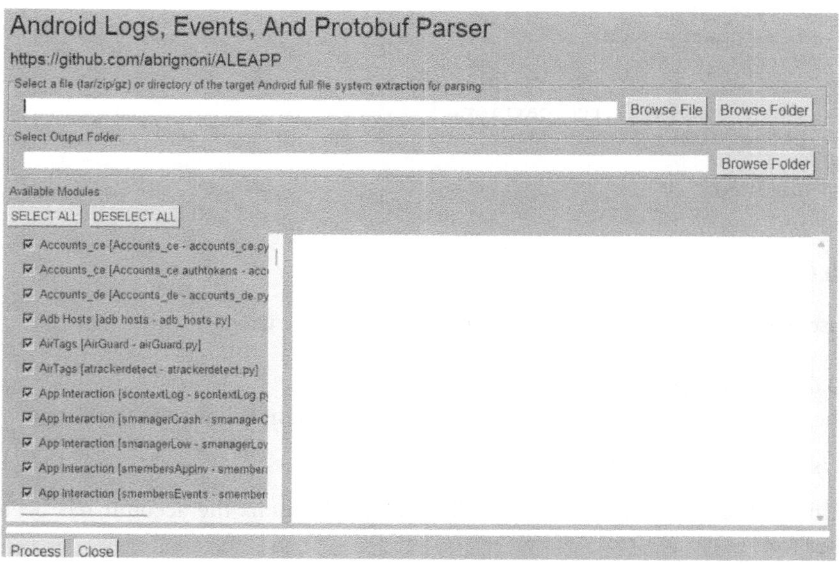

Figure 10.6 ALEAPP.

9 https://github.com/abrignoni/ALEAPP.

10.6 Evidence of Location

Due to the difficulty of obtaining a full file system without specialized tools. I have chosen to focus on evidence that can be extracted using *adb* and other open-source tools. This will include key evidence such as communication, location, network activity, and phone settings.

10.6.1 System Information

Includes what data exists within the device which stores general information about the device.

10.6.1.1 Sim Card Info

telephony.db contains information about the device's SIM card, which can be found here:

- /user_de/0/com.android.providers.telephony/databases/telephony.db

The SQL query used for retrieving SIM card info:

```
SELECT
    number,
    imsi,
    display_name,
    carrier_name,
    iso_country_code,
    carrier_id,
    icc_id,
    phone_number_source_carrier,
    phone_number_source_ims
FROM
    siminfo
```

10.6.2 User Settings

Discusses what setting provides information about the user.

10.6.2.1 Accounts

The _de.db can be used to identify what Google account is linked to the phone.

- /system_de/0/accounts_de.db

Inside the *Accounts* table, it also lists the applications the account has been used for.

The lastaccount.xml contains information about the last account used on the Google Play Store.

- /data/com.android.vending/shared_prefs/lastaccount.xml

10.6.2.2 Timezone

Used to determine the device's set timezone, the key to look for is persist.sys .timezone within /Property/persistent_properties.

10.6.2.3 Dump User Data with adb

Running the command "adb shell dumpsys user" provides a glimpse of the device and the user. Here, one can see the name of the device's user and the last login datetime.

```
adb shell dumpsys user
```

10.6.3 Communication

How the device has been used or communication

10.6.3.1 Call Logs

calllog.db stores the records of the phone calls the device has been used for.

- /data/com.android.providers.contacts/databases/calllog.db

The extract the phone calls from the database the following SQL query can be used:

```
SELECT
datetime(date /1000, 'unixepoch') as date,
phone_account_address,
number,
CASE
    WHEN type = 1 THEN 'Incoming'
    WHEN type = 2 THEN 'Outgoing'
    WHEN type = 3 THEN 'Missed'
    WHEN type = 4 THEN 'Voicemail'
    WHEN type = 5 THEN 'Rejected'
    WHEN type = 6 THEN 'Blocked'
    WHEN type = 7 THEN 'Answered Externally'
    ELSE 'Unknown'
    end as type,
duration,
CASE
    WHEN geocoded_location is NULL THEN ' '
    ELSE geocoded_location
    end as geocoded_location,
countryiso,
CASE
    WHEN transcription is NULL THEN ' '
    ELSE transcription
    END as content,
deleted
FROM
calls
```

10.6.3.2 SMS/MMS

SMS and MMS communication records on the device:

- /data/com.android.providers.telephony/databases/mmssms.db

When it comes to retrieving SMS/MMS data from the database, use the following:

```
SELECT _id as msg_id, thread_id, address as number, person,
   datetime(date/1000, 'UNIXEPOCH') as date,
   datetime(date_sent/1000, 'UNIXEPOCH') as date_sent,
   read,
   CASE WHEN type=1 THEN "Received"
        WHEN type=2 THEN "Sent"
        WHEN type=3 THEN "Draft"
        WHEN type=4 THEN "Outbox"
        WHEN type=5 THEN "Failed"
        WHEN type=6 THEN "Queued"
        ELSE type
   END as type,
   body as content
FROM sms
```

10.6.3.3 Email Information

Get information about email notifications and email subjects all saved in the *item* table.

- /data/com.google.android.gm/databases/bigTopDataDB.<user-id>

10.6.4 Application Usage

Store applications that have been used on the device.

10.6.4.1 APK Files Used for Installing Application

The location of the APK files used for installing applications can be found here: */app/*

10.6.4.2 Dumpsys Usagestats

Provides information about the daily statistics of the device's running applications:

```
adb shell dumpsys usagestats
```

Adb will now print out the activities that have happened on the device, into four different categories: daily, weekly, monthly, and yearly. The output provides a lot of information on the key such as Last time used, application lunch count, and much more, but these are the fields we are most often interested in. Here is an example of how stats are going to look like.

```
 In-memory monthly stats
timeRange="13/11/2023, 11:17 29/11/2023, 13:00"
package=com.google.android.youtube totalTimeUsed="12:05:58"
    lastTimeUsed="2023-11-29 11:29:20" totalTimeVisible="12:07:51"
     lastTimeVisible="2023-11-29 11:29:21" lastTimeComponentUsed
    ="2023-11-29 11:29:18" totalTimeFS="01:05" lastTimeFS
    ="2023-11-25 22:26:25" appLaunchCount=101
```

10.6.4.3 Application Traces

Frosting tracks the applications installed on the device, even if they are not installed from the Play Store. It can be used to prove the existence of applications on the system. It stores the application name, APK path, last update timestamp, and data location:

- /data/com.android.vending/databases/frosting.db

The database localappstate.db contains information about the installed packages; this also includes information about deleted apps:

- /data/com.android.vending/database/localappstate.db

10.6.4.4 install_requests

The install_queue.db database contains information about applications that have made update requests:

- /data/com.android.vending/databases/install_queue.db

For the data usage of applications, you should look at the data_usage.db that you can find here:

- /data/com.android.vending/databases/data_usage.db

10.6.4.5 Application Usage

The information that exists about the last usage of the application:

- /system/job/jobs.xml
- /system/users/0/app_idle_stats.xml

10.6.4.6 Application Notifications

This database contains notifications from applications. It can be used to prove application usage even if the app is deleted. This database contains the event, time, and package name:

- /system/notification_log.db

10.6.4.7 Application Permissions and Metadata

Identify the permissions an application had; this is useful in malware cases where you want to identify the access an application had:

- /system/packages.list
- /system/packages.xml

10.6.4.8 Application Snapshots

Contains snapshot images of applications, used by the phone when viewing running applications:

- /system_ce/snapshot/*.jpg

10.6.4.9 Downloads

Stores information about what has been downloaded on the device:

- /data/com.android.providers.downloads/databases/downloads.db

10.6.4.10 Calendar

User calendar events:

- /data/com.android.providers.calendar/databases/calendar.db

The SQL statement for retrieving data from the database:

```
select title,
description,
datetime(dtstart/1000,'unixepoch') as "start time",
datetime(dtend/1000,'unixepoch') as "start time",
eventTimezone,
case allDay when  0 then "No"
     when 1 then "Yes" end "all day",
rrule,
deleted from Events
```

10.6.4.11 Pictures

Contains information about the pictures on the device, including pictures and videos taken and saved, screenshots, and traces of SD card usage.

The downloaded table contains information about images that have been downloaded, such as name and resolution, the application used, and in some cases the URL of the image:

- /data/com.google.providers.media.module/databases/external.db

10.6.5 Wi-Fi

Stored information about what Wi-Fi the device has been connected to. Using the dumpsys command will display both the current Wi-Fi settings and historical Wi-Fi SSIDs that the device has been connected to. Together with wigle,[10] it can be used to geolocate users.

```
adb shell dumpsys wifi
```

10.6.6 Location

Without full file system access, Android phones do not provide location data. However, you may find some applications installed on the device that contain location information. I recommend trying to perform a Google takeout on the account linked to the phone, which can provide location data for the user.

10.6.7 Evidence Destruction

You can detect evidence destruction by looking at usage stats, which are logged every week. By examining the newest creation timestamp in the first week, you can determine when the device was first booted up.

- /data/system/powermanager
- /data/system/usagestats/0/weekly/

10.6.7.1 Factory Reset

Check the last modified timestamp of the files to identify when a factory reset of the device took place.

- /property/persistent_properties
- /misc/boostat/factory_Reset
- /misc/boostat/last_boot_time_utc

10.6.8 Summary

Android forensics is the process of extracting and analyzing data from Android devices. The handling of Android devices shares similarities with other smartphones, but it's essential to ensure that the device does not have access to the internet to prevent potential remote wiping of the device. The methods available to the general public require the device's passcode to access any information on the device. The advantage of Android over iPhone is the usage of standard file types that are easily handled by most programs.

---

10 https://wigle.net/.

Here is a summary of the evidence locations that provide essential information about the device, user activities, communication, and more.

- **Call logs**: /data/com.android.providers.contacts/databases/calllog.db this database stores information about incoming, outgoing, and missed calls.
- **SMS/MMS**: /data/com.android.providers.telephony/databases/mmssms.db this database contains SMS and MMS communication records.
- **Application usage**: Various locations provide insights into application usage, such as */data/com.android.vending/databases/frosting.db* for app installation tracking, and */system/users/0/app_idle_stats.xml* for app usage statistics.
- **Network connection**: Running *adb shell dumpsys wifi* displays both current Wi-Fi settings and historical Wi-Fi SSIDs, which can be used to geolocate users.
- **Location**: While Android devices may not provide direct location data without a full file system, installed apps or linked Google accounts may contain location information. Performing a Google Takeout on the linked account can provide user location data.
- **Evidence destruction**: Detecting potential evidence destruction can be done by examining usage stats (*/data/system/usagestats/0/weekly/*) or checking the last modified timestamp of files related to factory resets (e.g., */property/persistent_properties*, */misc/boostat/factory_Reset*, */misc/boostat/last_boot_time_utc*).

11

Network Forensics

The objective of network forensics is to deliver a comprehensive record of events that have transpired on a network, whether it involves cyber crime, illicit activities, or anything in between.

One of the most challenging aspects of network forensics is the collection phase. This is because of how rare it is for organizations to have a well-designed network data collection setup. It is extremely uncommon to arrive at a case where there is a complete PCAP of the entire incident. With some luck, there might be network flow data or firewall logs, and in the worst-case scenario, nothing at all. In cases where the organization has set up network capture, the next challenge is the sheer volume of data, making it difficult for investigators to identify data relevant to the case, as they must sift through large volumes of data to find the evidence they seek.

- Availability of data, not all networks have monitoring setups, making it difficult to get hold of the relevant data.
- The sheer volume of network data can be overwhelming, requiring advanced tools and techniques to effectively analyze the data.
- Networks are dynamic and constantly changing, making it difficult to maintain an accurate picture of network activity over time.
- Encryption and other security measures can complicate the analysis of network traffic, as they can obscure the content of network communications.

These are just some of the challenges you will be faced with.

11.1 Acquisition

Before any analysis can take place, data needs to be collected. The method of collection depends on the system and the type of data available. The different types of data include:

Practical Cyber Intelligence: A Hands-on Guide to Digital Forensics, First Edition. Adam Tilmar Jakobsen.

- Full-packet (PCAP)[1]
- Netflow traffic[2]
- Firewall logs
- Endpoint logs

Let's go into a little more detail about each type of data.

11.1.1 Pcap

Pcap is the capture of entire network packets. If the connection is not encrypted, it allows you to view the entire content of the packet. It is rare for an organization to have set up a pcap capturing device. One of the problems with pcap is the size of the files, making it hard to scale. Another concern of pcap is the privacy of employees.

Wireshark[3] seen in Figure 11.1, Tshark, and TCPdump[4] are all pcap capture and analysis tools. With Wireshark being GUI based, and Tshark and TCPDump CLI, these tools all have their pros and cons.

One such thing is with Wireshark and the limitation on the file size it can process. One way to over come, this is by filtering all the traffic away you do not care about using Tshark or TCPDump, thereby reducing the size of the file to something that can be loaded into Wireshark for analysis.

11.1.1.1 File Extraction from Network

The process of extracting files from pcap files can be done either manually by looking for the file header and/or file footer and carving out the data. There also exists an easier method using Wireshark or Tshark with this being executed using a simple command or using GUI interface. With Wireshark, the method of export file is done by going to: *Wireshark > File > Export Objects > protocol > destination* On the other hand if you would rather use a terminal to do the same the following command can be used.

```
tshark -r ${file} --export-object ${protocol},${path}
```

Table 11.1 shows what file types are supported for extraction by Wireshark.

This can also be achieved with Zeek, by executing the following command:

```
zeek -Cr sample.pcap /usr/local/zeek/share/zeek/policy/frameworks/
    files/extract-all-files.zeek
```

1 https://en.wikipedia.org/wiki/Pcap.
2 https://www.cisco.com/c/dam/en/us/td/docs/routers/asr920/configuration/guide/netmgmt/fnf-xe-3e-asr920-book.html.
3 https://www.wireshark.org/.
4 https://www.tcpdump.org/.

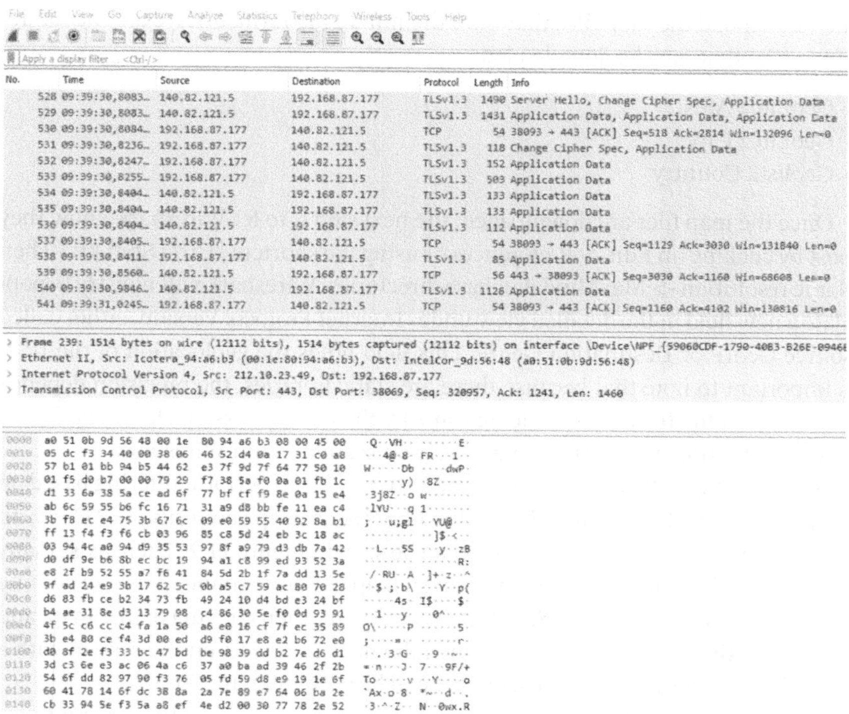

Figure 11.1 Wireshark.

Table 11.1 Supported file types by Wireshark (Tshark).

Protocol	Description
dicom	Medical image
HTTP	Web document
IMF	Email contents
smb	Windows network share file
tftp	Unsecured file

11.1.1.2 Geolocation with Wireshark

With Wireshark, it is also possible to geolocate IP addresses and draw nodes on a map to visually where connections are coming from. The first step to achieve this is to download the GeoIP lite database.[5] Start by creating an account on the site,

5 dev.maxmind.com/geoip/geolite2-free-geolocation-data.

then download the map files that have the.mmdb file format. Here are the names of the files that may be downloaded:

- GeoLite2 ASN
- GeoLite2 City
- Geolist2 Country

Once the map files are downloaded, the next step is to let Wireshark know they exist by clicking on Edit -> Preferences or using the shortcut "Ctrl+Shift+P." Then Name resolution -> MaxMind database directories. Wireshark will now try to populate a new field in the detailed view under Internet Protocol Version, either called Source GeoIP or Destination GeoIP. This field holds the geolocation of the IP. It is important to note that because these are static libraries, the precision depends on the age of the files. This is the reason why the newest version should be downloaded every time you perform a geolocation search within Wireshark.

With the map data imported, it is now also possible to perform filtering based on the geolocation of the connection, using filters such as ip.geoip.city == "City"; an example of the enrich packet analysis can be seen in Figure 11.2. There exist many other filters that can be used. Generating a map of where connections are coming from is done by first going to Statistics -> Endpoint, then clicking on the map, and opening in the browser. It will now open the native browser on the system with a map of all the connections. An example can be seen in Figure 11.3.

Although many network analysis courses go into detail about the different possibilities that having a full PCAP brings, it is worth noting that in forensic cases, pcap files are rarely available.

```
Source Address: 142.250.74.42
Destination Address: 10.105.10.67
v [Source GeoIP: Glen Cove, US, ASN 15169, GOOGLE]
    [Source GeoIP City: Glen Cove]
    [Source or Destination GeoIP City: Glen Cove]
    [Source GeoIP Country: United States]
    [Source or Destination GeoIP Country: United States]
    [Source GeoIP ISO Two Letter Country Code: US]
    [Source or Destination GeoIP ISO Two Letter Country Code: US]
    [Source GeoIP AS Number: 15169]
    [Source or Destination GeoIP AS Number: 15169]
    [Source GeoIP AS Organization: GOOGLE]
    [Source or Destination GeoIP AS Organization: GOOGLE]
    [Source GeoIP Latitude: 40.8627]
    [Source or Destination GeoIP Latitude: 40.8627]
    [Source GeoIP Longitude: -73.6351]
    [Source or Destination GeoIP Longitude: -73.6351]
```

Figure 11.2 Wireshark geo.

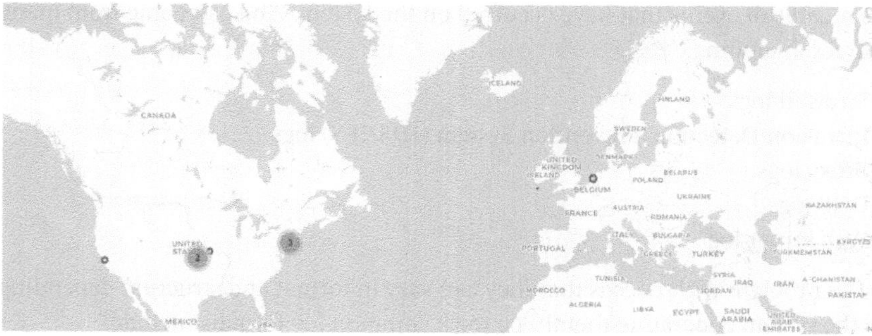

Figure 11.3 Wireshark map.

11.1.2 Netflow

Netflow is a protocol that collects and records network traffic metadata, such as IP addresses, ports, and timestamps. It does not capture the content of the packets themselves, which can be beneficial if privacy concerns are recording the packet of the network. Netflow data can be useful in understanding network activity, detecting anomalies, and identifying potential security threats. Netflow data is typically exported from routers, switches, and other network devices to a collector for further analysis.

There are several versions of Netflow, with versions 5 and 9 being the most common. Version 9, also known as IPFIX (IP Flow Information Export), is more flexible and extensible compared to the two versions. Some key fields in a Netflow record include:

- Source and destination IP addresses
- Source and destination ports
- Protocol (TCP, UDP, ICMP, etc.)
- Timestamps (start and end times of the flow)
- Number of packets and bytes exchanged

I am yet to find a good tool for analyzing NetFlow data; what I do is convert the Netflow data into CSV format which gets loaded into Python using Pandas[6] Dataframe, and from here I can analyze the data as I please.

11.1.3 Logs

Firewall logs are most commonly available as they are often enabled by default or setup because they used by the network administrators for debugging. The logs

6 https://pandas.pydata.org/.

are records of events that have occurred on the system. And can come from many sources, including:

- Firewall logs
- Intrusion Detection/Prevention System (IDS/IPS) logs
- Proxy logs
- DNS logs
- Web server logs

The problem with Logs is that they can vary in format and structure depending on the system generating them. The most common log formats include:

- **Syslog**[7]: A standard log format used by many network devices and Unix-based systems. Syslog messages contain a timestamp, a facility (source), a severity level, and a message.
- **W3C Extended Log File Format**[8]: A standard log format used by web servers, such as IIS and Apache. It contains information about client requests, server responses, and other transaction data.
- **Windows Event Log**: The native logging system in Windows operating systems. It records events from various sources, including the operating system, applications, and security components.

When it comes to analyzing logs, the first step is to parse and normalize them into a consistent format. From here the log can be imported into an analysis tool such as the ELK stack https://www.elastic.co/elastic-stack, allowing you to search through the data.

11.2 Analysis

When it comes to analyzing network data there are different methods that can be deployed to understand the traffic happening:

11.2.1 Connected Devices

Identifying connected devices: This is used to identify all devices connected to a network. Allows one to verify that all devices have been collected from a screen and that there are no hidden devices which are overlooked. I have seen NAS being stored within the walls of a house that only got identified because of network scans. A popular solution for this is Nmap[9]; it is free and open-source tool used for this

7 https://en.wikipedia.org/wiki/Syslog.
8 https://www.w3.org/TR/WD-logfile.html.
9 https://nmap.org/.

purpose. It is easy to use, offering both a GUI (Zenmap) and a command-line interface. Then to scan the IP range from 192.168.0.0 to 192.168.255.255, the following search can be performed:

```
nmap -T5 -Pn 192.168.0.0/16
```

Once finished it will print out all the devices that are connected which have an IP within the range that it can reach. Be aware this method does not always work, like with networks using subnets to segment devices from each other, and this will for the most only be a business network.

11.2.2 Statistical Analysis

Because of the large amount of data in network forensics, statistical analysis can be a helpful starting point. Visualization techniques, such as graphing data, can reveal outliers in data size or connection length. Frequency analysis can identify packets or devices that appear to communicate more often than expected. These are just some of the methods that can be deployed to understand the data and determine which packets require closer examination.

11.2.3 Expected Protocol and Connection Architecture

This is probably the most time-consuming way to analyze a network. It starts by identifying all expected protocols and connections on the network. Create a filter to sort out known good network connections, then categorize the remaining connections as good or bad.

11.2.4 Encrypted Network Activity Classification

Analyzing encrypted network traffic can be challenging. One effective approach is to examine traffic behavior and compare it to normal traffic patterns. This requires an in-depth understanding of each protocol and its behavior. Table 11.2 gives an example of the most common protocols and their associated characteristics:

11.2.5 Identifying Network Beacons Using Historical Network Data with RITA

This method of analysis is taken from RITA[10] created by "Active Countermeasures." The goal is to identify beacon traffic using historical data. I loved the idea of the project but found it to be too limiting, as it was designed as an add-on to Zeek.

10 https://github.com/activecm/rita.

Table 11.2 Network classification.

Protocol	Client volume	Server volume	Duration	Potential activity
HTTP	Small	Large	Short	HTTP download
HTTPS	Large	Small	Various	HTTP post upload
HTTP	Large	Large	Long	TLS VPN
SSH	Small	Large	Various	SCP
SSH	Various	Various	Long	shell
DNS	Large	Large	Long	Tunnel?

When trying to use RITA in an investigation, it's rare for people or organizations to have Zeek operating on the network. For that reason, I took the idea and implemented it into Python, to allow it to be used only with the type of evidence that is most often available: network logs and Netflow artifacts. This is meant mostly as a prototype script and will likely need to be cleaned up before being put into production.

The idea of RITA is that beacon traffic has a uniform distribution with a small deviation, while user traffic has a skewed distribution with a large deviation.

Here, we start by importing the necessary libraries needed for the program and defining the names of the columns we will be working with. This may need to be changed depending on the names of the columns used by your system. We start by filtering out the columns that we are not interested in and then group the connections by source and destination IP and destination port.

```
import math
import pandas as pd
import numpy as np

df= pd.DataFrame.from_csv("log.csv")

timestamp = 'bidirectional_first_seen_ms'
src_ip = 'src_ip'
dst_ip = 'dst_ip'
dst_host = 'requested_server_name'
dst_port = 'dst_port'
bytes_sent = 'src2dst_bytes'
# Filter out the unnecessary fields
filter = [timestamp, src_ip, dst_ip, dst_host, dst_port,
    bytes_sent]

#Group the connections that are the same.
groupby = [src_ip, dst_ip, dst_port]
```

```
df = df.loc[:,filter]

# In my case, I had to convert the milliseconds that my system
    used for timestamp to datetime, this might not be necessary
    depending on the system
df[timestamp] = pd.to_datetime(df[timestamp], unit='ms')

df = df.groupby(groupby).agg(list) # group the sample by source
    and destination IP and destination port
df.reset_index(inplace=True)
```

Once we have grouped the connections, we calculate the number of times there has been a connection to the destination IP and port from a given IP, and the delta time between connections.

```
#ConnectionCount is by taking each row in the timestamp column,
    and getting the about of connections that have been made
df['ConnectionCount'] = df[timestamp].apply(lambda x: len(x))

#Remove all connections with less than 22 connections, the idea
    is that the malware will probably try to connect at least once
    per hour.
df = df.loc[df['ConnectionCount'] > 22]

# Sort by timestamp
df[timestamp] = df[timestamp].apply(lambda x: sorted(x))
# Calculate the delta time between connections
df['delta_time'] = df[timestamp].apply(lambda x: pd.Series(x).
    diff().dt.seconds.dropna().tolist())
```

Then we calculate the Bowley skewness[11] measure, formula: "(Q3 + Q1 – 2*Q2) / (Q3 – Q1)." This allows us to identify if we have a negative or positive skewed distribution. Beaconing traffic should have a symmetric distribution; this goes for both the delta time and data size distributions.

Next we will also calculate the Median Absolute Deviation (MAD) to check the spread of the distribution, using the median value. The formula for MAD is $\text{median}(|x_i - \text{median}(X)|)$.

A simpler explanation from Wikipedia[12] is:

> Consider the data (1, 1, 2, 2, 4, 6, 9). It has a median value of 2. The absolute deviations about 2 are (1, 1, 0, 0, 2, 4, 7) which in turn have a median value of 1 (because the sorted absolute deviations are (0, 0, 1, 1, 2, 4, 7)). So the median absolute deviation for this data is 1.

---

11 https://www.statisticshowto.com/bowley-skewness/.

12 https://en.wikipedia.org/wiki/Median_absolute_deviation.

```
# Find the quartiles for the dataset.
df['tsLow'] = df['delta_time'].apply(lambda x: np.percentile(np.
    array(x),25))
df['tsMid'] = df['delta_time'].apply(lambda x: np.percentile(np.
    array(x), 50))
df['tsHigh'] = df['delta_time'].apply(lambda x: np.percentile(np.
    array(x), 75))

# Calculate the skewness, using the formula
df['tsBowleyNum'] = df['tsLow'] + df['tsHigh'] - 2 * df['tsMid']
df['tsBowleyDen'] = df['tsHigh'] - df['tsLow']

# tsSkew should equal zero if the denominator equals zero
# Bowley skew is unreliable if Q2 = Q1 or Q2 = Q3
df['tsSkew'] = df[['tsLow', 'tsMid', 'tsHigh', 'tsBowleyNum','
    tsBowleyDen']].apply(
        lambda x: x['tsBowleyNum'] / x['tsBowleyDen'] if x['
          tsBowleyDen'] !=0 and x['tsMid'] != x['tsLow'] and x['
          tsMid'] != x['tsHigh'] !=0 else 0.0, axis=1)

df['tsMadm'] = df['delta_time'].apply(lambda x: np.median(np.
    absolute(np.array(x) - np.median(np.array(x)))))
df['tsConnDiv'] = df[timestamp].apply(lambda x: (x[-1].
    to_pydatetime() - x[0].to_pydatetime()).seconds / 90)
```

Once we have calculated the necessary variables, it's time for the time delta score.

```
# Calculate the Time delta score
df['tsConnCountScore'] = df.apply(lambda x: 0.0 if x['tsConnDiv']
    == 0 else x['ConnectionCount'] / x['tsConnDiv'] if x['
    ConnectionCount'] / x['tsConnDiv'] < 1.0 else 1.0, axis=1)

df['tsSkewScore'] = 1.0 - abs(df['tsSkew'])
df['tsMadmScore'] = df['tsMadm'].apply(lambda x: 0 if 1.0 - (x /
    30.0) < 0 else 1.0 - (x / 30.0))

# Calculate the score of time delta using
df['tsScore'] = (((df['tsSkewScore'] + df['tsMadmScore'] + df['
    tsConnCountScore']) / 3.0) * 1000) / 1000
```

ds stands for data size. Here we do the same thing as we did with delta time, now just for data size.

```
# Variables for data size dispersion
df['dsLow'] = df[bytes_sent].apply(lambda x: np.percentile(np.
    array(x), 25))
df['dsMid'] = df[bytes_sent].apply(lambda x: np.percentile(np.
    array(x), 50))
df['dsHigh'] = df[bytes_sent].apply(lambda x: np.percentile(np.
    array(x), 75))
df['dsBowleyNum'] = df['dsLow'] + df['dsHigh'] - 2 * df['dsMid']
df['dsBowleyDen'] = df['dsHigh'] - df['dsLow']
```

```
# dsSkew should equal zero if the denominator equals zero
# Bowley skew is unreliable if Q2 = Q1 or Q2 = Q3
df['dsSkew'] = df[['dsLow','dsMid','dsHigh','dsBowleyNum','
    dsBowleyDen']].apply(
        lambda x: x['dsBowleyNum'] / x['dsBowleyDen'] if x['
            dsBowleyDen'] != 0 and x['dsMid'] != x['dsLow'] and x['
            dsMid'] != x['dsHigh'] else 0.0, axis=1)

df['dsMadm'] = df[bytes_sent].apply(lambda x: np.median(np.
    absolute(np.array(x) - np.median(np.array(x)))))

# data size score
df['dsSkewScore'] = 1.0 - abs(df['dsSkew'])
df['dsMadmScore'] = df['dsMadm'].apply(lambda x: 0 if x/ 128.0 <
    0 else x/ 128.0)
df['dsSmallnessScore'] = df['dsMid'].apply(lambda x: 0 if 1.0 - x
    / 8192.0 < 0 else 1.0 - x / 8192.0)

# Calculate the score using the sum of
df['dsScore'] = (((df['dsSkewScore'] + df['dsMadmScore'] + df['
    dsSmallnessScore']) / 3.0) * 1000) / 1000
```

Once we have the score for both, the overall beaconing score is calculated by taking the sum of the data size and delta time score and dividing by 2.

```
df['Score'] = (df['dsScore'] + df['tsScore']) / 2
df.sort values(by= 'Score', ascending=False, inplace=True)

df.to_csv("output.csv")
```

There you have it, a quick overview of the algorithm behind *RITA*. It is quite simple once you start understanding the components, and it is very effective for identifying beaconing traffic.

To use the code, there are a few things you have to do. The first step is acquiring the necessary log files or NetFlow in CSV format. The data must be bidirectional for this program to work.

Once you have the CSV file of the network traffic, the next step is to ensure that the defined columns in the program match the columns in the CSV file. The program should now read the data and output a CSV file with the probability of the different network connections being beaconing.

Remember that beaconing traffic is not necessarily *evil*; it can just as well be a program that frequently checks for update packets such as antivirus. This is why the next step should be to verify if any of the connections are malicious.

11.2.6 Domain Analysis

The goal of domain analysis is to analyze the domains the network has been connected to and identify if they are malicious or not. Common strategies include looking for newly registered domains or checking if they have been part of any previous scams. In this analysis approach, I'd like to focus on a tactic frequently employed by cybercriminals: typosquatting. This involves using domain names that appear similar to the target domain they are trying to impersonate (e.g., *fbi.com* and *fbi.com*). What I did was compared the domains the organization was connected to in the past seven days against the Majestic Million.[13]

For the comparison of domains, I used the Levenshtein distance,[14] a method for calculating the distance between two strings. Below is one example of implementing the math into code.

```
import pandas as pd

def levenshtein(s, t):
        if s == t: return 0
        elif len(s) == 0: return len(t)
        elif len(t) == 0: return len(s)
        v0 = [None] * (len(t) + 1)
        v1 = [None] * (len(t) + 1)
        for i in range(len(v0)):
            v0[i] = i
        for i in range(len(s)):
            v1[0] = i + 1
            for j in range(len(t)):
                cost = 0 if s[i] == t[j] else 1
                v1[j + 1] = min(v1[j] + 1, v0[j + 1] + 1, v0[j] +
                     cost)
            for j in range(len(v0)):
                v0[j] = v1[j]
        if v1[len(t)] < 3:  % Not necessary to output domains
            that are widely different, which is why I set it at 3.
            return s,t,v1[len(t)]

domain = pd.read_csv("majestic.csv")
target = pd.read_csv("domin.csv")

leven = pd.DataFrame()
leven = [levenshtein(trow,drow) for drow in domain for trow in
    target]

leven. columns = ["domain","target","score"]
leven.to_csv("Levenshtein_result.csv")
```

The idea of the code is to loop through the two dataframes: one with the domains the network has connected to and the other with the Majestic Million list. The goal is to find a domain with a distance of 1 or 2 character from the domains in Majestic list. This method is especially useful for threat-hunting for possible malicious domains used in cyberattacks. While the Levenshtein distance is an effective

13 https://majestic.com/reports/majestic-million.
14 https://en.wikipedia.org/wiki/Levenshtein_distance.

way to identify typosquatting domains, there are other techniques you can use to further refine your domain analysis and increase the accuracy of identifying malicious domains. Some of these techniques include:

Entropy analysis: Entropy[15] is a measure of randomness in a sequence of characters. In the context of domain analysis, higher entropy values for a domain name may indicate the use of randomly generated strings, which are commonly seen in malicious domains. You can calculate the entropy of a domain and compare it against a threshold to flag potentially suspicious domains.

Reverse IP lookup: Malicious actors may use the same IP address for multiple malicious domains. By performing a reverse IP lookup, you can identify all the domains hosted on a given IP address. If several suspicious domains are found on the same IP address, the IP address is likely associated with malicious activities.

WHOIS information analysis: WHOIS information includes the registration details of a domain, such as the registrant's name, address, and contact information. Malicious actors often provide fake or incomplete WHOIS information. By analyzing this data, you can identify domains with suspicious registration details.

Blacklist check: There are several publicly available blacklists, such as Google Safe Browsing,[16] PhishTank,[17] and Spamhaus,[18] that contain a known malicious domain. By checking if a domain is listed in one or more of these blacklists, you can quickly identify if it has been involved in malicious activities.

Domain age: Malicious domains are often short-lived, as attackers frequently change domain names to evade detection. By analyzing the age of a domain, you can flag recently registered domains that may be associated with malicious activities.

Top-level domain (TLD) analysis: Some TLDs are more commonly associated with malicious activities. Knowing which TLDs are frequently used by adversaries can help in the process of predicting if the domain is malicious.

By combining the techniques mentioned above, you can create a very comprehensive system that can be used to predict the probability of a domain being malicious or not.

11.3 Summary

Network forensics is a vital aspect of cybersecurity investigations, especially when dealing with cybercrimes. The effectiveness of network forensics depends on the evidence available and how relevant the network data is to the case. It is rare

15 https://en.wikipedia.org/wiki/Entropy_(information_theory).
16 https://developers.google.com/safe-browsing.
17 https://phishtank.org/.
18 https://www.spamhaus.com/.

for analysts to have access to packet capture (PCAP), which provides the most information. However, more often than not, analysts must rely on default logging policies and data from network devices. However, it's essential to start with NetFlow artifacts and understand the evidence that can be extracted from them. A recommended resource for learning about network flow analysis is the book Network Flow Analysis.[19] Although the book is old, it remains a valuable resource for understanding network forensics.

19 Network Flow Analysis 1st edition by Lucas, Michael W.

12

Malware Analysis

Malware analysis is the study of malware, aiming to understand its behavior. What sets malware analysis apart from other forms of reverse engineering is that malware typically tries to take control of a system. This is why it's important to use an isolated environment separate from the rest of the network, ensuring that the malware doesn't accidentally infect the entire network.

Like other reverse engineering disciplines, malware analysis requires a high level of technical expertise, as well as a deep understanding of computer systems and security. Malware analysis is an essential tool in cybersecurity, allowing practitioners to develop countermeasures and protect against attacks. It's also used by researchers and law enforcement to study and investigate malware developers, as each piece of malware leaves behind clues about its creator. In some cases, malware developers may even intentionally leave such clues. The analysis process involves using various tools and techniques, such as disassemblers, debuggers, and sandbox environments, to reverse engineer the malware's code and behavior, and identify its capabilities, techniques, and potential weaknesses. Most of my experience is with Windows malware, so this discussion will primarily focus on that perspective.

Malware can come in many forms, including documents with macros, scripts, and executable files. Malware can also use multiple technologies to achieve its goals. For example, a phishing email might contain a link to a macro-embedded Word file, followed by shell code that downloads the next module, and finally, a PowerShell command to download the final payload. This is just one example; the possibilities are endless, and it's up to the malware author to be as creative as possible to evade anti-virus detection.

When analyzing malware, it's crucial to be knowledgeable about various technologies and the tricks that malware authors use to bypass security controls. In this discussion, I will go over the basics of malware analysis, how to set up a secure environment for analysis, and some common practices for handling different types of malware.

Practical Cyber Intelligence: A Hands-on Guide to Digital Forensics, First Edition. Adam Tilmar Jakobsen.

12.1 Acquiring Malware Samples

Before you can begin analyzing malware, you need samples to analyze. A good starting point is using malware samples that others have already analyzed, allowing you to compare your results. There are several websites with extensive collections of malware samples available for download; example of malware bazaar can be seen in Figure 12.1.

Here is a list of some sites where you can go find malware samples:

- Vx-underground[1]
- Malshare[2]
- Malware bazaar[3]

For Mac-specific malware, I recommend going to objective-see[4]

Please note that these samples are live and can be harmful to your system if executed. For this reason, I recommend that you always exercise caution and ensure that you are working in a secure and isolated environment when handling malware samples.

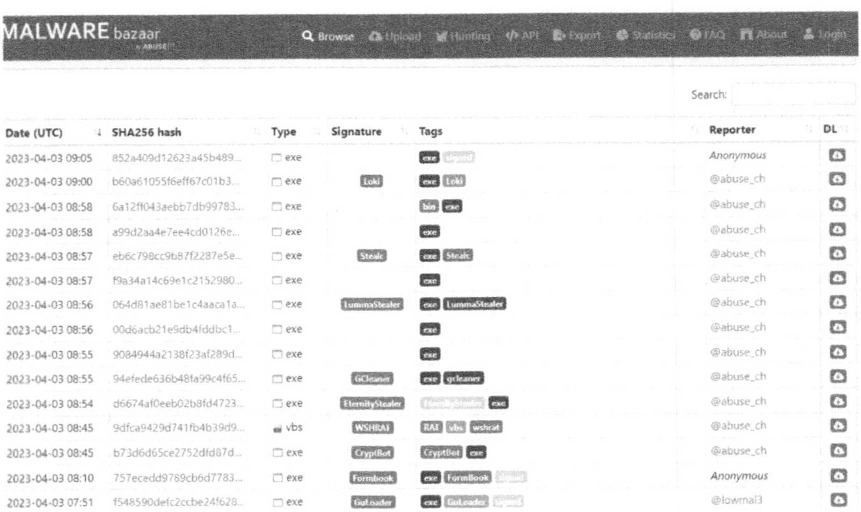

Figure 12.1 Malware bazaar.

1 https://www.vx-underground.org/.
2 https://malshare.com/.
3 https://bazaar.abuse.ch/.
4 https://objective-see.com/malware.html.

12.2 Handling Malware Samples

When acquiring malware samples, it is crucial to avoid infecting your machine. A common method for transferring samples between devices is to contain them within a password-protected archive. This prevents accidental execution and stops antivirus software from scanning the file and containing it.

Another approach on Windows is to defang the sample which can be done by simply removing the extension; that way windows will not know what to do with the sample if you were to execute it.

12.2.1 Virtual Environment

Active analysis of malware involves executing the malware in a controlled environment to monitor its activity. Since we are working with live malware that can take control of the computer and spread itself to other systems, analysis must be done inside a contained environment. Virtual machines can be used to create these isolated environments to prevent further injection, and software such as VMware[5] or VirtualBox[6] can be used to create and manage these virtual environments; example of a setup can be seen in Figure 12.2.

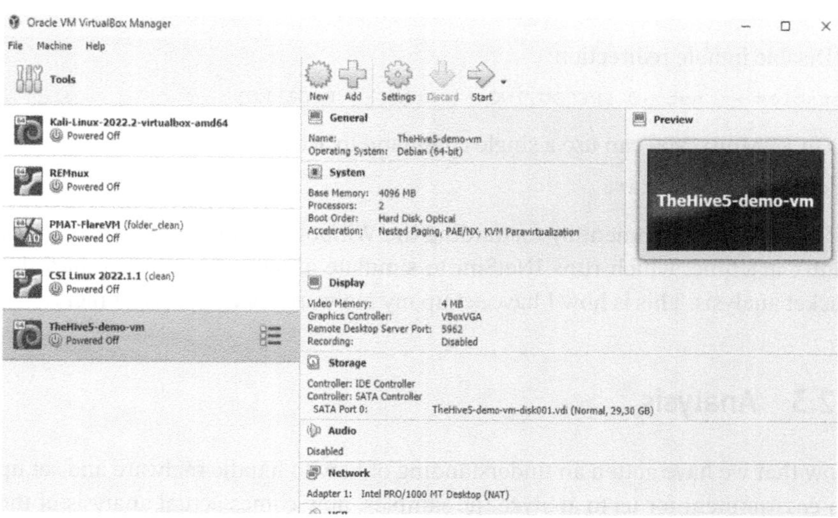

Figure 12.2 Virtual box.

5 https://www.vmware.com/.
6 https://www.virtualbox.org.

As most malware targets Windows, it's a good idea to have two virtual machines: a Windows machine for executing and monitoring malware without risking infecting the whole network, and a Linux machine for analyzing the malware without the risk of infection. Linux is chosen because malware is less likely to be designed for it, and many malware analysis tools are developed for the Linux systems.

When it comes to creating the environment for executing malware within it must be Windows-based as they have been designed for that environment. Luckily Microsoft provides virtual images for evaluation purposes, like the Windows 10 image.[7] For Linux forensic images, REMnux[8] is my go-to malware analysis image as it comes pre-installed with malware analysis tools. Remember to take a snapshot of the image before executing any samples, or you risk having to reinstall the environment anew.

Many malware samples perform an internet check to see if they are on an internet-connected host and identify if they are within a sandbox. If they cannot connect, they might self-destruct. To set up a fake network for the malware to connect to, use either Fakenet-ng[9] or INetSim.[10] Both solutions simulate a network for the malware to connect to.

If the sample instead connects to hardcoded IP addresses, it is possible to change the iptable on the Linux machine to accept all IP requests. Enable iptables redirection:

```
iptables -t nat -A PREROUTING -i eth0 -j REDIRECT
```

Disable iptable redirection:

```
iptables -t nat -D PREROUTING -i eth0 -j REDIRECT
```

On REMnux, you can use a single command to accept-all-ips service:

```
accept-all-ips start
```

Set up the environment by forwarding the Windows machine's network to the Linux machine, which runs INetSim to simulate a network and Wireshark for packet analysis. This is how I have set up my malware analysis environment.

12.3 Analysis

Now that we have gotten an understanding of how to handle malware and set up an environment for us to analyze the samples, now comes actual analysis of the malware, with the goal of extracting intel. This will be a very light fly-by on the

---

7 https://developer.microsoft.com/en-us/microsoft-edge/tools/vms/.
8 https://remnux.org.
9 https://github.com/mandiant/flare-fakenet-ng.
10 https://www.inetsim.org/.

different methods that are used for analysis. I will at the end of this chapter provide you with additional resources you can use to go deeper into malware analysis if this section piques your interest.

12.3.1 Dynamic Analysis

Dynamic analysis involves systematically interacting with an application at runtime and observing its behavior. Virtual environments are often used for this purpose, as they allow for greater control over variables. The process involves comparing the system before and after interactions and documenting any changes observed.

This process allows the malware to be safely executed, monitored, and recorded, including the files and resources it accesses, the network connections it establishes, and any other actions it performs. Dynamic analysis can be performed using a sandbox or a debugger. Both tools hook into the program, allowing you to control the application's flow and perform code patches at runtime, providing valuable insights into the malware's behavior and characteristics.

12.3.1.1 Sandbox with Cuckoo

A sandbox automates the entire process of dynamically analyzing samples by setting up a virtual environment that hooks into the sample and observes its behavior. Cuckoo Sandbox[11] is a widely recommended open-source project that generates a report outlining the sample's behavior. To experiment with Cuckoo without installing it, try using cert cuckoo,[12] a visual of the program can be seen in Figure 12.3. Keep in mind that anything you upload to a public sandbox can be viewed by everyone.

Installation To install Cuckoo on your system without worrying about samples becoming publicly available, use Vagrant, which simplifies the process. Ensure you have Vagrant and Packer installed on your machine by visiting vagrantup[13] and packer.[14]

A project called BoomBox has set up Cuckoo using Vagrant, but it is no longer up-to-date. To resolve compatibility issues with newer Vagrant versions, use this fork of the project:

```
git clone https://github.com/Paradoxxs/BoomBox
```

11 https://github.com/cuckoosandbox/cuckoo.
12 https://cuckoo.cert.ee.
13 https://www.vagrantup.com/.
14 https://www.packer.io/.

Figure 12.3 Cuckoo.

Set everything up on Windows:

```
./build.ps1 -ProviderName virtualbox -VagrantOnly
```

If only the sandbox is set up, run the following command to bring up the cuckoo image. Ensure you run the command inside the Vagrant folder, or it will fail.

```
vagrant up cuckoo
```

Once completed, access Cuckoo at http://192.168.30.100:8080 with the username and password "vagrant." Upload samples using the web interface and make REST API queries to the server, which should be available on port 8090. You can find the available API calls in the Cuckoo documentation.[15]

12.3.1.2 Capa

Capa[16] is a binary emulator with detection capabilities and tries to identify the program function. For example, it might suggest that the file is a backdoor, is capable of installing services, or relies on HTTP to communicate. To set Capa start by downloading the bin file for your OS. Run Capa with very verbose output on the sample and save it to a text file:

```
capa -vv sample.exe > capa.txt
```

Output to JSON:

```
capa -vv -j sample.exe > capa.json
```

By utilizing these dynamic analysis tools and techniques, you can gain a deeper understanding of the behavior and characteristics of a given malware sample.

15 https://cuckoo.readthedocs.io/en/latest/usage/api/#resources.
16 https://github.com/mandiant/capa.

This knowledge can be invaluable in developing effective countermeasures and mitigation strategies to protect your systems from potential threats.

12.3.2 Code Analysis

Code analysis involves disassembling or decompiling the malware to understand its inner workings. This is typically done using disassemblers or decompilers, depending on the language the malware was written in.

12.3.2.1 Disassemblers and Decompilers

Disassemblers are tools that translate the machine code of a binary into a human-readable assembly language. They are commonly used to analyze malware samples written in low-level languages like C or C++.

- **Ghidra**[17]: Ghidra is an open-source software reverse engineering (SRE) suite developed by the National Security Agency (NSA)[18] of the United States. It includes a disassembler, decompiler, and various other analysis tools; an image can be seen in Figure 12.4.
- **Ida**[19]: Ida is a popular commercial disassembler that supports a wide range of processor instructions and executable formats. It also includes a built-in debugger, making it a powerful tool for reverse engineering and malware analysis.

Both these tools include decompilers which are tools that translate the compiled code back into a high-level language, such as C, C#, or Java. The process will never

Figure 12.4 Ghidra.

17 https://ghidra-sre.org/.
18 https://www.nsa.gov/.
19 https://hex-rays.com/.

be perfect, but it can give a general idea of the functionality of the code, as long it is not too obfuscated. There exist two tools I would like to mention that can almost revert the compiled code C# and Java, back to its original state.

- **dnSpy**[20]: is a powerful open-source .NET debugger and assembly editor, which also includes a decompiler. It can be used to analyze malware samples written in .NET languages like C# or VB.NET.
- **Jadx**[21]: is an open-source Java decompiler, which can be used to analyze malware samples written in Java. It can convert Android APK files, DEX files, or Java class files back into Java source code.

When starting on code analysis here are a few good starting points:

- What API calls does the program make, and what are the parameters that are passed to the API calls?
- Is there any logic flow based on the returns from the calls? If there isn't a test after a call, it most likely is not of interest as the function called does not have a return value and most likely is a utility function.
- If the same function is called multiple times, there is a high possibility it is a decryption function.

12.4 Summary

The method used for analyzing malware can be applied to the analysis of any kind of system. The tools might be slightly different depending on the system, but the approach is always the same: using a combination of static and dynamic analysis of the target in question.

For those interested in deepening their knowledge of malware analysis, there are many resources available. TCM-Security's "Practical Malware Analysis & Triage"[22] offers an excellent balance of depth and value, covering the basics of dynamic and code analysis and a section on automation.

When it comes to books, *Practical Malware Analysis*[23] by Michael and Andrew is considered one of the best in the field. It covers a wide range of topics, from the basics to more complex issues. However, it focuses on IDA Pro, an expensive tool, which may not be accessible for everyone. To supplement this, *The Ghidra Book*[24]

---

20 https://github.com/dnSpy/dnSpy.
21 https://github.com/skylot/jadx.
22 https://academy.tcm-sec.com/p/practical-malware-analysis-triage.
23 https://nostarch.com/malware.
24 https://nostarch.com/GhidraBook.

by Chris and Kara can be a valuable resource, as it allows readers to tackle the problems presented in the book without relying on costly tools.

Overall, malware analysis requires advanced technical skill which requires a deep understanding of the operation system the malware is targeting. The good thing is there are numerous resources available to help you develop your expertise in this area.

13

OSINT

Open-source intelligence (OSINT) is the process of collecting, processing, and analyzing information that is publicly available to everyone. The degree to which something is available to everyone is up to your organization; the question is a 5$ price to access data still considered part of OSINT?

With the constantly increasing amount of information available on the open internet has made OSINT a critical skill for various types of investigations. It allows the investigator to access a wide range of information, with relative ease, that might otherwise be overlooked. This information can be used for various purposes, such as threat intelligence, user profiling and much more. OSINT can be quite diverse, depending on the specific context and circumstances of the case, ranging from passive collection of social media data to HUMINT operations, where you directly interact with the target. Because data exists everywhere on the internet this means we will be using a wide range of sources, such as social media and network infrastructure to gather information about a specific topic or target.

To ensure the effectiveness of an OSINT investigation, it is essential to have a well-defined request for information (RFI). This helps analysts focus their efforts and create a plan to answer the question at hand. OSINT is an ever-changing field, as sources of information are continuously being added or removed. Therefore, it is crucial to prepare the work environment, identify and organize resources, and set up sock puppet accounts on social media before you start the investigation, I like to do this in-between cases.

There are numerous resources available for OSINT, and it is impossible to list them all. However, some popular resources include:

- Intel techniques[1] tools and techniques by Michael Bazzell, author of *OSINT Techniques*.

1 Inteltechniques.com/tools/index.html.

- My version of intel techniques[2] tools, these are the ones that are most frequently used by me.
- Awesome-osint[3] is a curated list of OSINT resources.

By utilizing these resources and staying up-to-date with the latest developments in OSINT, investigators can gather valuable information and evidence to support their investigations.

13.1 Methodology

Having a process or methodology helps you to ensure you are on track and not aimlessly search for information. There are several steps involved in the OSINT methodology, which can be grouped into three main phases: planning, collection, and analysis.

13.1.1 Planning

Identifies the specific topic or issue they want to study and develops a plan for collecting that will yield the best results, and answers the question set forth by the customer. Having a clear plan allows you to move forward with intention rather than haphazardly browsing the internet. To make this step easier, it is a good idea to have a set workflow that describes how you are going to conduct the investigation based on the information available.

13.1.2 Collection

The process of collecting the information from different sources. This can involve using various tools and techniques, such as search engines, social media platforms, and databases, to access and gather information. The collected information may be in a variety of formats, such as text, images, or audio and video.

13.1.3 Analysis

The analysis phase is about extracting insights, patterns, and connections from the data you have collected. This may involve using various techniques, such as natural language processing, data mining, and visualization, to process and analyze the information. The results of the analysis are then disseminated to relevant stakeholders and decision-makers.

---

2 adamtilmar.com/tools.
3 github.com/jivoi/awesome-osint.

Overall, the OSINT methodology involves three main phases: planning, collection, and analysis. It involves identifying the specific topic or issue to be studied, collecting the relevant information from open sources, and analyzing and synthesizing the information to extract insights from the data. Within a single investigation, you will perform this loop continually throughout the process, as new data is presented.

13.2 Documentation

Documentation is a crucial aspect of any OSINT investigation and should be done throughout the OSINT methodology. It is essential to keep track of the information you discover, as any websites or sources may be taken down or become inaccessible over time. Proper documentation helps to maintain the integrity of your research and ensures that you have a complete record of your findings.

Creating a workspace environment for each case you are working on can help you stay organized and prevent different cases from getting mixed up. Since most investigations involve extensive use of the browser, browser extensions can be helpful tools for documentation. One popular extensions include GoFullPage for capturing full-page screenshots. Here is a list of commonly used tools for documentation:

- Hunchly[4]
- Windows Game Bar (Win + G)
- OneNote
- XMind
- HTTrack[5]
- Snipping Tool (Win + Shift + S)

One of the tools I would like to point out is HTTrack is an open-source tool for creating a backup of an entire website. It is an excellent choice for preserving the content of a site, especially if it may be taken down or become inaccessible in the future.

Installation:

```
sudo apt-get install httrack
```

Using HTTrack to create a copy of a website:

```
httrack https://test.org/
```

4 https://www.hunch.ly.
5 https://www.httrack.com.

In summary, proper documentation is vital to the success of any OSINT investigation. Organizing your workspace, utilizing browser extensions, and leveraging documentation tools can help you maintain an accurate and complete record of your findings.

13.3 Securing Yourself (OPSEC)

Operational security (OPSEC) is crucial when conducting OSINT investigations. It helps protect your identity, prevents targets from realizing they are being researched, and safeguards your devices from potential malware or browser exploits. Implementing OPSEC measures can also prevent infections from spreading within an organization.

Securing your OSINT environment typically involves:

1. **Virtual environment**: Using virtual machines (VMs) enables you to discard your system if it becomes infected and quickly spins up a new one. Common virtualization software includes VMware Workstation Player and VirtualBox. You can use pre-configured OSINT VMs like Trace Labs, CSI Linux, or Kali Linux, or start with a base image like Ubuntu and create your OSINT image.
2. **VPN or Tor**[6]: Utilizing a virtual private network (VPN) or the Tor network helps, will give some sense of privacy by making it harder for you to be tracked. While VPNs offer more control and faster speeds, Tor provides a higher level of anonymity. For maximum control, consider setting up your own VPN, and this can be done using Streisand; the downside is that you will not have as many nodes as larger VPN providers have.
3. **Strong, unique passwords**: Use complex, unique passwords for each account and service to minimize the risk of unauthorized access.
4. **Two-factor authentication**: Implementing two-factor authentication (2FA) adds an extra layer of security to your accounts.
5. **Reusage of information**: One of the fastest ways for adversaries to identify and link your sock puppets together is when you reuse the same information across multiple sites and accounts. For this reason, I recommend using fake information for everything and a unique email and username for each. One option is to setup unique emails across the site using fastmail[7]; for the price of *5$*/month you get 600 alias emails, and this is an easy way to handle all the emails as everything will get forwarded to the real email. It even allows you to reply using the alias mail, so the target will ever only know that mail.
6. **Regular software updates**: Keep your software and devices updated to patch vulnerabilities and reduce the risk of exploitation.

---

6 https://www.torproject.org.
7 fastmail.com.

By employing these OPSEC measures, you can secure your OSINT environment, protect your data and information, and prevent unauthorized access to your accounts and devices.

13.3.1 Sock Puppet

Sock puppets are synthetic identities or personas created to examine content on sites that only allow access to authenticated users. They are used to conceal one's true identity and intentions, appearing as an average user on a site. When creating a long-term sock puppet, it's crucial to develop a believable character and blend in with the platform's typical user base. Here some of the considerations one should make when creating a convincing sock puppet:

1. **Generate a believable persona**: Use tools like "fake name generator"[8] to create a complete persona with a realistic name, address, and other personal details; an example can be seen in Figure 13.1. Remember to save this information in a secure location.
2. **Think like a normal user**: Interact with the platform as an average user would, including outside of typical working hours.
3. **Use an unmodified browser**: Access the site with a standard browser to avoid raising suspicion.
4. **Avoid VPNs when possible**: While VPNs can protect your identity, they can also appear suspicious. Use public Wi-Fi or cellular networks when appropriate.
5. **Use common services**: Register accounts with popular services like Gmail to appear more like an average user.
6. **Don't reuse information across sock puppets**: Avoid sharing information like phone numbers between different personas.

13.3.2 Picture Generation

When creating a new long-term sock puppet that will interact with a target, it's essential to make the persona appear genuine. Using tools like "this person does not exist"[9] generates a unique, AI-generated face that can be used as profile pictures; example can be seen in Figure 13.2.

To further avoid detection, modify the image by mirroring, resizing, or changing the file name; the main problem with this is that it only generates a single picture. Another possibility is to generate images using tools like midjourney[10]; I have yet to try using these tools for profile images. **Note**, never use random pictures from

8 fakenamegenerator.com.
9 thispersondoesnotexist.com.
10 https://www.midjourney.com.

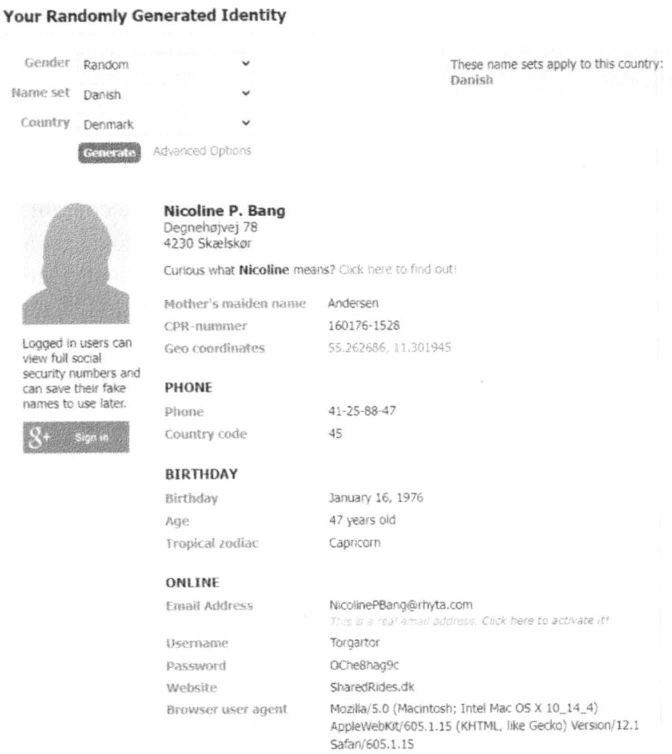

Figure 13.1 Fake name generator example.

the internet, as they may belong to real people who could be contacted by your target if they perform a reverse image search.

By following these guidelines and using the right tools, you can create convincing sock puppets that blend in with the platform's user base and protect your true identity during OSINT investigations.

13.4 Search Engines

Search engines enable users to search for content on the World Wide Web using a basic query language. OSINT relies heavily on search engines to locate information online. It is important to understand how to effectively use them by incorporating operators to optimize search results. Some common operators include:

- Using quotes to search for specific phrases
- Expanding the usage of quotes by adding * to the quote

Figure 13.2 This person does not exist.

- Using "-" to remove search results (e.g., jaguar -car)
- Using filetype: to search for specific file types

These operators can be combined to search for specific objects on the internet. Various search engines serve different purposes and offer different capabilities. Google is the most widely used search engine and has many applications for OSINT. To utilize Google effectively, you need to understand its search operators; an example can be seen in Table 13.1.

Below is a list of other useful search engines, each specializing in its area:

- Bing, Microsoft's search engine, is particularly useful for reverse image searches and can be used to search for domains hosted on a specific IP using the `ip:` operator.

Table 13.1 Search operators.

Operator	Description
site:	Search only on the specified site
filetype:	Search for file type
cache:	Google cache of a page (add &strip=1 at the end of the URL to ensure only resources from Google cache are loaded)
inurl:	Search for strings in the URL
link:	Find pages that link to the website

- Tineye[11] specializes in reverse image searches.
- Pimeyes[12] uses AI for face recognition in images.
- Yandex[13] is a Russian search engine useful for Russian-specific searches.
- Shodan[14] is a search engine for Internet-connected devices. It allows users to search for technology.
- Grayhatwarfare[15] indexes public buckets and link shorteners, making them searchable.
- Scamsearch[16] is a search engine for finding scams related to email, usernames, etc.
- Censys[17] is a search engine for identifying the devices and networks that make up the internet. The platform provides users with a wealth of information about internet-connected devices, including web servers, Internet of Things (IoT) devices, and industrial control systems. They have recently launched a chatbot on gpt.censys.io that will create search queries for you based on text prompts, helping you create better search queries.

13.5 Profiling

Profiling involves gathering information about an account or individual to identify the person behind online activities. This process is crucial for building a threat profile.

11 tineye.com.
12 pimeyes.com.
13 yandex.com.
14 shodan.io.
15 grayhatwarfare.com.
16 scamsearch.io.
17 search.censys.io.

13.5.1 Building Threat Profile

Identifying the actor behind a profile, whether it's an individual or a group, can be a challenging task. They often take measures to hide their identity, while you are trying to identify key information they may have left behind. As you gather information, insert it into your document to see how different accounts are linked together through information reuse. Some techniques for gathering information include:

13.5.1.1 Username

Usernames are the way we identify ourselves on the internet. Some people choose to have the same username across multiple platforms, allowing them to establish a stronger online identity. Others opt for using unique username for each account they create to protect their privacy and make themselves more difficult to track.

To identify if a particular username has been used on various websites, you can use open-source tools. It's essential to use multiple tools, as they each cover different sites; an example of username search using what my name can be seen in Figure 13.3.

Sherlock Sherlock[18] is a Python tool that hunts down social media accounts by username. You can see the sites it currently searches here.[19]

To search for a single user:

```
python3 sherlock username
```

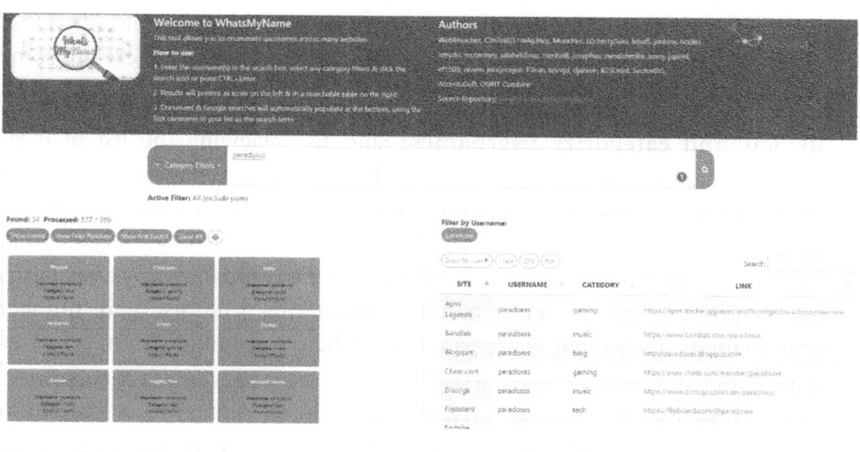

Figure 13.3 What my name.

18 https://github.com/sherlock-project/sherlock.
19 https://github.com/sherlock-project/sherlock/blob/master/sherlock/resources/data.json.

To search for multiple users, use the following command:

```
python3 sherlock username username2 username3
```

Maigret Maigret[20] is a fork of the Sherlock project that also collects information from social media by username. It currently supports more than 2500 sites.

To search for a single user:

```
python3 maigret username
```

To search for a single user and export the report as HTML:

```
python3 maigret username --HTML
```

If you prefer not to use scripts or command lines, some websites will perform the search for you. Here is a list of the best sites for username searches that I have found:

- whatsmyname.app
- instantusername.com
- sersearch.org/results_normal.php

My go-to tool is whatsmyname.app for performing username searches, as it is the most extensive search and provides a link to the profile page.

13.5.1.2 Username Analysis

Once you have gathered a list of usernames associated with your target using the tools and techniques mentioned earlier, it's time to analyze the results. Username analysis helps you identify patterns, connections, and additional information that can help you build a more comprehensive profile of your target. Here are some steps to follow when analyzing usernames:

1. **Review and categorize usernames**: Start by reviewing the list of usernames you have collected. Categorize them based on their origin (social media, forums, websites, etc.) and the type of information they might provide (personal, technical, financial, etc.).
2. **Look for patterns and connections**: Analyze the usernames for any patterns or connections, such as similar naming conventions, word usage, or number combinations. Identifying these patterns can help you link different accounts or profiles to the same individual or group.
3. **Cross-reference usernames**: Cross-reference the usernames with other information you have collected about your target, such as email addresses, phone

20 https://github.com/soxoj/maigret.

numbers, or IP addresses. This can help you establish connections between different online personas and reveal additional information about your target.

4. **Analyze account activity**: Investigate the accounts associated with the usernames, focusing on their activity, connections, and content. Analyzing account activity can provide insights into your target's interests, habits, and online behavior.
5. **Perform sentiment analysis**: Examine the content and tone of the messages, posts, or comments associated with the usernames. Sentiment analysis can help you identify the target's emotional state, attitudes, and intentions.
6. **Identify common themes and topics**: Look for common themes and topics in the content associated with the usernames. Identifying these can help you understand your target's interests, expertise, and motivations.
7. **Create a visual representation**: Create a visual representation of the relationships between the usernames and the associated accounts, profiles, or websites. This can help you better understand the connections between different online personas and reveal potential areas for further investigation.
8. **Update your threat profile**: As you analyze the usernames and gather new information, update your threat profile to reflect your findings. Continuously refine your profile as you discover more about your target.

13.5.1.3 Email

Email is one of the most common ways we communicate with each other and register for services. The unique nature of email addresses makes them a great search parameter when doing OSINT work. An email consists of two parts: username and domain.

```
username@domain.tld
```

First, you have the username of the email, which can be checked for reuse by the method described in the username section.

The domain name is another key information, if not a cloud service, that can be used to identify if there is any infrastructure for the domain. The infrastructure mapping section will go into detail on how to do this.

Epieos[21] is an amazing tool when you want to identify a person behind an email address or see what other sites it is registered to; example of the search result can be seen in Figure 13.4. The way it does this is by using a tool called holehe.[22] This tool goes out and tries to register or log in with that email and see what response it gets back from the different sites. Most sites will tell you if an account with that email already exists. Epieos will also see if any Google or Skype profile is registered using the email and provide you with a link to the profile, which can contain the real name of the person.

21 epieos.com.
22 github.com/megadose/holehe.

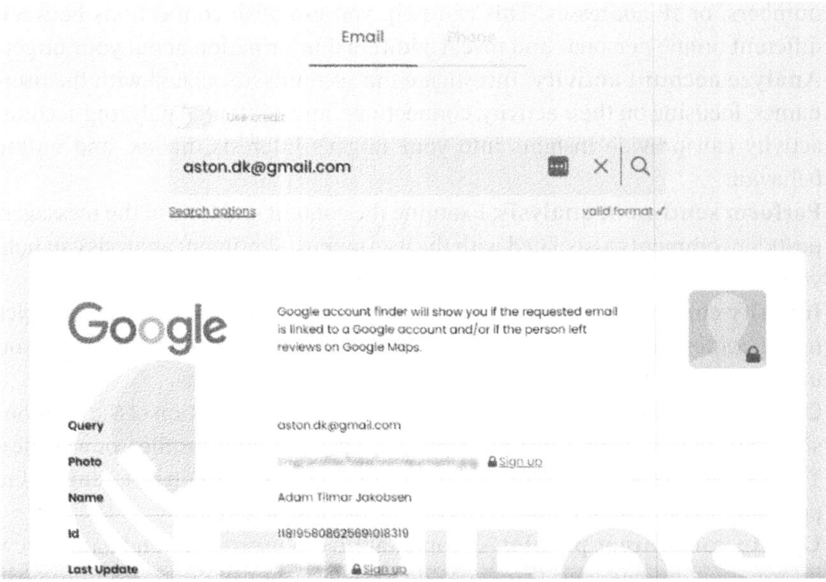

Figure 13.4 Epieos.

13.5.1.4 Forgot Password

Using the "forgot password" function on websites can provide additional information about a profile. Many sites have a second factor for account recovery, such as a phone number or an additional email. By knowing your target's username, email, or phone number, you can use the "forgot password" feature, which potentially will reveal part of their second factor; an example can be seen in Figure 13.5.

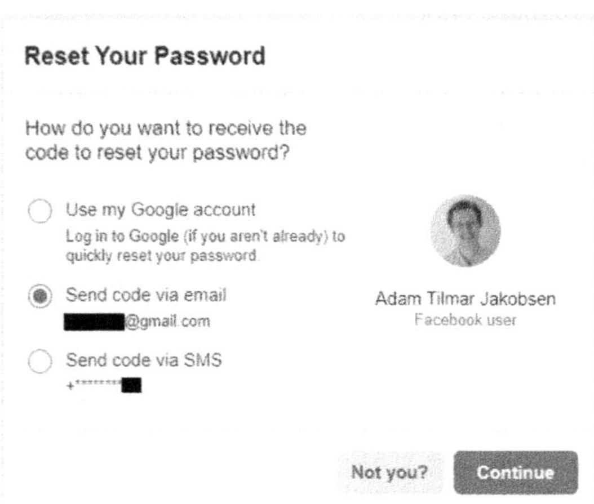

Figure 13.5 Forgot password.

Be cautious, as this might also alert the user that something is going on, so use it as a last resort.

When I do this link of searchesI would normally test each site before doing this, to understand if the site sends a message to the user when performing the *password reset* request. The sites I have frequently used this method are *Facebook, Paypal, Google, and Outlook* and often with great success. Remember this can change at any moment; one moment it might give information, the other nothing.

13.5.1.5 Data Breaches

Another option is to see if the email has been part of any breaches or leaks. Using sites such as "have I been pwned"[23] will tell you if the email has appeared anywhere. If this is the case, the next step is to locate the leaked data and see if it provides any new information about the target. An easier way is to use data services such as intelX[24] as they will collect, parse, and present the information for you. This information, of course, does not come for free.

13.5.1.6 Identify Domain Emails

If you only have a domain, it is also possible to search for emails belonging to the domain. Services such as Skymem[25] and Hunter[26] use the internet to try and identify emails for you. Another approach is to perform Google Dorks on LinkedIn to identify accounts that have their email in the profile.

```
site:linkedin.com domain.tld email
```

13.5.1.7 Reputation/Scam

A final place to look is if the email has been part of any scams or anything similar. Here services such as Emailrep[27] and Scamsearch[28] can be used, as they collect information about scams including the email used. This allows you to see if they have reused the email in previous scams.

13.6 Hunt for Data

This section is about hunting for data. We will be looking at different sources and tools that can be used to collect information. The amount of data uploaded every day to public forums continues to increase. It is essential to verify any data that

23 haveibeenpwned.com.
24 intelx.io.
25 skymem.info.
26 hunter.io.
27 https://emailrep.io.
28 http://scamsearch.io.

is legit and not generated, especially large combo lists from data breaches. The question is always how much of it is just duplicated data.

The best way to handle this is to collect all the data in one place and remove any duplicate files. These data leaks contain more than just usernames and passwords. They can include information such as IP addresses that the user has connected from and account verification information.

One of the simplest ways to identify if an email or domain has been part of any breaches is to use the "Have I been pwned"[29] service. It will also tell you what breaches the credentials have appeared in.

The possession of this kind of information and exercising the method described in this section can be seen as illegal in some countries. Make sure to verify becomes starting on the journey of leaks collections.

These leaks are useful for us because they contain information that would otherwise not be available. It allows us to pivot from one account to another account by identifying information reuse or taking control of the accounts. Threat actors are just like everyone else and might reuse information such as email and password on multiple sites. This allows us to link multiple accounts together, allowing us to create a diagram of their internet activity.

13.6.1 Data Brokers

Let's start with the simplest method of acquiring data, which is from data brokers. These services collect and index data and make it all searchable for you. All of this work does not come for free. However, many of the services will provide a limited amount of information for free.

IntelX[30] is my go-to site for looking up what data is available. What IntelX does is collect and index it all; data comes from sources such as the darknet, document-sharing platforms, whois, public data leaks, and others. Using the free service only allows you to view a limited amount of information, but you might still find something useful; an example of a data search can be seen in Figure 13.6.

Another site, Breach Directory,[31] allows you to check if the information is part of a data breach. What makes it different is that it provides both a partial password and the SHA1 hash of the password, which we can use to crack and identify the entire password.

Leak Peek is a similar service that indexes breaches and leaks. What makes Leak Peek unique is it returns a partial password and the source of the data.

---

29 https://haveibeenpwned.com.
30 https://intelx.io.
31 https://breachdirectory.org.

Figure 13.6 Index.

13.6.2 Leak and Dumps Collection

Instead of relying on data brokers that have automated the whole process for a premium, you also have the option to collect the information yourself. In the following section, we will go over where and how to collect data from a wide array of sources. This information has been made publicly available either through misconfigured services or hacking attacks. This is not about using hacking techniques to gain access to systems.

13.6.3 Hacker Forums

Hacker forums are gateways to the underground market that attract hackers with varying levels of experience. Newcomers to the field may leave a trail of information that can be traced back to their real identity. More experienced hackers can also be identified by linking their current profiles to previously used accounts, where operational security (opsec) was not a priority.

These forums are marketplaces for leads, exploits, dumps, and much more.

What is useful for us is that leaks and dumps are frequently released to the public on these forums. This allows us to download any leaks that can be used in investigations. Many of these forums require you to collect points, which are used for access to data. The way you acquire points is by posting on the site.

Some of these sites have public ban lists, which contain information on every banned user and their registration details, and can be another useful source. Feuds between users can also lead to key information if they decide to dox each other.

Don't limit your search to just hacker forums; consider other platforms like Bitcoin forums or StackOverflow as well. Use the "insite:" operator on Google to search for username appearances within a site:

```
username insite:domain.tld
```

Figure 13.7 Telegram.

13.6.4 Telegram

Telegram[32] is quickly becoming a popular place to exchange information; example can be seen in Figure 13.7. These channels are publicly available and used for both communication and sharing leaks. These channels are used as marketplaces to sell their leaks, and it is common for them to provide sample data to entice users. Some channels share publicly available dumps for you to download. The good thing about this is that you do not have to go through the trouble of earning forum points to gain access to the data.

There is no official method to search for channels, but with a bit of Google-fu, you can identify channels.

Examples of identifying channels:

```
site:telegram.me "breach"
```

```
site:t.me "breach"
```

32 https://telegram.org.

Luckily the following sites try to index Telegram channels and make them searchable:

- Telemetr[33]
- Telegramchannels[34]
- Telegram-group[35]

13.6.5 Paste

Paste sites are places where people can post text they want to share anonymously. Pastes are publicly available to everyone; example can be seen in Figure 13.8. These pastes might not exist forever because they can be taken down for violating the terms of service; you might be able to find archives of removed pastes. Using sites such as archive.org which could have saved a copy of the paste site.

The first tool I would like to point to is PasteHunter,[36] an open-source tool that will query publicly available pasted data. Another excellent online tool is Psbdmp[37] indexes paste from Pastebin, making it searchable for you.

Paste sites:

- pastebin[38]
- 0bin[39]
- Justpaste.it[40]

Figure 13.8 psbdmp.

---

33 https://telemetr.io/en/channels?channel=leak+data.
34 https://telegramchannels.me/search?type=all&search=breach.
35 https://www.telegram-group.com/en?s=breach.
36 https://github.com/kevthehermit/PasteHunter.
37 https://www.psbdmp.ws.
38 https://pastebin.com.
39 https://0bin.net.
40 https://justpaste.it.

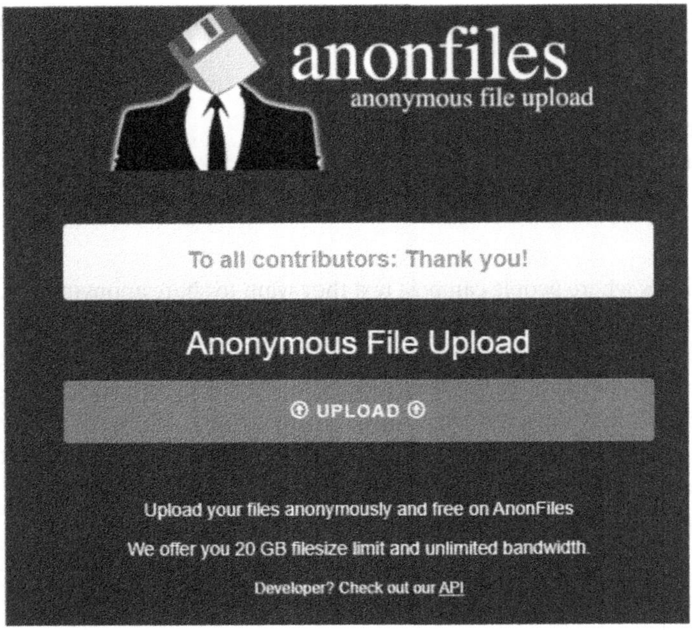

Figure 13.9 Anonfiles.

13.6.6 Anonymous Upload Sites

These sites allow users to upload data anonymously. They are frequently utilized by hacker groups to dump information on a target when they do not pay for the ransomware. Below in Figure 13.9 is just one of the many sites that exist.

The most common upload site is Anonfiles.

13.7 Infrastructure Mapping

Various types of cybercrime require some form of infrastructure to operate. This can include phishing sites, command and control (C2) servers, revenge porn sites, leak sites, and more. The goal of this chapter is to help you map out the infrastructure of a target, identify new leads, and discover hidden services to be aware of.

13.7.1 IP Address

Internet Protocol (IP) is part of the OSI model and is used to route packets between network endpoints. IP was designed as a unique number that pointed to a device. The most widely used version is still IPv4, with its 32-bit address allowing for 2^{32} unique IPs. Due to this limitation, Network Address Translation (NAT) has been developed to enable more computers to access the internet using the same IP. NAT allows multiple devices to use the same IP by distinguishing between endpoints using port numbers instead. This makes it nearly impossible to attribute network activities with just the IP address. One option is to ask the Internet Service Provider (ISP) to which the IP is registered; this will also require information about the source port and the specific time of day of the connection, as IP and port assignments get shuffled between endpoints.

IPv6, a new version of IP, uses a 128-bit address and allows for 3.4×10^{34} addresses. IPv6 is still in the adoption phase in most parts of the world. Primarily smartphones and IoT devices use IPv6 exclusively. Due to the large increase in address space, NAT is no longer required, allowing us to use IP for attribution again. However, the probability of encountering IPv6 remains low, even for smart devices.

A similar issue arises with websites and related services, as many of them are hosted by hosting providers. These providers can use a single IP address to host a large number of websites, up to tens of thousands, for both IPv4 and IPv6. This forces us to use other attribution methods to group websites together.

IP addresses are used to define the computer we want to communicate with, and then ports are used to define what service on the device we would like to interact with. Think of ports as virtual endpoints used for sending and receiving data across computer networks. They serve as doors for services, providing a method for directly communicating with a service hosted on a network. The most commonly used ports are HTTP (80) and HTTPS (443).

Despite these challenges, IP addresses can still provide valuable information, such as geolocation, previous usage as a Tor node, and VPN usage. One of my go-to services is ipinfo[41] which identifies location, VPN, services, domains, and more; an image can be seen in Figure 13.10. If you prefer to use a command-line interface (CLI) that is also an option, look at the documentation[42] on how to get started.

13.7.1.1 Shodan

Shodan[43] is an excellent service that scans the entire internet, looking for devices and attempting to fingerprint the services running on the different ports. It is used as a search engine for network devices, allowing users to query both services and versions running on the internet; an example can be seen in Figure 13.11.

Shodan is one of the best options for searching for devices that connect to the internet and try to fingerprint the services running on their ports. It is also possible to search for an organization, allowing you to identify any services they have

41 https://ipinfo.io.
42 https://github.com/ipinfo/cli.
43 https://www.shodan.io.

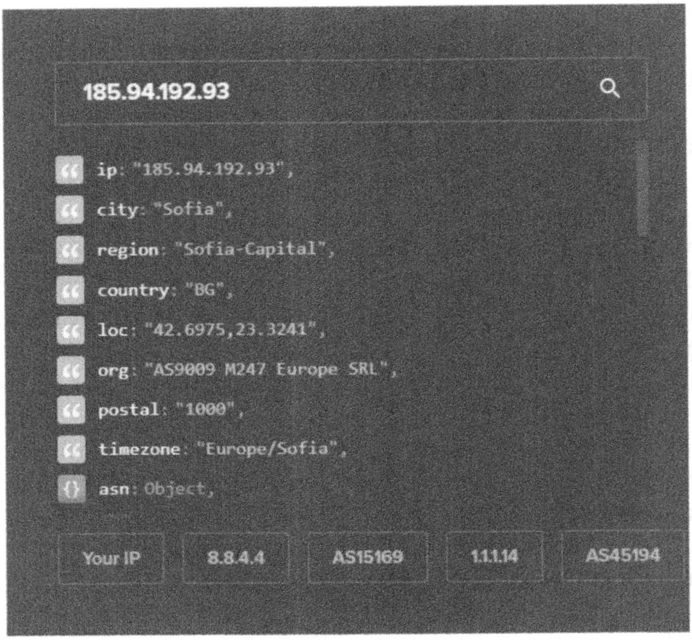

Figure 13.10 Ip info.

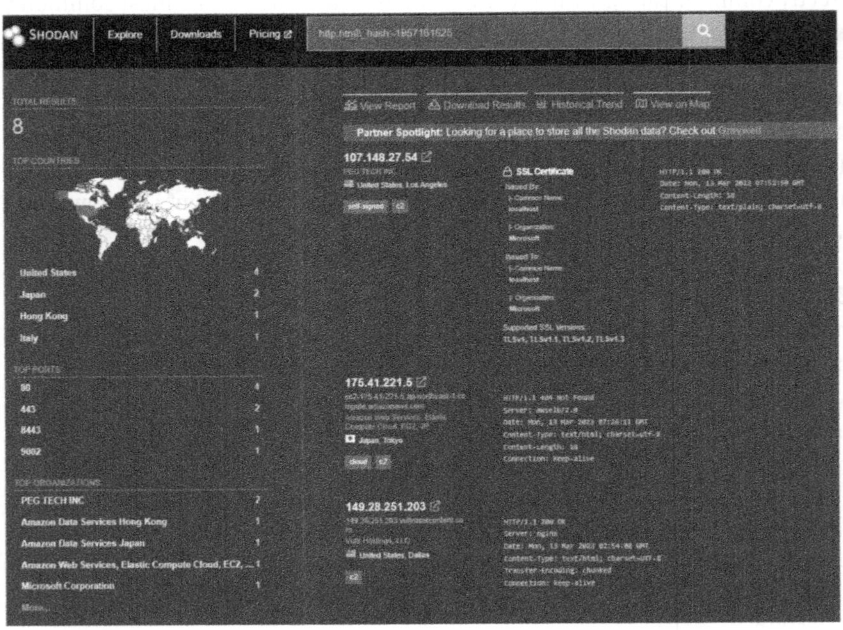

Figure 13.11 Shodan.

running on the internet that they may have forgotten about. It is recommended to purchase a membership, as it allows you to perform additional queries and increases the number of API requests you have. The regular price is $50, but it is frequently on sale for just $5.

Shodan can be used for many different kinds of threat research such as searching for adversary command and control (C2) infrastructure. Let's take a look at one of the most commonly used C2, Cobalt strike.[44] With a simple search query using the product parameter, we can have Shodan display all current active Cobalt strike instance.[45] Shodan also indexes Cobalt Strike configurations, which can be used to identify Cobalt Strike instances using the same watermark configuration settings.[46] It of course not just limited to the correct query; you can almost identify any kind of C2 that exists.

Shodan is not limited to just the website; we can optimize and automate the process of searching on Shodan by using their Shodan cli,[47] and export the data to a format we can use later. Let's start by setting up Shodan CLI.

Download Shodan:

```
apt install python3-shodan
```

Setup API key

```
shodan init {api_key}
```

Now to search for results using the Shodan cli, the following download query structure is used:

```
Shodan download --limit {# of results} {filename}.json {query}
```

Once the data has been downloaded it needs to be parsed for us to extract information. This will take the JSON output from the previous command and output it to a CSV format.

```
Shodan parse --fields ip_str,port,org --seperator, data.json
```

You are also able to perform historical information on IP.

```
shodan host --history --format pretty {IP}
```

We are not limited to just the cli; there is also an official python library,[48] which we can use. The installation is done using the pip command: "pip install shodan".

44 https://www.cobaltstrike.com.
45 https://www.shodan.io/search?query=product%3A%22Cobalt+Strike+Beacon%22.
46 https://www.shodan.io/search?query=watermark%3A1234567890.
47 https://cli.shodan.io.
48 https://github.com/achillean/shodan-python.

13.7.1.2 Nmap

If you prefer to conduct the search on your own, tools such as Nmap, and a port scanner, can be used. Nmap is commonly used by hackers to discover open ports, and service versions, and perform OS fingerprinting. The benefit of using Nmap instead of an online tool is that you can search an IP range relatively easily. Nmap also supports scanning of IPv6 but is limited to a single address at a time. It has a scripting engine that allows for more advanced scans, such as vulnerability scanning for the most common vulnerabilities that exist. See the documentation at nsedoc.[49]

A list of the different options that exist can be found at man-briefoptions.[50]

13.7.2 Domain

Domains are text strings that can be translated into IP addresses. Domains were created because they are more memorable than IP addresses. Before a domain can be used, it must be registered with the Internet Corporation for Assigned Names and Numbers (ICANN).

13.7.2.1 Domain Name System (DNS)

The Domain Name System (DNS) is a system that translates domain names, like "google.com," into IP addresses used by computers to identify each other on the internet. This translation occurs through a distributed network of DNS servers, which store and manage domain name and IP address information. When you enter a domain name in your web browser, your computer sends a request to a DNS server to resolve the domain name into an IP address and then uses that IP address to connect to the website you requested. DNS is used for various purposes, such as web and mail services.

Below is a list of different types of DNS entries that exist:

- **A record (Address Record)**: This type of DNS entry maps a domain name to an IP address.
- **CNAME (Canonical Name record)**: This type of DNS entry creates an alias for a domain name, pointing it to another domain name.
- **MX (mail exchange record)**: This type of DNS entry specifies the mail server responsible for accepting email messages for a particular domain.
- **NS (name server record)**: This type of DNS entry identifies the authoritative name servers for a particular domain.
- **PTR (pointer record)**: This type of DNS entry maps an IP address to a domain name, the opposite of an A record.

---

49 https://nmap.org/nsedoc.
50 https://nmap.org/book/man-briefoptions.html.

- **SOA (start of authority record)**: This type of DNS entry contains information about the domain name's primary name server, administrative contact, and other metadata.
- **TXT (text record)**: This type of DNS entry is used to store arbitrary text data associated with a domain name, such as SPF records for email authentication.

There are tools available to help you perform DNS queries. Some recommended ones include dnsview[51] and dnsdumpster[52] which can be seen in Figure 13.12.

These tools can be used to find additional information about a domain, which can then be used as a pivot point. This is especially useful for locating services that hide behind Content Delivery Networks (CDNs) like Cloudflare.

By using the information obtained from DNS queries, hosting data, and other sources, you can gain a deeper understanding of a domain's infrastructure and possibly uncover additional domains, services, or even potential security vulnerabilities.

13.7.2.2 Reverse Domain Names Lookup

Using hosting providers is common, as they often host multiple domain names on a single IP address. Reverse DNS lookup makes it possible to identify all domains hosted on a given IP address.

View DNS Reverse IP[53] offers an excellent tool for this. Another option is using the Bing search engine; simply use the query parameter **IP:ip address**,[54] and will return all the domains hosted on the IP.

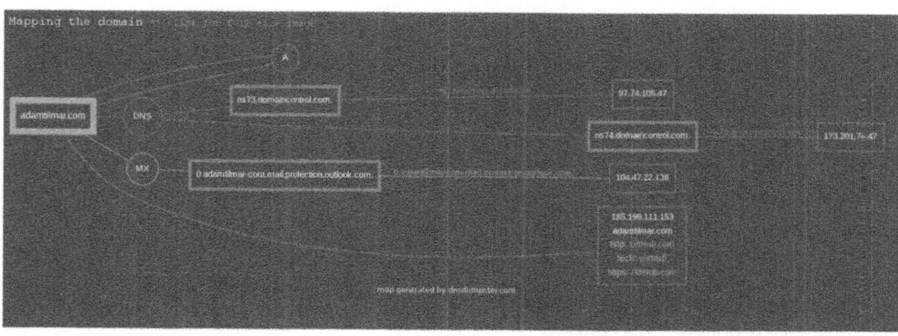

Figure 13.12 DNS dumpster.

---

51 dnsview.info.

52 dnsdumpster.com.

53 https://viewdns.info/reverseip.

54 https://www.bing.com/search?q=ip%3a+204.93.177.100.

13.7.3 Whois

WHOIS[55] information provides details about the registration and ownership of a domain or IP, including the registrant's name, address, phone number, and email address. This information can be useful for identifying the individuals or organizations responsible for managing a website, as well as any potential connections between websites.

Some popular tools for querying WHOIS information include:

- DomainTools[56]: A comprehensive suite of tools for researching domains, IP addresses, and DNS records, including a powerful WHOIS search tool.
- Whois.com[57]: A simple and friendly tool for querying WHOIS information for a specific domain.
- ICANN WHOIS[58]: The official WHOIS lookup tool provided by the Internet Corporation for Assigned Names and Numbers (ICANN).
- domainiq[59]
- ViewDNS[60]
- ipinfo[61]

As information can change over time, having a lookup method for historical data can be crucial. This can be useful in cases where the operator of a site had poor operational security and the domain was registered with their real name and address.

13.7.3.1 Historical Whois Data Sources

Having access to historical Whois information can be essential for identifying a domain's previous owner, but it often comes at a price. You can try your luck on *intelx* to see if they have any historical Whois information that is available for free. Otherwise, you have to use paid services such as:

- whoisology[62]
- whoxy[63]
- domainiq[64]

---

55 https://en.wikipedia.org/wiki/WHOIS.
56 https://www.domaintools.com.
57 https://www.whois.com/whois.
58 https://lookup.icann.org.
59 https://www.domainiq.com.
60 https://viewdns.info/whois.
61 https://ipinfo.io.
62 https://whoisology.com.
63 https://www.whoxy.com.
64 https://www.domainiq.com.

13.7.3.2 Reverse Whois

It is also possible to do a reverse lookup on registrant information, allowing users to identify other domains that are using the same registration information; this can be done on viewdns reverse whois.[65]

13.7.4 Website

Websites are services we visit using our browsers, frequently hosted on port 80 or 443. They can be used for various types of fraud, such as fake organization fronts, webshops, and more. The goal of many website investigations is to identify the person behind the site. A good starting point is examining the domain whois registration data.

Analyzing the content of a website can provide valuable information about its owner, activities, and potential connections to other websites or services. Some key aspects to consider when investigating website content include:

- **Text content**: Look for names, email addresses, phone numbers, or other identifiable information that could be used to trace the identity of the website owner or administrator.
- **Monitoring**: To track changes in a website's appearance over time, Visualping[66] can monitor websites and notify you of any visual changes.
- **Images and multimedia**: Examine images, videos, and other media for metadata, watermarks, or other identifiers that could be used to trace their origin or ownership.
- **Source code**: Inspect the website's HTML, CSS, and JavaScript source code for comments, authorship information, or other clues about the site's creation and maintenance.
- **Links and references**: Analyze the website's internal and external links to identify connections to other websites, services, or individuals that could be related to the site's owner or activities.
- **Backlinks**: Websites that link to the target domain. Host.io[67] can help identify these.
- **Redirects**: Websites can send HTTP codes 301 or 302, directing browsers to new locations. Host.io can help identify these.

By examining the content of a website in detail, you can uncover valuable information about the owner, activities, and potential connections to other websites or services. This information can be used to build an understanding of the website's

65 viewdns.info/reversewhois.
66 https://visualping.io.
67 https://host.io.

purpose, infrastructure, and potential involvement in fraudulent activities or other cybercrime, and if it is part of a larger network of websites used to scam

You can also ask the hosting provider for information. To determine where the site is hosted you can use `nslookup` commands and perform an IP lookup on a service like `ipinfo.io`. However, with the rise of content delivery networks (CDNs) like Cloudflare, this has become a dead-end. CDNs act as a middle-man between the site and the user, providing security and preventing attacks and downtime. When you perform a lookup of a website IP, you'll often see the CDN provider's IP instead.

Fortunately, there are multiple methods to identify the actual IP address used behind the CDN:

- **SSL certificate**: Each SSL certificate is unique and has its fingerprint. By examining historical data, you can identify which websites have been associated with the certificate. Censys, Shodan, ZoomEye, and crt.sh are tools that can be used for this purpose. The goal is to identify the IP used when the certificate was active.
- **Historical DNS records**: These can help identify which IP addresses the domain resolved to in the past.
- **Subdomains**: Is not always protected by CDNs; often only the main domain is protected. By identifying subdomains, you may discover other IP addresses.
- **Favicon**: The icon displayed in the browser tab is often found at example.com/favicon.ico. Each favicon has a unique hash, which can be identified using faviconhash.[68] Tools like Shodan.io can search for sites with similar favicons using the query: `http.favicon.hash:hash`.
- **Analytic ID**: Look for websites that share the same Google Analytics ID.

To verify if the domain resolves to the IP address you found, use the `curl` command by forcing `curl` to resolve the website at the defined IP address: `curl -k domain --resolve domain:port:ip`.

For example:

```
curl -k https://gmgroup.pro --resolve gmgroup.pro:443:
    185.150.117.30
```

13.7.4.1 Hosting

Websites need to be hosted on one or more IP addresses. To identify a website's current IP address, you can use the **nslookup** command. IP addresses can change over time, which is why looking at historical IP information can be valuable.

68 faviconhash.com.

Historical domain IP addresses sources:

- Viewdns iphistory[69]
- PassiveDNS[70]
- Shodan.io[71]

Commonly, the first time a malicious domain appears on the internet it is in a more insecure setting that might be closer to where they live, or the current IP of the domain points to Cloudflare, but is still hosted in the same place when it first appeared.

13.7.4.2 Domain Analytics

To track users' activity when visiting a site, domain analytics can be used; it works by having a script with an ID loaded onto the site, which will collect data and send it to a analytics database site like Google analytic. We can use this to identify other sites that share the same analytic ID. It is common for people who own multiple sites to use the same analytic ID to track them all and to have everything on a single dashboard. The site I use for these kinds of search is AnalyzeID[72] as it cross-references multiple attributes, such as IP and analytics ID, to identify other websites owned by the same person. Below are some of the other sites that perform the same kind of search:

- Spy On Web[73] searches domain names and identifies multiple sources of information, cross-referencing websites with shared attributes. This helps identify sites potentially owned by the same person.
- Domainiq Reverse Analytics[74] also performs reverse searches on Google Analytics IDs.
- Hacker Target Reverse Analytics Search[75] is unique because it also provides historical analytics ID data.

13.7.4.3 SSL Certificates

SSL certificates are used to create secure communications between a website and its users. Analyzing a website's SSL certificate can reveal information about the organization that owns the domain, as well the certificate authority that issued it. I have seen threat actors be lazy about their infrastructure and copy/paste the same website and use it multiple times and forget to create a new SSL certification,

69 https://viewdns.info/iphistory.
70 https://passivedns.mnemonic.no.
71 https://www.shodan.io.
72 https://analyzeid.com.
73 https://spyonweb.com.
74 https://www.domainiq.com/reverse_analytics.
75 https://hackertarget.com/reverse-analytics-search.

which I used to find all the websites they hosted by searching on censys.io on all the websites sharing the same certificate.

Some popular tools for analyzing SSL certificates include:

- **SSL Labs**[76]: A free online service that provides a deep analysis of a website's SSL configuration, including information about the certificate, encryption protocols, and potential vulnerabilities.
- **Censys**[77]: Also allows you to explore SSL/TLS certificates, and to search for certificates associated with a particular domain, organization, or IP address.

Here are some Censys search query examples:

Domain:

```
services.tls.certificates.leaf_data.names: "*.example.com"
```

Organization name:

```
services.tls.certificates.leaf_data.subject.organization: "Google"
```

13.7.4.4 Robots.txt

Most websites have a robots.txt[78] file in the root directory. This is used to instruct search engine crawlers which pages they are allowed to crawl and index. This file can reveal sensitive information, help identify parts of the site that are under development, or uncover hidden sub-directories. Example of a robots.txt is `https://www.dr.dk/robots.txt`

13.7.4.5 Web Archive

Web archives are sites such as the Wayback Machine,[79] which can be seen in Figure 13.13 and webarchive,[80] which record and preserve the history of websites that exist on the internet. They allow you to look back in time to see how the internet used to look like. They can be very valuable in finding information that is no longer available.

It is frequently used in cases to look into the past for information that is no longer available.

13.7.4.6 Website Fingerprinting

Website fingerprinting is a technique used to gather information about a website's technology stack, server software, content management systems (CMS), and more.

76 https://www.ssllabs.com/ssltest.
77 https://censys.io.
78 https://developers.google.com/search/docs/crawling-indexing/robots/intro.
79 https://web.archive.org.
80 https://archive.ph.

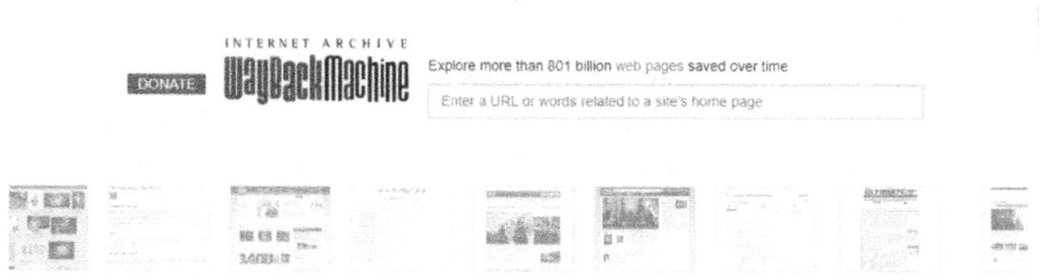

Figure 13.13 Way back machine.

This information can provide valuable insights into potential security vulnerabilities, as well as how the website is built and maintained. Some popular tools for website fingerprinting include:

- **BuiltWith**[81]: A comprehensive web technology profiler that provides insights into the technology stack used by a website, including web servers, CMS, JavaScript libraries, and analytics tools.
- **Wappalyzer**[82]: A browser extension and web service that detects and displays the technologies used on websites, such as server software, CMS, and programming languages.
- **WhatCMS**[83]: A service that identifies the CMS used by a website, which can be useful in discovering potential vulnerabilities or weak spots in a site's infrastructure.

By analyzing the technology stack, framework, and software used by the website, you can gain insights to the building blocks and possibly identify websites created by the same person or organization. I once used this technique to identify a network of websites used as fronts for money laundering, all because they shared the same unique bootstrap template, which had hidden data about the origin of the template which I used to pivot and find the other websites used by the same criminal network.

13.7.4.7 Directory and Subdomain Identification

Discovering hidden directories and subdomains within a website can provide valuable insights into its structure and organization. Several tools can be used to perform dictionary discovery against sites, allowing you to identify directories and subdomains. Common methods are using a wordlist of typical directories and subdomains, brute-forcing, or crawling the website looking for hidden or forgotten directories.

---

81 https://builtwith.com.
82 https://www.wappalyzer.com.
83 https://whatcms.org.

Censys Subdomain Finder

- dmns.app identifies subdomains using DNS records.
- Dirhunt[84] is an atypical web crawler that identifies files and directories using open sources like Google and VirusTotal, rather than making requests to the server.

  ```
  dirhunt example.tld
  ```

  Use the "-e" switch to search for specific files and potentially uncover forgotten ones:

  ```
  dirhunt example.tld -e zip,sh,z7
  ```

  The "-f" switch allows you to search for specific filenames:

  ```
  dirhunt example.com -f wp_admin,/etc/passwd
  ```

- Wfuzz[85] is a web fuzzer that uses a wordlist to iterate over directories, files, subdomains, and more. It replaces any instance of "FUZZ" with the payload from the wordlist.
  Installing Wfuzz can be done using the Python module pip:

  ```
  pip install wfuzz
  ```

  When it comes to directory fuzzing put */FUZZ* at the end of the URL:

  ```
  wfuzz -w worldlist.txt --hc 404 example.tld/FUZZ
  ```

  The *-hc* flag tells wfuzz to hide results with the HTTP response code of 404. You can do the same with subdirectories domains within a fixed directory *"example.tld/upload/FUZZ"*.
  The same kind of search can be done with the subdomain:

  ```
  wfuzz -w worldlist.txt --hc 404 FUZZ.example.tld/
  ```

13.7.4.8 Documents

Documents are often available on websites which can also contain metadata, which is often not purged before upload. This can provide information about the document's creator, such as the author, program used, and creation date. This can give valuable information about the creator of the website. One way to perform a document search is with search engine operators, such as using Google to search for specific file types. Here is an example of searching for the typical files found.

```
site:domain.tld filetype:pdf,xlsx,docx
```

---

84 https://github.com/Nekmo/dirhunt.
85 https://github.com/xmendez/wfuzz.

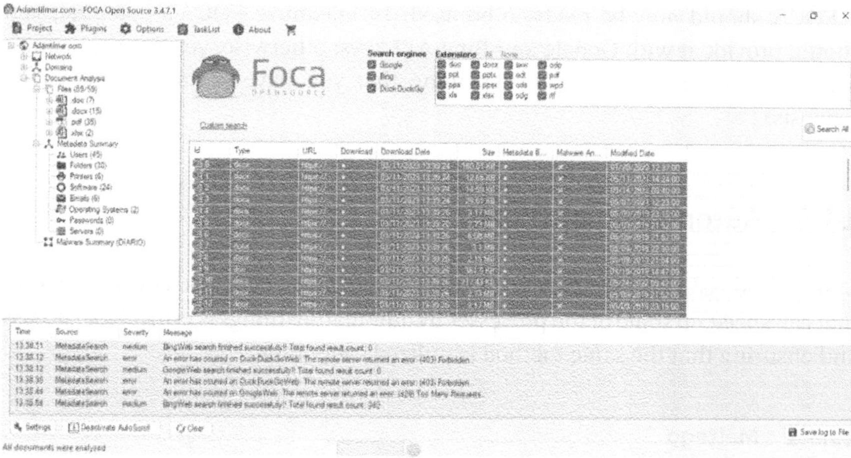

Figure 13.14 FOCA.

The process can be extensive due to the large number of file types, and once identified the documents must be downloaded, thereafter the metadata extracted and parsed, for further analysis. This is why you should use a tool called FOCA, which will automate the process. FOCA is a Windows GUI tool that automates the process of finding documents, extracting, and parsing metadata. FOCA aims to identify as many documents as possible using search engines, download them, and categorize metadata by type; an example of the application can be seen in Figure 13.14. You can download the application on their GitHub page.[86]

One of the requirements to run FOCA is an SQL server; my preferred way is using a docker as it is quick to set up and easy to replicate. The first step is to download docker over at docker.[87] Once you have installed docker you can set up the SQL express database using the following command

```
docker run -e "ACCEPT_EULA=Y" -e "MSSQL_SA_PASSWORD=yourStrong(!)
    Password" -e "MSSQL_PID=Express" -p 1433:1433 -d mcr.microsoft
    .com/mssql/server:2019-latest
```

When you start FOCA you will be prompted with a login portal to the SQL database, switch over to "SQL server authentication" and insert the following.

- Server name: localhost
- Username: SA
- Password: yourStrong(!)Password

---

86 https://github.com/ElevenPaths/FOCA.
87 docker.com.

FOCA should now be ready to be used. To maximize FOCA's potential, you should provide it with Google and Bing API keys; otherwise, you may encounter the HTTP response code 429, informing that you have performed too many requests.

13.8 Automation of OSINT Tasks

Many of the tasks within OSINT can be quite repetitive, which is why having tools that can speed up some of the processes by automating things is critical for success and ensuring that the same method is utilized every time.

13.8.1 Maltego

This would not be an OSINT chapter without mentioning Maltego, developed by Paterva, which is a powerful OSINT and data visualization tool that enables digital forensics professionals to collect, correlate, and analyze information from a myriad of open sources. With its intuitive interface and robust features, Maltego streamlines the often complex and time-consuming process of data gathering, transforming it into a dynamic, interactive, and visually informative experience. In Figure 13.15 you can see an example of a search using Maltego What makes Maltego so great is the combination of the transformer that is responsible for API calls and parsing of the data and their graph visualization tools.

This allows people that are new to OSINT to perform advanced searches with ease. Of course, it is not all positive; there are some challenges using Maltego: the automated data gathering can sometimes lead to a lack of direct attribution for the sources of information. This can be a challenge in terms of accountability and

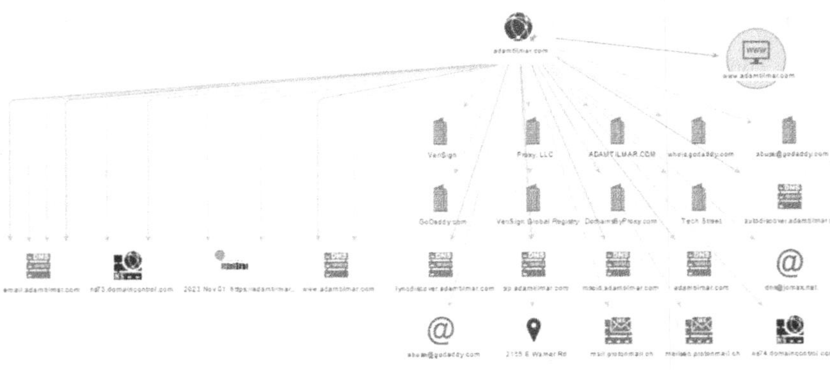

Figure 13.15 Maltego.

validation of the gathered data. The other thing to be aware of is that all queries you do within Maltego will be performed on their server, which could raise some privacy concerns.

Other than these concerns, Maltego is an excellent tool, which can take a novice OSINT investigator to a much higher level. The good thing is the community version is free of charge and is an excellent way to give it a spin you can find it over at Maltego.[88] They even have free training available on how to use the platform over at Maltego courses.[89]

13.9 Summary

OSINT (Open-Source Intelligence) is a vast field with endless possibilities for collecting information about almost anything. The key to mastering OSINT is understanding which information is relevant and which is noise. When pivoting from one data point to another, it's essential to have at least two or more connections between the points. This approach helps ensure that you don't go down the wrong path and filter out irrelevant information.

Mastering OSINT is challenging, as it is constantly changing, and you must be prepared for your tools and methodologies to become obsolete at any time. Although this guide only scratches the surface, there are valuable resources available to help you dive deeper into the world of OSINT. Two recommended books are *OSINT Techniques* by Michael Bazzell and *Hunting Cyber Criminals* by Vinny Troia. While both books may already be outdated upon release, they serve as excellent starting points for learning the tools and strategies necessary to excel in the field of OSINT. Remember, continuous learning and adaptation are crucial to staying ahead in this ever-evolving domain.

88 maltego.com.
89 https://spark.maltego.com/courses.

14

Case Studies

14.1 Case of "The Missing Author"

To provide a practical example of using OSINT and digital forensics together, let's explore a high-level case I've worked on in the past. This case involved a website used to spread illegal material, and the primary goal of the investigation was to identify the suspect(s) responsible for creating and maintaining the site.

Starting with just the domain name, I first looked at the *whois* registration information, which was unfortunately redacted for privacy. I then sought out historical *whois* data from data brokers and found contact information from a few years back that was not redacted. This led us to a suspect, and after obtaining a warrant, we raided the suspect's residence and found two Windows computers and an iPhone.

Upon analyzing the data on these devices, we discovered that the suspect had set up their devices to perform forensic cleanups at every shutdown, which removed files typically used in digital forensics. However, we were able to find multiple pieces of evidence pointing to the suspect as the hostmaster of the site through shellbags, previous access to the domain email using Outlook, and some old deleted documents.

The challenge was to find evidence that the suspect was the author of the articles posted on the site. To do this, I applied naive Bayes classifier, similar to the method used by email programs to classify spam. By calculating the probability of words appearing in known texts and random samples, we could determine the likelihood of the articles on the website being written by the suspect or a random person.

One of the insights gained through this process was that all the articles had the same spelling mistake. This method did allow us to identify that a majority of the articles had a very high probability of being written by the suspect, because of similar word usage and the same spelling mistake in both texts. Although this evidence alone might not be enough to convict someone, it provided valuable information for the investigator, which was used in the interrogation process to get a confession.

Practical Cyber Intelligence: A Hands-on Guide to Digital Forensics, First Edition. Adam Tilmar Jakobsen.

In summary, this case study demonstrates how OSINT, digital forensics, and data analytics can work together to solve complex problems. We used OSINT to identify a suspect through historical *whois* information, digital forensics to analyze data on the devices, and data analytics to gain new insights into the information available.

14.2 The Insider Threat

A large multinational corporation noticed unusual activity on its network, including unauthorized access to sensitive data and confidential documents. The company's internal cybersecurity team initiated an investigation to identify the source of the breach.

The initial investigation led to the discovery of an employee's compromised credentials. However, further analysis of the employee's computer and digital behavior revealed that the employee himself was responsible for the unauthorized access. It turned out that he had been disgruntled after being passed over for a promotion and had decided to leak sensitive information to a competitor.

Using digital forensics techniques, investigators were able to trace the unauthorized access to specific devices and locations, ultimately proving the employee's involvement. They also uncovered email correspondence and file transfers to the competitor, which were used as evidence to take legal action against the employee and recover the stolen data.

15

Ending

As we come to the end of this book on "cyber investigation," I hope you have gained new insights into the techniques and methods used in this field. The aim was to provide a comprehensive and valuable resource for anyone interested in learning about cyber investigation, covering topics from the basics of digital forensics to advanced techniques for tracking down criminals and organizations.

The hands-on approach and practical examples presented throughout the book should make it an ideal guide for both beginners and experienced investigators. The clear and concise writing style ensures that the content is accessible, even for those with no prior knowledge of the cyber investigation domain.

15.1 What's the Next Step?

So, where do you go from here? If you find digital investigation intriguing and want to further develop your skills, consider participating in Capture the Flag (CTF) events that include both hacking and forensics challenges. Some great resources for practice include Hack the Box,[1] CyberDefenders,[2] and TryHackMe.[3]

Thank you for reading this book. I hope you found the information interesting and useful. Any feedback is greatly appreciated, so please feel free to share your thoughts on what worked well and what could be improved, especially if you come across any inaccuracies.

1 https://app.hackthebox.com/.
2 https://cyberdefenders.org/.
3 https://tryhackme.com.

Index

Practical Cyber Intelligence: A Hands-on Guide to Digital Forensics, First Edition. Adam Tilmar Jakobsen.

Printed and bound by CPI Group (UK) Ltd, Croydon, CR0 4YY

17/09/2026

14964331-0001